My Life in France

My Life in France

Julia Child

WITH ALEX PRUD'HOMME

ALFRED A. KNOPF  NEW YORK 2006

THIS IS A BORZOI BOOK
PUBLISHED BY ALFRED A. KNOPF

Material on pages 113 to 114 first appeared in somewhat
different form as "In Praise of Partridge," *The New York
Times Magazine Sophisticated Traveler,* October 21, 1990.

ISBN 1-4000-4346-8

Printed in the United States of America

To Paul

CONTENTS

✤ ✤ ✤

FOREWORD

⚜ ⚜ ⚜

IN AUGUST 2004, Julia Child and I sat in her small, lush garden in Montecito, California, talking about her life. She was thin and a bit stooped, but more vigorous than she'd been in weeks. We were in the midst of writing this book together. When I asked her what she remembered about Paris in the 1950s, she recalled that she had learned to cook everything from snails to wild boar at the Cordon Bleu; that marketing in France had taught her the value of "*les human relations*"; she lamented that in her day the American housewife had to juggle cooking the soup and boiling the diapers—adding, "if she mixed the two together, imagine what a lovely combination that would make!"

The idea for *My Life in France* had been gestating since 1969, when her husband, Paul, sifted through hundreds of letters that he and Julia had written his twin brother, Charles Child (my grandfather), from France in 1948–1954. Paul suggested creating a book from the letters about their favorite, formative years together. But for one reason or another, the book never got written. Paul died in 1994, aged ninety-two. Yet Julia never gave up on the idea, and would often talk about her intention to write "the France book." She saw it, in part, as a tribute to her husband, the man who had swept her off to Paris in the first place.

I was a professional writer, and had long wanted to work on a collaborative project with Julia. But she was self-reliant, and for years had politely resisted the idea. In December 2003, she once again mentioned "the France book," in a wistful tone, and I again offered to assist her. She was ninety-one, and her health had been waxing and waning. This time she said, "All right, dearie, maybe we *should* work on it together."

My job was simply to help Julia tell her story, but it wasn't always easy. Though she was a natural performer, she was essentially a private person who didn't like to reveal herself. We started slowly, began to work in sync, and eventually built a wonderfully productive routine. For a few days every month, I'd sit in her living room asking questions, reading from family letters, and listening to her stories. At first I taped our conversations, but when she began to poke my tape recorder with her long fingers, I realized it was distracting her, and took notes instead. The longer we talked about "little old France," the more she remembered, often with vivid intensity—"Ooh, those lovely roasted, buttery French chickens, they were so good and *chickeny*!"

Many of our best conversations took place over a meal, on a car ride, or during a visit to a farmers' market. Something would trigger a memory, and she'd suddenly tell me about how she learned to make baguettes in Paris, or bouillabaisse in Marseille, or how to survive a French dinner party—"Just speak very loudly and quickly, and state your position with utter conviction, as the French do, and you'll have a marvelous time!"

Almost all of the words in these pages are Julia's or Paul's. But this is not a scholarly work, and at times I have blended their voices. Julia encouraged this approach, pointing out that she and Paul often signed their letters "PJ" or "Pulia," as if they were two halves of one person. I wrote some of the exposition and transitions, and in so doing tried to emulate Julia's idiosyncratic word choices—"Plop!," "Yuck!," "Woe!," "Hooray!" Once I had gathered enough material, I would write up a vignette; she would avidly read it, correct my French, and add things as they occurred to her in small, rightward-slanting handwriting. She loved this process, and was an exacting editor. "This book energizes me!" she declared.

Julia and I shared a sense of humor, and appetite, and she thought I looked like Paul, which probably helped our collaboration. As for me, I was grateful for the chance to reconnect with her and to be part of such an interesting project. Some writers find that the more they learn about their co-authors the less they like them, but I had the opposite experience: the more I learned about Julia Child, the more I came to respect her. What impressed me most was how hard she worked, how devoted she was to the "rules" of *la cuisine française* while keeping herself open to creative exploration, and how determined she was to persevere in the face of setbacks. Julia never lost her sense of wonder and inquisitiveness. She was, and is, a great inspiration.

Another great inspiration has been our editor, Judith Jones, who worked with Julia for more than forty years. With patience and a deep understanding of our subject, she was indispensable in helping to shape this book. Judith's assistant, Ken Schneider, was also a great help.

On August 13, 2004—just after our conversation in her garden, and only two days before her ninety-second birthday—Julia died of kidney failure in her sleep. Over the next year, I finished *My Life in France*, but every day wished I could call her up and ask her to clarify a story, or to share a bit of news, or just to talk. I miss her. But through her words in these pages, Julia's voice remains as lively, wise, and encouraging as ever. As she would say, "We had such fun!"

Alex Prud'homme
August 2005

My Life
in France

Me in the middle, surrounded by my brother, John, and younger sister, Dorothy

Introduction

THIS IS A BOOK about some of the things I have loved most in life: my husband, Paul Child; *la belle France*; and the many pleasures of cooking and eating. It is also something new for me. Rather than a collection of recipes, I've put together a series of linked autobiographical stories, mostly focused on the years 1948 through 1954, when we lived in Paris and Marseille, and also a few of our later adventures in Provence. Those early years in France were among the best of my life. They marked a crucial period of transformation in which I found my true calling, experienced an awakening of the senses, and had such fun that I hardly stopped moving long enough to catch my breath.

Before I moved to France, my life had not prepared me for what I would discover there. I was raised in a comfortable, WASPy, upper-middle-class family in sunny and non-intellectual Pasadena, California. My father, John McWilliams, was a conservative businessman who managed family real-estate holdings; my mother, Carolyn, whom we called Caro, was a very warm and social person. But, like most of her peers, she didn't spend much time in the kitchen. She occasionally sallied forth to whip up baking-powder biscuits, or a cheese dish, or finnan haddie, but she was not a cook. Nor was I.

As a girl I had zero interest in the stove. I've always had a healthy appetite, especially for the wonderful meat and the fresh produce of California, but I was never encouraged to cook and just didn't see the point in it. Our family had a series of hired cooks, and they'd produce heaping portions of typical American fare—fat roasted chicken with buttery mashed potatoes and creamed spinach; or well-marbled porterhouse steaks; or aged leg of lamb cooked medium gray—not pinky-red rare, as the French do—and always accompanied by brown gravy and green mint sauce. It was delicious but not refined food.

Paul, on the other hand, had been raised in Boston by a rather

bohemian mother who had lived in Paris and was an excellent cook. He was a cultured man, ten years older than I was, and by the time we met, during World War II, he had already traveled the world. Paul was a natty dresser and spoke French beautifully, and he adored good food and wine. He knew about dishes like *moules marinières* and *boeuf bourguignon* and *canard à l'orange*—things that seemed hopelessly exotic to my untrained ear and tongue. I was lucky to marry Paul. He was a great inspiration, his enthusiasm about wine and food helped to shape my tastes, and his encouragement saw me through discouraging moments. I would never have had my career without Paul Child.

Introduction

We'd first met in Ceylon (Sri Lanka) during the Second World War and were married in September 1946. In preparation for living with a new husband on a limited government income, I decided I'd better learn how to cook. Before our wedding, I took a bride-to-be's cooking course from two Englishwomen in Los Angeles, who taught me to make things like pancakes. But the first meal I ever cooked for Paul was a bit more ambitious: brains simmered in red wine! I'm not quite sure why I picked that particular dish, other than that it sounded exotic and would be a fun way to impress my new husband. I skimmed over the recipe, and figured it wouldn't be too hard to make. But the results, alas, were messy to look at and not very good to eat. In fact, the dinner was a disaster. Paul laughed it off, and we scrounged up something else that night. But deep down I was annoyed with myself, and I grew more determined than ever to learn how to cook well.

In our first year as young marrieds, we lived in Georgetown, in Washington, D.C., in a small white clapboard house on Olive Avenue. While Paul worked on mounting exhibits for the State Department, I worked as a file clerk. In the evening, I would approach the stove armed with lofty intentions, the *Joy of Cooking* or *Gourmet* magazine tucked under my arm, and little kitchen sense. My meals were satisfactory, but they took hours of laborious effort to produce. I'd usually plop something on the table by 10:00 p.m., have a few bites, and collapse into bed. Paul was unfailingly patient. But years later he'd admit to an interviewer: "Her first attempts were not altogether successful. . . . I was brave because I wanted to marry Julia. I trust I did not betray my point of view." (He did not.)

In the winter of 1948, Paul was offered a job running the Visual Presentation Department for the United States Information Service (USIS) in Paris, and I tagged along. I had never been to Europe, but once we had settled in Paris, it was clear that, out of sheer luck, I had landed in a magical city—one that is still my favorite place on earth. Starting slowly, and then with a growing enthusiasm, I devoted myself to learning the language and the customs of my new home.

In Paris and later in Marseille, I was surrounded by some of the best food in the world, and I had an enthusiastic audience in my husband, so it seemed only logical that I should learn how to cook *la cuisine bourgeoise*—good, traditional French home cooking. It was a revelation. I simply fell in love with that glorious food and those marvelous chefs. The longer we stayed there, the deeper my commitment became.

IN COLLABORATING on this book, Alex Prud'homme and I have been fortunate indeed to have spent hours together telling stories, reminiscing, and thinking out loud. Memory is selective, and we have not attempted to be encyclopedic here, but have focused on some of the large and small moments that stuck with me for over fifty years.

Alex was born in 1961, the year that our first book, *Mastering the Art of French Cooking*, which I wrote with Simone Beck and Louisette Bertholle, was published. How appropriate, then, that he and I should work together on this volume, which recounts the making of that book.

Our research has been aided immeasurably by a thick trove of family letters and datebooks kept from those days, along with Paul's photographs, sketches, poems, and Valentine's Day cards. Paul and his twin brother, Charlie Child, a painter who lived in Bucks County, Pennsylvania, wrote to each other every week or so. Paul took letter writing seriously: he'd set aside time for it, tried to document our day-to-day lives in a journalistic way, and usually wrote three to six pages a week in a beautiful flowing hand with a special fountain pen; often he included little sketches of places we'd visited, or photos (some of which we have used in these pages), or made mini-collages out of ticket stubs or newsprint. My letters were usually one or two pages, typed, and full of spelling mistakes, bad grammar, and exclamation points; I tended to focus on what I was cooking at the time, or the human dramas boiling around us. Written on thin pale-blue or white airmail paper, those hundreds of letters have survived the years in very good shape.

When I reread them now, the events those letters describe come rushing back to me with great immediacy: Paul noticing the brilliant sparkle of autumn light on the dark Seine, his daily battles with Washington bureaucrats, the smell of Montmartre at dusk, or the night we spied wild-haired Colette eating at that wonderful Old World restaurant Le Grand Véfour. In my letters, I enthuse over my first taste of a toothsome French duck roasted before an open fire, or the gossip I'd heard from the vegetable lady in the Rue de Bourgogne marketplace, or the latest mischief of our cat, Minette, or the failures and triumphs of our years of cookbook work. It is remarkable that our family had the foresight to save those letters—it's almost as if they knew Alex and I were going to sit down and write this book together one day.

We tip our hats in gratitude to the many people and institutions who have helped us with *My Life in France*, especially to my dear friend and lifelong editor at Knopf, Judith Jones, she of the gimlet eye and soft editorial touch. And to my beloved French "sisters," Simone Beck and Louisette Bertholle, with whom I collaborated; to my sister, Dorothy, my enthusiastic niece, Phila Cousins, and her brother, Sam; to my invaluable assistant, Stephanie Hersh, and my attorney Bill Truslow. We also sing the praises of the Schlesinger Library at the Radcliffe Institute, which has graciously housed the bulk of my papers and Paul's photographs; the Museum of American History at the Smithsonian Institution, which has been kind enough to display artifacts from my career, including my entire kitchen from our house in Cambridge, Massachusetts; to WGBH, Boston's public television station; to my alma mater,

Smith College; also to the many family members and friends who have aided us with memories, photos, good company, and fine meals as we pieced together this volume.

What fun and good fortune I had living in France with Paul, and again in writing about our experiences with Alex. I hope that this book is as much fun for you to read as it was for us to put together—*bon appétit!*

Julia Child
Montecito, California
August 2004

PART I

CHAPTER I

La Belle France

1. SEA CHANGE

AT FIVE-FORTY-FIVE in the morning, Paul and I rousted ourselves from our warm bunk and peered out of the small porthole in our cabin aboard the SS *America*. Neither of us had slept very well that night, partially due to the weather and partially due to our rising excitement. We rubbed our eyes and squinted through the glass, and could see it was foggy out. But through the deep-blue dawn and swirling murk we spied rows of twinkling lights along the shore. It was Wednesday, November 3, 1948, and we had finally arrived at Le Havre, France.

I had never been to Europe before and didn't know what to expect. We had been at sea for a week, although it seemed a lot longer, and I was more than ready to step onto terra firma. As soon as our family had seen us off in fall-colored New York, the *America* had sailed straight into the teeth of a North Atlantic gale. As the big ship heeled and bucked in waves as tall as buildings, there was a constant sound of bashing, clashing, clicking, shuddering, swaying, and groaning. Lifelines were strung along the corridors. Up . . . up . . . up . . . the enormous liner would rise, and at the peak she'd teeter for a moment, then down . . . down . . . down . . . she'd slide until her bow plunged into the trough with a great shuddering spray. Our muscles ached, our minds were weary, and smashed crockery was strewn about the floor. Most of the ship's passengers, and some of her crew, were green around the gills.

Paul and I were lucky to be good sailors, with cast-iron stomachs: one morning we counted as two of the five passengers who made it to breakfast.

I had spent only a little time at sea, on my way to and from Asia during the Second World War, and had never experienced a storm like this before. Paul, on the other hand, had seen every kind of weather imaginable. In the early 1920s, unable to afford college, he had sailed from the United States to Panama on an oil tanker, hitched a ride on a little ferry from Marseille to Africa, crossed the Mediterranean and Atlantic from Trieste to New York, crewed aboard a schooner that sailed from Nova Scotia to South America, and served briefly aboard a command ship in the China Sea during World War II. He'd experienced waterspouts, lightning storms, and plenty of the "primordial violence of nature," as he put it. Paul was a sometimes macho, sometimes quiet, willful, bookish man. He suffered terrible vertigo, yet was the kind to push himself up to the top of a ship's rigging in a fierce gale. It was typical that aboard the tossing SS *America* he did most of the worrying for the two of us.

Paul had been offered the job of running the exhibits office for the United States Information Service (USIS), at the American embassy in Paris. His assignment was to help promote French-American relations through the visual arts. It was a sort of cultural/propaganda job, and he was well suited for it. Paul had lived and worked in France in the 1920s, spoke the language beautifully, and adored French food and wine. Paris was his favorite city in the world. So, when the U.S. government offered him a job there, he jumped at the chance. I just tagged along as his extra baggage.

Travel, we agreed, was a litmus test: if we could make the best of the chaos and serendipity that we'd inevitably meet in transit, then we'd surely be able to sail through the rest of life together just fine. So far, we'd done pretty well.

We had met in Ceylon in the summer of 1944, when we'd both been posted there by the Office of Strategic Services (OSS), the precursor to the CIA. Paul was an artist, and he'd been recruited to create war rooms where General Mountbatten could review the intelligence that our agents had sent in from the field. I was head of the Registry, where, among other things, I processed agents' reports from the field and other top-secret papers. Late in the war, Paul and I were transferred to Kunming, China, where we worked for General Wedemeyer and continued our courtship over delicious Chinese food.

Although we had met abroad, we didn't count our wartime in Asia as real living-time abroad: we were working seven days a week, sleeping in group quarters, and constantly at the beck and call of the military.

But now the war was over. We had been married in 1946, lived for two years in Washington, D.C., and were moving to Paris. We'd been so busy since our wedding day, September 1, 1946, that we'd never taken a proper honeymoon. Perhaps a few years in Paris would make up for that sorry state of affairs and give us a sort of working honeymoon. Well, it *sounded* like a good plan.

As I GAZED through the porthole at the twinkling lights of Le Havre, I realized I had no idea what I was looking at. France was a misty abstraction for me, a land I had long imagined but had no real sense of. And while I couldn't wait to step ashore, I had my reasons to be suspicious of it.

In Pasadena, California, where I was raised, France did not have a good reputation. My tall and taciturn father, "Big John" McWilliams, liked to say that all Europeans, especially the French, were "dark" and "dirty," although he'd never actually been to Europe and didn't know any Frenchmen. I had met some French people, but they were a couple of cranky spinster schoolteachers. Despite years of "learning" French, by rote, I could neither speak nor understand a word of the language. Furthermore, thanks to articles in *Vogue* and Hollywood spectaculars, I suspected that France was a nation of icky-picky people where the women were all dainty, exquisitely coiffed, nasty little creatures, the men all Adolphe Menjou–like dandies who twirled their mustaches, pinched girls, and schemed against American rubes.

I was a six-foot-two-inch, thirty-six-year-old, rather loud and unserious Californian. The sight of France in my porthole was like a giant question mark.

The *America* entered Le Havre Harbor slowly. We could see giant cranes, piles of brick, bombed-out empty spaces, and rusting half-sunk hulks left over from the war. As tugs pushed us toward the quay, I peered down from the rail at the crowd on the dock. My gaze stopped on a burly, gruff man with a weathered face and a battered, smoldering cigarette jutting from the corner of his mouth. His giant hands waved about in the air around his head as he shouted something to someone. He was a porter, and he was laughing and heaving luggage around like a happy bear, completely oblivious to me. His swollen belly and thick shoulders were encased in overalls of a distinctive deep blue, a very attractive color, and he had an earthy, amusing quality that began to ease my anxiety.

So THAT'S what a real Frenchman looks like, I said to myself. *He's hardly Adolphe Menjou. Thank goodness, there are actual blood-and-guts people in this country!*

By 7:00 a.m., Paul and I were ashore and our bags had passed through customs. For the next two hours, we sat there smoking and yawning, with our collars turned up against the drizzle. Finally, a crane pulled our large sky-blue Buick station wagon—which we'd nicknamed "the Blue Flash"—out of the ship's hold. The Buick swung overhead in a sling and then dropped down to the dock, where it landed with a bounce. It was immediately set upon by a gang of *mécaniciens*, men dressed in black berets, white butcher's aprons, and big rubber boots. They filled the Flash with *essence*, oil, and water, affixed our diplomatic license plates, and stowed our fourteen pieces of luggage and half a dozen trunks and blankets away all wrong. Paul tipped them, and restowed the bags so that he could see out the back window. He was very particular about his car-packing, and very good at it, too, like a master jigsaw-puzzler.

As he finished stowing, the rain eased and streaks of blue emerged from the gray scud overhead. We wedged ourselves into the front seat and pointed our wide, rumbling nose southeast, toward Paris.

II. *SOLE MEUNIÈRE*

THE NORMAN COUNTRYSIDE struck me as quintessentially French, in an indefinable way. The real sights and sounds and smells of this place were so much more particular and interesting than a movie montage or a magazine spread about "France" could ever be. Each little town had a distinct character, though some of them, like Yvetot, were still scarred by gaping bomb holes and knots of barbed wire. We saw hardly any other cars, but there were hundreds of bicyclists, old men driving

Paul's photographs of the French countryside

horses-and-buggies, ladies dressed in black, and little boys in wooden shoes. The telephone poles were of a different size and shape from those in America. The fields were intensely cultivated. There were no bill-boards. And the occasional pink-and-white stucco villa set at the end of a formal *allée* of trees was both silly and charming. Quite unexpectedly, something about the earthy-smoky smells, the curve of the landscape, and the bright greenness of the cabbage fields reminded us both of China.

Oh, *la belle France*—without knowing it, I was already falling in love!

AT TWELVE-THIRTY we Flashed into Rouen. We passed the city's ancient and beautiful clock tower, and then its famous cathedral, still pockmarked from battle but magnificent with its stained-glass windows. We rolled to a stop in la Place du Vieux Marché, the square where Joan of Arc had met her fiery fate. There the *Guide Michelin* directed us to Restaurant La Couronne ("The Crown"), which had been built in 1345 in a medieval quarter-timbered house. Paul strode ahead, full of antici-pation, but I hung back, concerned that I didn't look chic enough, that I wouldn't be able to communicate, and that the waiters would look down their long Gallic noses at us Yankee tourists.

It was warm inside, and the dining room was a comfortably old-fashioned brown-and-white space, neither humble nor luxurious. At the far end was an enormous fireplace with a rotary spit, on which some-thing was cooking that sent out heavenly aromas. We were greeted by the maître d'hôtel, a slim middle-aged man with dark hair who carried himself with an air of gentle seriousness. Paul spoke to him, and the maître d' smiled and said something back in a familiar way, as if they were old friends. Then he led us to a nice table not far from the fire-place. The other customers were all French, and I noticed that they were treated with exactly the same courtesy as we were. Nobody rolled their eyes at us or stuck their nose in the air. Actually, the staff seemed happy to see us.

As we sat down, I heard two businessmen in gray suits at the next table asking questions of their waiter, an older, dignified man who ges-ticulated with a menu and answered them at length.

"What are they talking about?" I whispered to Paul.

"The waiter is telling them about the chicken they ordered," he whispered back. "How it was raised, how it will be cooked, what side dishes they can have with it, and which wines would go with it best."

"*Wine?*" I said. "At *lunch?*" I had never drunk much wine other than some $1.19 California Burgundy, and certainly not in the middle of the day.

In France, Paul explained, good cooking was regarded as a combination of national sport and high art, and wine was always served with lunch and dinner. "The trick is moderation," he said.

Suddenly the dining room filled with wonderfully intermixing aromas that I sort of recognized but couldn't name. The first smell was something oniony—"shallots," Paul identified it, "being sautéed in fresh butter." ("What's a shallot?" I asked, sheepishly. "You'll see," he said.) Then came a warm and winy fragrance from the kitchen, which was probably a delicious sauce being reduced on the stove. This was followed by a whiff of something astringent: the salad being tossed in a big ceramic bowl with lemon, wine vinegar, olive oil, and a few shakes of salt and pepper.

My stomach gurgled with hunger.

I couldn't help noticing that the waiters carried themselves with a quiet joy, as if their entire mission in life was to make their customers feel comfortable and well tended. One of them glided up to my elbow. Glancing at the menu, Paul asked him questions in rapid-fire French. The waiter seemed to enjoy the back-and-forth with my husband. Oh, how I itched to be in on their conversation! Instead, I smiled and nodded uncomprehendingly, although I tried to absorb all that was going on around me.

We began our lunch with a half-dozen oysters on the half-shell. I was used to bland oysters from Washington and Massachusetts, which I had never cared much for. But this platter of *portugaises* had a sensational briny flavor and a smooth texture that was entirely new and surprising. The oysters were served with rounds of *pain de seigle*, a pale rye bread, with a spread of unsalted butter. Paul explained that, as with wine, the French have "crus" of butter, special regions that produce individually flavored butters. *Beurre de Charentes* is a full-bodied butter, usually recommended for pastry dough or general cooking; *beurre d'Isigny* is a fine, light table butter. It was that delicious *Isigny* that we spread on our rounds of rye.

Rouen is famous for its duck dishes, but after consulting the waiter

Paul had decided to order *sole meunière*. It arrived whole: a large, flat Dover sole that was perfectly browned in a sputtering butter sauce with a sprinkling of chopped parsley on top. The waiter carefully placed the platter in front of us, stepped back, and said: "*Bon appétit!*"

I closed my eyes and inhaled the rising perfume. Then I lifted a forkful of fish to my mouth, took a bite, and chewed slowly. The flesh of the sole was delicate, with a light but distinct taste of the ocean that blended marvelously with the browned butter. I chewed slowly and swallowed. It was a morsel of perfection.

In Pasadena, we used to have broiled mackerel for Friday dinners, codfish balls with egg sauce, "boiled" (poached) salmon on the Fourth of July, and the occasional pan-fried trout when camping in the Sierras. But at La Couronne I experienced fish, and a dining experience, of a higher order than any I'd ever had before.

Along with our meal, we happily downed a whole bottle of Pouilly-Fumé, a wonderfully crisp white wine from the Loire Valley. Another revelation!

Then came *salade verte* laced with a lightly acidic vinaigrette. And I tasted my first real baguette—a crisp brown crust giving way to a slightly chewy, rather loosely textured pale-yellow interior, with a faint reminder of wheat and yeast in the odor and taste. Yum!

We followed our meal with a leisurely dessert of *fromage blanc*, and ended with a strong, dark *café filtre*. The waiter placed before us a cup topped with a metal canister, which contained coffee grounds and boiling water. With some urging by us impatient drinkers, the water eventually filtered down into the cup below. It was fun, and it provided a distinctive dark brew.

Paul paid the bill and chatted with the maître d', telling him how much he looked forward to going back to Paris for the first time in eighteen years. The maître d' smiled as he scribbled something on the back of a card. "*Tiens,*" he said, handing it to me. The Dorin family, who owned La Couronne, also owned a restaurant in Paris, called La Truite, he explained, while Paul translated. On the card he had scribbled a note of introduction for us.

"Mairci, monsoor," I said, with a flash of courage and an accent that sounded bad even to my own ear. The waiter nodded as if it were nothing, and moved off to greet some new customers.

Paul and I floated out the door into the brilliant sunshine and cool air. Our first lunch together in France had been absolute perfection. It was the most exciting meal of my life.

BACK IN THE FLASH, we continued to Paris along a highway built by the U.S. Army Corps of Engineers. With double roadways on each side of a grass median, and well-engineered overpasses and underpasses, it reminded us of the Hutchinson River Parkway, outside of New York City. That impression faded as dusk came on and the unmistakable silhouette of the Eiffel Tower loomed into sight, outlined with blinking red lights.

Paris!

At nightfall, we entered the city via the Porte de Saint-Cloud. Navigating through the city was strange and hazardous. The streetlights had been dimmed, and for some reason (wartime habit?) Parisians drove with only their parking lights on. It was nearly impossible to see pedestrians or road signs, and the thick traffic moved slowly. Unlike in China or India, where people also drove by parking light, the Parisians would constantly flash on their real headlights for just a moment when they thought there was something in the road.

Across the Pont Royal, up the Rue du Bac, nearly to Boulevard Saint-Germain, and then we pulled over at 7 Rue Montalembert in front of the Hôtel Pont Royal. We were exhausted, but thrilled.

Paul unloaded the Flash and drove off into the misty dark in search of a garage that was reputedly five minutes away. We'd been told that it wasn't safe to leave the car on the street at night. The Buick wagon was considerably bulkier than the local Citroëns and Peugeots, and Paul was anxious to find a safe berth for what the *garagistes* called our "*autobus américain.*" I accompanied our bags up to our room, but noticed that the hotel seemed to be swaying from side to side, like the *America:* I had yet to regain my land legs.

An hour later, and still no sign of Paul. I was hungry and growing concerned. Finally, he reappeared in a lather, saying: "I had a hell of a time. I went *up* instead of *down* the Boulevard Raspail, then came back via Saint-Germain thinking it was Raspail, then got stuck on a one-way street. So I parked the car and walked. Eventually I found the garage, but then I couldn't find the car—I thought I'd left it on Raspail, but it was on Saint-Germain! Nobody knew where the garage was, or the

Me looking out at Paris from the Hôtel Pont Royal

hotel. Finally, I brought car to garage and me to you at the hotel. . . . Let's eat!"

We went to a little place on Saint-Germain where the food was fine, although nothing compared with La Couronne (the standard by which I would now measure every eatery), and disappointingly packed with tourists. I had only been in Paris for a few hours but already considered myself a native.

Paul's job at the USIS was to "inform the French people by graphic means about the aspects of American life that the [United States] government deems important." The idea was to build goodwill between our nations, to reinforce the idea that America was a strong and reliable ally, that the Marshall Plan was designed to help France get back on its feet (without telling Paris how to run its affairs), and to insinuate that rapacious Russia was not to be trusted. It seemed straightforward.

On his first day of work, Paul discovered that the USIS exhibits office had been leaderless for months and was a shambles. He was to oversee a staff of eight, all French—five photographers, two artists, and one secretary—who were demoralized, overworked, underpaid, riven with petty jealousies, and hobbled by a lack of basic supplies. There was little or no photographic film, paper, developer, or flashbulbs. Even essentials like scissors, bottles of ink, stools—or a budget—were missing. The lights in his office would conk out three or four times a day. Because there were no proper files, or shelves, most of his unit's fifty thousand photographic prints and negatives were stuffed into ragged manila envelopes or old packing boxes on the floor.

In the meantime, the ECA, the Economic Cooperation Administration, which administered the Marshall Plan, was sending orders in big, thoughtless clumps: Prepare hundreds of exhibit materials for a trade fair in Lyon! Introduce yourself to all the local politicians and journalists! Send posters to Marseille, Bordeaux, and Strasbourg! Be charming at the ambassador's champagne reception for three hundred VIPs! Put on an art show for an American ladies' club! Et cetera. Paul had endured far worse during the war, but he fumed that such working conditions were "ridiculous, naïve, stupid, and incredible!"

I wandered the city, got lost, found myself again. I engaged the garage man in a lengthy, if not completely comprehensible, discussion about retarding the Flash's spark to reduce the "ping." I went into a big department store and bought a pair of slippers. I went into a boutique and bought a chic green-feathered hat. I got along "*assez bien.*"

At the American embassy I collected our ration books, pay information, commissary tickets, travel vouchers, leave sheets, *cartes d'identité*, and business cards. Mrs. Ambassador Caffrey had let it be known that she felt protocol had slipped around the embassy, and insisted that people like us—on the bottom of the diplomatic totem pole—leave our cards with everyone of equivalent or superior rank: that meant I had to leave over two hundred cards for Paul and over one hundred for me. Phooey!

ON NOVEMBER 5, a banner headline in the *International Herald Tribune* proclaimed that Harry S. Truman had been elected president, defeating Thomas Dewey at the eleventh hour. Paul and I, devoted Democrats, were exultant. My father, "Big John" McWilliams, a staunchly conservative Republican, was horrified.

Pop was a wonderful man on many counts, but our different worldviews were a source of tension that made family visits uncomfortable for me and miserable for Paul. My mother, Caro, who had died from the effects of high blood pressure, and now my stepmother, Philadelphia McWilliams, known as Phila, were apolitical but went along with whatever Pop said for the sake of domestic harmony. My brother, John, the middle sibling, was a mild Republican; my younger sister, Dorothy, stood to the left of me. My father was pained by his daughters' liberal leanings. He had assumed I would marry a Republican banker and settle in Pasadena to live a conventional life. But if I'd done that I'd probably have turned into an alcoholic, as a number of my friends had. Instead, I had married Paul Child, a painter, photographer, poet, and mid-level diplomat who had taken me to live in dirty, dreaded France. I couldn't have been happier!

Reading about Truman's election victory, I imagined the doom and gloom around Pasadena: it must have seemed like the End of Life as Big John knew it. *Eh bien, tant pis*, as we Parisians liked to say.

PARIS SMELLED OF SMOKE, as though it were burning up. When you sneezed, you blew sludge onto your handkerchief. This was partly due to some of the murkiest fog on record. It was so thick, the newspapers reported, that airplanes were grounded and transatlantic steamers were stuck in port for days. Everyone you met had a "fog drama" to tell. Some people were so terrified of getting lost that they spent all night in their cars, others missed plunging into the Seine by a centimeter, and several people drove for hours in the wrong direction, only to find themselves at a metro stop on the outskirts of town; they abandoned their cars and took the train home, but, upon emerging from the metro, got lost on foot. The fog insinuated itself everywhere, even inside the house. It was disconcerting to see clouds in your rooms, and it gave you a vague sense of being suffocated.

But on our first Saturday in Paris, we awoke to a brilliant bright-blue sky. It was thrilling, as if a curtain had been pulled back to reveal a mound of jewels. Paul couldn't wait to show me around his city.

We began at the Deux Magots café, where we ordered *café complet.* Paul was amused to see that nothing had changed since his last visit, back in 1928. The seats inside were still covered with orange plush, the brass light fixtures were still unpolished, and the waiters—and probably the dust balls in the corners—were the same. We sat outside, on wicker seats, munching our croissants and watching the morning sun illuminate the chimney pots. Suddenly the café was invaded by a mob of camera operators, soundmen, prop boys, and actors, including Burgess (Buzz) Meredith and Franchot Tone, costumed and grease-painted as shabby "Left Bank artists." Paul, who had once worked as a busboy/scenery-painter in Hollywood, chatted with Meredith about his movie, and how people in the film business were always the same agreeable type, whether in Paris, London, or Los Angeles.

We wandered up the street. Paul—mid-sized, bald, with a mustache and glasses, dressed in a trench coat and beret and thick-soled shoes—strode ahead, eyes alert and noticing everything, his trusty Graflex camera strapped around his shoulder. I followed, eyes wide open, mouth mostly shut, heart skipping with excitement.

At Place Saint-Sulpice, black-outfitted wedding guests were kissing each other on both cheeks by the fountain, and the building where Paul's mother had lived twenty years earlier was unchanged. Glancing up at a balcony, he spied a flower box she had made, now filled with marigolds. But at the corner, a favorite old building had disappeared. Not far away, the house where Paul's twin, Charlie, and his wife, Fredericka, known as Freddie, had once lived was now just a rubble-strewn lot (had it been blown to bits by a bomb?). Next to the theater on Place de l'Odéon we noticed a small marble plaque that read: "In memory of Jean Bares, killed at this spot in defense of his country, June 10, 1944." There were many of these somber reminders around the city.

We wended our way across the Seine and through the green Tuileries and along dank backstreets that smelled of rotting food, burned wood, sewage, old plaster, and human sweat. Then up to Montmartre and Sacré-Coeur, and The View over the whole city. Then down again, back over the Seine and, via Rue Bonaparte, to lunch at a wonderful old restaurant called Michaud.

Parisian restaurants were very different from American eateries. It was such fun to go into a little bistro and find cats on the chairs, poodles under the tables or poking out of women's bags, and chirping birds in the corner. I loved the crustacean stands in front of cafés, and began to order boldly. *Moules marinières* was a new dish to me; the mussels' beards had been removed, and the flesh tasted lovely in a way I had never expected it to. There were other surprises, too, such as the great big juicy pears grown right there in Paris, so succulent you could eat them with a spoon. And the grapes! In America, grapes bored me, but the Parisian grapes were exquisite, with a delicate, fugitive, sweet, ambrosial, and irresistible flavor.

As we explored the city, we made a point of trying every kind of cuisine, from fancy to hole-in-the-wall. In general, the more expensive the establishment, the less glad they were to see us, perhaps because they could sense us counting our centimes. The red-covered *Guide Michelin* became our Bible, and we decided that we preferred the restaurants rated with two crossed forks, which stood for medium quality and expense. A meal for two at such an establishment would run us about five dollars, which included a bottle of *vin ordinaire*.

Michaud became our favorite place for a time. Paul had learned about it through friends at the embassy, and it was just around the corner from Rue du Bac, where Rue de l'Université turns into Rue Jacob. It was a relaxed, intimate two-forker. The proprietress, known simply as Madame, stood about four feet three inches tall, had a neat little French figure, red hair, and a thrifty Gallic "save everything" quality. A waiter would take your order and bring it to Madame's headquarters at the bar. In one motion, she'd glance at the ticket, dive into a little icebox, and emerge with the carefully apportioned makings of your meal—meat, fish, or eggs—put it on a plate, and send it into the kitchen to be cooked. She poured the wine in the carafes. She made change at the register. If sugar ran low, she'd trot upstairs to her apartment to fetch it in a brown cardboard box; then she'd measure just the right amount into a jar, with not a single grain wasted.

Despite her frugality, Madame had an intimate and subtle charm. In a typical evening, you'd always shake her hand three times: upon entering, when she dropped by your table in the midst of your meal, and at the door as you left. She was happy to sit down with a cup of coffee to talk, but only for a moment. She'd join in a celebration with a glass of champagne, but for just long enough. The waiters at Michaud were all around sixty years old and carried themselves with the same intimate yet reserved manner she did. The clientele seemed to be made up of Parisians from the *quartier* and a smattering of foreigners who'd stumbled over this little prize and had kept it to themselves.

That afternoon, Paul ordered *rognons sautés au beurre* (braised kidneys) with watercress and fried potatoes. I was tempted by many things, but finally succumbed once again to *sole meunière*. I just couldn't get over how good it was, the sole crisp and bristling from the fire. With a carafe of *vin compris* and a perfectly soft slice of Brie, the entire lunch came to 970 francs, or about $3.15.

Computing *l'addition* all depended on which exchange rate you used. We U.S. Embassy types were only allowed to exchange dollars for francs at the official rate, about 313 francs to the dollar. But on the black market the exchange was 450 francs to the dollar, an improvement of more than 33 percent. Though we could have used the extra money, it was illegal, and we didn't dare risk our pride, or our posting, to save a few sous.

After more wandering, we had a very ordinary dinner, but finished the evening on a high note with dessert at Brasserie Lipp. I was feeling buoyant, and so was Paul. We discussed the stereotype of the Rude Frenchman: Paul declared that, in Paris of the 1920s, 80 percent of the people were difficult and 20 percent were charming; now the reverse was true, he said—80 percent of Parisians were charming and only 20 percent were rude. This, he figured, was probably an aftereffect of the war. But it might also have been due to *his* new outlook on life. "I am less sour now than I used to be," he admitted. "It's because of you, Julie." We analyzed one another, and concluded that marriage and advancing age agreed with us. Most of all, Paris was making us giddy.

"Lipstick on my belly button and music in the air—thaat's Paris, son," Paul wrote his twin, Charlie. "What a lovely city! What *grenouilles*

Paul's scenes of Paris

à la provençale. What Châteauneuf-du-Pape, what white poodles and white chimneys, what charming waiters, and *poules de luxe*, and maîtres d'hôtel, what gardens and bridges and streets! How fascinating the crowds before one's café table, how quaint and charming and hidden the little courtyards with their wells and statues. Those garlic-filled belches! Those silk-stockinged legs! Those mascara'd eyelashes! Those electric switches and toilet chains that never work! *Holà! Dites donc! Bouillabaisse! Au revoir!*"

III. Roo de Loo

"It's easy to get the feeling that you know the language just because when you order a beer they don't bring you oysters," Paul said. But after seeing a movie about a clown who cried through his laughter, or laughed through his tears—we couldn't tell which—even Paul felt discombobulated. "So much for my vaunted language skills," he griped.

At least he could communicate. The longer I was in Paris, the worse my French seemed to get. I had gotten over my initial astonishment that anyone could understand what I said at all. But I loathed my gauche accent, my impoverished phraseology, my inability to communicate in any but the most rudimentary way. My French "u"s were only worse than my "o"s.

This was brought home at Thanksgiving, when we went to a cocktail party at Paul and Hadley Mowrer's apartment. He wrote a column for the *New York Post* and did broadcasts for the Voice of America. She was a former Mrs. Ernest Hemingway, whom Paul had first met in Paris in the 1920s. Hadley was extremely warm, not very intellectual, and the mother of Jack Hemingway, who had been in the OSS during the war and was called Bumby. At the Mowrers' Thanksgiving party, more than half the guests were French, but I could barely say anything interesting at all to them. I am a talker, and my inability to communicate was hugely frustrating. When we got back to the hotel that night, I declared: "I've had it! I'm going to learn to speak this language, come hell or high water!"

A few days later, I signed up for a class at Berlitz: two hours of private lessons three times a week, plus homework. Paul, who was a lover of word games, made up sentences to help my pronunciation: for the rolling French "r"s and extended "u"s, he had me repeat the phrase "*Le serrurier sur la Rue de Rivoli*" ("The locksmith on the Rue de Rivoli") over and over.

IN THE MEANTIME, I had discovered an apartment for rent that was large, centrally located, and a bit weird. It was two floors of an old four-story *hôtel particulier*, at 81 Rue de l'Université. A classic Parisian building, it had a gray cement façade, a grand front door about eight feet high, a small interior courtyard, and an open-topped cage elevator. It was situated in the Seventh Arrondissement, on the Left Bank, an ideal location, one block in from the Seine, between the Assemblée Nationale and the Ministry of Defense. Paul's office at the U.S. Embassy was just across the river. Day and night, the bells of the nearby Church of Sainte-Clothilde tolled the time; it was a sweet sound, and I loved hearing it.

On December 4, we moved out of the Hôtel Pont Royal and into 81 Rue de l'Université. On the first floor lived our landlady, the distinguished Madame Perrier. She was seventy-eight, thin, with gray hair and a lively French face; she dressed in black and wore a black choker around her neck. With her lived her daughter, Madame du Couédic; son-in-law, Hervé du Couédic; and two grandchildren. On the ground floor, a concierge, whom I thought of as an unhappy crone, occupied a little apartment.

Madame Perrier was a cultured woman, an amateur bookbinder and photographer. The widow of a World War I general, she had also lost a son and a daughter within three months of each other. Yet she glistened like an old hand-polished copper fire-hood. It gave me great pleasure to see someone as fully mature and mellow but also as lively and aglow as she was. Madame Perrier became the model for how I wanted to look in my dotage. Her daughter, Madame du Couédic, looked like a typical French gentry-woman, with a spare frame, dark hair, and a somewhat formal manner. Her husband was also pleasant, but had an air of cool formality; he ran a successful paint business. By unspoken consent, we all got to know each other slowly, and eventually considered each other dear friends.

Paul and I were given the second and third floors. The elevator opened into a large, dark *salon* on the second floor. Madame Perrier's taste dated to the last century, and the *salon* looked faintly ridiculous:

decorated in Louis XVI style, it was high-ceilinged, with gray walls, four layers of gilded molding, inset panels, an ugly tapestry, thick curtains around one window, fake electric sconces, broken electric switches, and weak light. Sometimes I'd blow a fuse in there simply by plugging in the electric iron, which made me curse. But the *salon's* proportions were fine, and we improved things by editing out most of the chairs and tables.

We turned an adjacent room into our bedroom. The walls in there were covered in green cloth and so many plates, plaques, carvings, and whatnots that it looked like the inside of a freshly sliced plum cake. We removed most of the wall hangings, as well as a clutter of chairs, tables, cozy-corners, and hassocks, and stored them in an empty room upstairs that we named the *oubliette* (forgettery). Sensitive to the feelings of Madame Perrier, and in typically organized fashion, Paul drew up a diagram showing where each artifact had hung, so when it came time for us to leave we could re-create her decor exactly.

The kitchen was on the third floor, and was connected to the *salon* by a dumbwaiter that worked only some of the time. The kitchen was large and airy, with an expanse of windows along one side, and an immense stove—it seemed ten feet long—which took five tons of coal every six months. On top of this monster stood a little two-burner gas contraption with a one-foot-square oven, which was barely usable to heat plates or make toast. Then there was a four-foot-square shallow soapstone sink with no hot water. (We discovered we couldn't use it in the winter, because the pipes ran along the outside of the building and froze up.)

The building had no central heating and was as cold and damp as Lazarus's tomb. Our breath came out in great puffs indoors. So, like true Parisians, we installed an ugly little potbellied stove in the *salon* and sealed ourselves off for the winter. We stoked that bloody stove all day, and it provided a faint trace of heat and a strong stench of coal gas. Huddled there, we made quite a pair: Paul, dressed in his Chinese winter jacket, would sit midway between the potbellied stove and the forty-five-watt lamp, reading. I, charmingly outfitted in a thick padded coat, several layers of long underwear, and some dreadfully huge red leather shoes, would sit at a gilt table attempting to type letters with stiff fingers. Oh, the glamour of Paris!

I didn't mind living in primitive conditions with Charlie and Freddie Child at their hand-built cabin in the Maine woods, but I saw no sense in being even *more* primitive while living in the "cultural center of the world." So I set up a makeshift hot-water system (i.e., a tub of water set over a gas geyser), a dishwashing station, and covered garbage cans. Then I hung a nice row of cooking implements on the kitchen wall, including my Daisy can-opener and a Magnagrip, which made me feel at home.

Saying "81 Rue de l'Université" proved too much of a mouthful, and we quickly dubbed our new home "Roo de Loo," or simply "81."

Rue de Loo came with a *femme de ménage* (maid) named Frieda. She was about twenty-two, a farm girl who had been kicked around by life; she had a darling, illegitimate nine-year-old daughter whom she boarded in the country. Frieda lived on the fourth floor at Roo de Loo, in appallingly primitive conditions. She had no bathroom or hot water, so I set aside a corner of our bathroom on the third floor for her to use.

I was not used to having domestic help, and the arrangement with Frieda took some adjustment for the both of us. She made a decent soup but was not a skilled cook, and she had the annoying habit of dumping the silverware on the table in a great crashing pile. One evening, I sat her down before dinner for a little consultation. In my inadequate French, I tried to explain how to arrange a table, how to serve from the

left, how she should take time and care to do things right. No sooner had I commenced my well-intentioned instruction than she broke into sniffles, snorts, and sobs and rushed upstairs murmuring tragic French phrases. I followed her up there and tried again. Using my Berlitz-enhanced subjunctive, I explained how I wanted her to enjoy life, to work well but not too hard, and so on. This brought more sobs, tears, and blank stares. Eventually, after a few fits and starts, we got the hang of each other.

It was French law that an employer pay for an employee's Social Security, which worked out to about six to nine dollars every three months; we also paid for Frieda's health insurance. It was a fair system, and we were happy to help her. But I held on to my very mixed feelings about living with domestic help. Part of the problem was that I found I rather enjoyed shopping and homekeeping.

Feeling nesty, I went to Le Bazar de l'Hôtel de Ville, known as "le B.H.V.," an enormous market filled with aisle upon aisle of cheaply made merchandise. It took me two hours just to walk around and get my bearings. Then I bought pails, dishpans, brooms, soap rack, funnel, light plugs, wire, bulbs, and garbage cans. I filled the back of the Flash with my loot, drove it to 81, then returned to le B.H.V. for more. I even bought a new kitchen stove for ninety dollars. On another jaunt, I loaded up with a frying pan, three big casserole dishes, and a potted flower.

Paris was still recovering from the war, and coffee rations ran out quickly, cosmetics were expensive, and decent olive oil was as precious as a gem. We didn't have an icebox, and like most Parisians just stuck our milk bottles out the window to keep cool. Luckily, we had brought plates, silver, linen, blankets, and ashtrays with us from the States, and we were able to shop for American goods at the embassy PX.

I made up a budget, but immediately grew depressed. Paul's salary was $95 a week. After I'd divided our fixed costs into separate envelopes—$4 for cigarettes, $9 for auto repairs and gas, $10 for insurance, magazines, and charities, and so forth—we'd have about $15 left for clothes, trips, and amusements. It wasn't much. We were trying to live like civilized people on a government salary, which simply wasn't possible. Fortunately, I had a small amount of family money that produced a modest income, although we were determined to save it.

PAUL'S FIRST USIS EXHIBIT—a series of photographs, maps, and text explaining the Berlin Airlift—was hung in the window of the TWA office on the Champs-Élysées. It proved very popular with passersby. In the meantime, he was feeling his way slowly through the embassy bureaucracy, taking care not to step on people's toes or Achilles' heels.

His French staff was increased to ten, and by all accounts they loved "M'sieur Scheeld." But his American colleagues were not quite sure what to make of my husband. Paul was a very accomplished exhibits man, took great pride in a job well done, and knew the importance of establishing reliable channels of communication ("the channels, the *channels*," he'd mutter). But he wasn't professionally ambitious. For those who cared about vaulting up the career ladder, having lunch or socializing with the right people was terribly important; Paul often had a sandwich alone with his camera on the banks of the Seine. Or he'd come home for leftovers with me—chicken soup, sausages, herring, and warm bread—followed by a brief nap. This habit was probably not good for his career, but that wasn't the point. We were enjoying life together in Paris.

Paul *was* ambitious for his painting and photography, which he did on evenings or weekends, but even those ambitions were more aesthetic than commercial. He was a physical person, a black belt in judo, a man who loved to tie complicated knots or carve a piece of wood. Naturally, he would have loved recognition as an Important Artist. But his motivation for making paintings and photographs wasn't fame or riches: his pleasure in the act of creating, "the thing itself," was reward enough.

Understaffed, running out of film, and facing a raft of promises unkept by the State Department, Paul was forced to cancel an early-winter vacation in order to cover for others at the embassy. In the meantime, I had volunteered to create a cataloguing system for the USIS's fifty thousand orphaned photographs. I had done similar file-work during the war, but this was a real struggle. Not only was cross-referencing all of the prints close to impossible, I was trying to design an idiot-proof system for other people—*French* people—to use. In the hope of finding a standard approach to cataloguing, I visited five big photo libraries, only to discover that no standard existed. Photo cataloguing in France was generally left to ladies who'd been doing the job for thirty years and could recognize every print by its smell or something.

OUR DOMESTIC CIRCLE was completed when we were adopted by a *poussiequette* we named Minette (Pussy). We assumed she was a mutt, perhaps a reformed alley cat—a sly, gay, mud-and-cream-colored little thing. I had never been much of an animal person, although we'd had small dogs in Pasadena. But Paul and Charlie liked cats and were devoted to the briard, a wonderfully woolly, slobbery French sheepdog they referred to as "the Noblest Breed of All." (We'd had one in Washington—Maquis—who had died tragically young by choking on a sock.)

"Mini" soon became an important part of our lives. She liked to sit in Paul's lap during meals, and paw tidbits off his plate when she thought he wasn't looking. She spent a great deal of time playing with a brussels sprout tied to a string, or peering under our radiators with her tail switching. Once in a while, she'd proudly present us with a mouse. She was my first cat ever, and I thought she was marvelous. Soon I began to notice cats everywhere, lurking in alleys or sunning themselves on walls or peering down at you from windows. They were such interesting, independent-minded creatures. I began to equate them with Paris.

IV. ALI-BAB

PAUL AND I were intent on meeting French people, but that was not as easy as one might think. For one thing, Paris was crawling with Americans, most of them young, and they liked to cling together in great expat flocks. We knew quite a few of these Yanks, and liked them well enough, but as time went on, I found that they grew less and less interesting to me—and I, no doubt, to them. There were two ladies from Los Angeles, for instance, whom I once considered "just wonderful," and who lived not far from us on the Left Bank, but who completely faded from my life within a few months. This wasn't an intentional separation from my past—it was just the natural evolution of things.

Upon departing the States we'd been given many letters of introduction to friends-of-friends we "must meet." But we were so busy, and so excited, that it took a long time to get to the list. Plus we didn't have a telephone.

You forget how much you rely on something as simple as a phone until you don't have one. After we'd moved into 81, we had placed an order for a phone, and waited. First a man came by to see if we lived where we said we did. Then two men visited to make a "study" of our situation. Then another man appeared to find out if we *really* wanted a phone. The process was very French, and made me laugh, especially when I thought of how quickly such a transaction would have taken place in the States. In the meantime, I was making phone calls at the post office, the PTT ("Postes, Télégraphes et Téléphones"), where there were only two pay phones, and one could only buy one *jeton*, or token, at a time. It took hours to make a three-minute call, but I enjoyed it because I was able to practice my French on the two ladies at the counter. They were curious about how things were done in America, and filled me in on all the local gossip about who had done what during the war, how *la grippe* (the flu) was spreading like wildfire, and where to find the best prices in the *quartier*.

When we finally did get to calling on our friends-of-friends, one of the first couples we met was Hélène and Jurgis Baltrusaitis. He was a taciturn, inward-looking Lithuanian art historian who had just returned from a sabbatical year at Yale and New York University. Hélène was an outgoing enthusiast, the stepdaughter of Henri Foçillon, a famed art historian who had been Jurgis's mentor. They had a fourteen-year-old boy named Jean, who distressed his parents by madly chewing American bubble gum. We hit it off immediately, especially with dear Hélène, who was a "swallow-life-in-big-gulps" kind of person. Whereas Jurgis saw Sunday as an opportunity to burrow deeply into his books,

Hélène couldn't wait to join Paul and me for a jaunt through the countryside.

One December Sunday, the three of us drove out to the Fontainebleau forest. The cloudy gray sky broke open and turned blue, the air was vigorously cool, and the sun shone brightly. After an hour or so of hiking, we broke out a picnic basket brimming with sausages, hardboiled eggs, baguettes, pâtisseries, and a bottle of Moselle wine. We ate lying against twisted gray rocks covered with emerald-green moss. Except for the yawping crows in the beech trees, we were the only ones in that enchanted place. On the way home, we stopped in the little town of Étampes. At a café next to a twelfth-century church, a mob of locals, all red in the face from wine, were celebrating something with expansive singing in hoarse, quavering voices. It was a lovely scene.

The longer I was in France, the stronger and more ecstatic my feel-

ings for it became. I missed my family, of course, and things like certain cosmetics or really good coffee. But the U.S. seemed like an increasingly distant and dreamlike place.

The Baltrusaitises—the Baltrus—introduced us to *le groupe Focillon:* fifteen or twenty art historians, many of whom had been disciples of Hélène's stepfather. They met once a week *chez* Baltru for wine, a nibble of something, and impassioned debate over, say, whether or not a certain false transept in a certain church was built *before* or *after* 1133. Regulars at these meetings included Louis Grodecki, a violently opinionated Pole, and Verdier, a smooth and witty Frenchman, who were constantly attacking and counterattacking each other over medieval arcana; Jean Asche, a husky former Resistance hero who'd been captured and sent to Buchenwald by the Nazis, and whose wife, Thérèse, became a dear friend of mine; and Bony, a university lecturer. It was a sociable, intellectually vigorous, and very French circle—exactly the sort of friends Paul and I had been hoping to find, but would never have discovered on our own.

Among all of these accomplished art historians, Paul was the only practicing artist. He had learned stained-glass making in the 1920s, when he'd worked on the windows at the American Church in Paris. Although he suffered terrible vertigo, he had forced himself to climb high into the eaves to work on some of the trickiest windows, thereby earning the nickname Tarzan of the Apse. To show his appreciation for *le groupe Focillon*, Paul designed a stained-glass medallion, about ten inches round, showing each of the group's members in a symbolic pose. It was a characteristic gesture, one that helped us gain quick acceptance into this unusual group.

SURROUNDED BY GORGEOUS FOOD, wonderful restaurants, and a kitchen at home—and an appreciative audience in my husband— I began to cook more and more. In the late afternoon, I would wander along the quay from the Chambre des Députés to Notre Dame, poking my nose into shops and asking the merchants about everything. I'd bring home oysters and bottles of Montlouis–Perle de la Touraine, and would then repair to my third-floor *cuisine*, where I'd whistle over the stove and try my hand at ambitious recipes, such as veal with turnips in a special sauce.

But I had so much more to learn, not only about cooking, but about shopping and eating and all the many new (to me) foods. I hungered for more information.

It came, at first, from Hélène, my local guide and language coach. She was a rather knowing instructor, and soon I began to use her French slang and to see Paris as she saw it. Although she wasn't very interested in cooking, Hélène loved to eat and knew a lot about restaurants. One day she loaned me a great big old-fashioned cookbook by the famed chef Ali-Bab. It was a real *book:* the size of an unabridged dictionary, printed on thick paper, it must have weighed eight pounds. It was written in old French, and was out of print, but was full of the most succulent recipes I'd ever seen. And it was also very amusingly written, with little asides about cooking in foreign lands and an appendix on why gourmets are fat. Even on sunny days, I'd retreat to my bed and read Ali-Bab—"with the passionate devotion of a fourteen-year-old boy to *True Detective* stories," Paul noted, accurately.

I had worked on my French diligently, and was able to read better and say a little more every day. At first my communications in the marketplace had consisted of little more than finger-pointing and simplistic grunts: "*Bon! Ça! Bon!*" Now when I went to L'Olivier, the olive-oilery on the Rue de Rivoli—a small shop filled with crocks of olives and bottles of olive oil—I could actually carry on a lengthy conversation with the jolly olive man.

My tastes were growing bolder, too. Take snails, for instance. I had never thought of eating a *snail* before, but, my, tender escargots bobbing in garlicky butter were one of my happiest discoveries! And truffles, which came in a can, and were so deliciously musky and redolent of the earth, quickly became an obsession.

I shopped at our neighborhood marketplace on la Rue de Bourgogne, just around the corner from 81. My favorite person there was the vegetable woman, who was known as Marie des Quatre Saisons because her cart was always filled with the freshest produce of each season. Marie was a darling old creature, round and vigorous, with a crease-lined face and expressive, twinkling eyes. She knew everyone and everything, and she quickly sized me up as a willing disciple. I bought mushrooms or turnips or zucchini from her several times a week; she taught me all about shallots, and how to tell a good potato from a bad one. She took great pleasure in instructing me about which vegetables were best to eat, and when; and how to prepare them correctly. In the meantime, she'd fill me in on so-and-so's wartime experience, or where to get a watchband fixed, or what the weather would be tomorrow. These informal conversations helped my French immeasurably, and also gave me the sense that I was part of a community.

We had an excellent *crémerie*, located on the *place* that led into the Rue de Bourgogne. It was a small and narrow store, with room for just five or six customers to stand in, single-file. It was so popular that the line would often extend out into the street. Madame la Proprietress was robust, with rosy cheeks and thick blond hair piled high, and she presided from behind the counter with cheerful efficiency. On the wide wooden shelf behind her stood a great mound of freshly churned, sweet, pale-yellow butter waiting for pieces to be carved as ordered. Next to the mound sat a big container of fresh milk, ready to be ladled out. On the side counters stood the cheese—boxes of Camembert, large hunks of Cantal, and wheels of Brie in various stages of ripeness—some brand-new and almost hard, others soft to the point of oozing.

The drill was to wait patiently in line until it was your turn, and then give your order clearly and succinctly. Madame was a whiz at judging the ripeness of cheese. If you asked for a Camembert, she would cock an eyebrow and ask at what time you wished to serve it: would you be eating it for lunch today, or at dinner tonight, or would you be enjoying it a few days hence? Once you had answered, she'd open several boxes, press each cheese intently with her thumbs, take a big sniff, and—*voilà!*—she'd hand you just the right one. I marveled at her ability to calibrate a cheese's readiness down to the hour, and would even order cheese when I didn't need it just to watch her in action. I never knew her to be wrong.

The neighborhood shopped there, and I got to know all the regulars. One of them was a properly dressed maid who shopped in the company of her household's proud, prancing black poodle. I saw her on a regular basis, and she was always dressed in formless gray or brown clothes. But one day I noticed that she had arrived without the poodle and dressed in a new, trim black costume. I could see the eyes of everyone in line shifting to observe her. As soon as Madame spotted the new finery, she summoned the maid to the front of the line and served her with great politesse. When she swept by me and out the door with a slight Mona Lisa smile on her lips, I asked my neighbor in line why the maid had been given such deferential treatment.

"She has a new job," the woman explained, with a knowing look. "She works for *la comtesse*. Did you see how she's dressed today? Now she's practically a *comtesse* herself!"

I laughed, and as I approached Madame to give my order, I thought: "So much for the French Revolution."

IN MID-DECEMBER, a little snow flurry sugared the cobblestones, and Paul and I were struck by the almost total lack of holiday commercialism in the streets. Occasionally you'd see a man dragging a fir tree across the Place de la Concorde, a sprig of holly over a doorway, or kids lined up in front of a department store watching the animated figures. But in comparison with the crass Christmas ballyhoo in Washington or Los Angeles, Paris was wonderfully calm and picturesque.

We shared Christmas Day with the Mowrers. They were a good deal older and wiser than me, and I thought of them as semi-parental figures. Their big news was that Bumby Hemingway was engaged to marry a tall Idaho girl named Byra "Puck" Whitlock.

PARIS WAS WONDERFULLY WALKABLE. There wasn't much car traffic, and one could easily hike from the Place de la Concorde to the top of Montmartre in a half-hour. We carried a pocket-sized map-book with a brown cover called *Paris par Arrondissement*, and would intentionally wander off the beaten path. Paul, the mad photographer, always carried his trusty camera slung over his shoulder and had a small sketchpad stuffed in his pocket. I discovered that when one follows the artist's eye one sees unexpected treasures in so many seemingly ordinary scenes. Paul loved to photograph architectural details, café scenes, hanging laundry, market women, and artists along the Seine. My job was to use my height and long reach to block the sun over his camera lens as he carefully composed a shot and clicked the shutter.

In our wanderings we had discovered La Truite, the restaurant owned by the cousins of the Dorins who ran La Couronne in Rouen. La Truite was a cozy place off le Faubourg Saint-Honoré, behind the American embassy. The chef was Marcel Dorin, a distinguished old-schooler, assisted by his son. They did a splendid roast chicken: suspended on a string, the bird twirled in front of a glowing electric grill;

every few minutes, a waiter would give it a spin and baste it with the juices that dripped down into a pan filled with roasting potatoes and mushrooms. Oh, those were such fine, fat, full-flavored birds from Bresse—one taste, and I realized that I had long ago forgotten what *real* chicken tasted like! But La Truite's true glory was its *sole à la normande*, a poem of poached and flavored sole fillets surrounded by oysters and mussels, and napped with a wonder-sauce of wine, cream, and butter, and topped with fluted mushrooms. "Voluptuous" was the word. I had never imagined that fish could be taken so seriously, or taste so heavenly.

One cold afternoon just before New Year's, Paul and I strolled up to the Buttes-Chaumont park. At the top of the hill, by the little Greek temple, we looked back at Sacré-Coeur on Montmartre, now silhouetted through layers of mist by the declining sun. In a little bistro, we warmed ourselves with coffee and stared at the city through dirty windows. Behind Paul's head, a fat white cat slept on a pile of ledgers. Beside me, a large dog made up of many breeds gave a big "Woof!," then settled into a deep snooze. Two little monkeys gobbled peanuts and wrestled furiously over a folding chair, filling the air with clatter and squeals. Three boys played dice at a nearby table. An old man wrote a letter. At the bar, a frowsy blonde gossiped with a horn-rimmed man in a beret. A fat white dog dressed in a green turtleneck waddled by, and the blonde cooed: "*Ah, qu'il est joli, le p'tit chou.*"

v. PROVENCE

"I FEEL IT IS my deep-seated duty to show you the *rest* of France," Paul said one day. And so, at the end of February 1949, he, Hélène, and I drove out of cold, gray Paris down to bright, warm Cannes.

The tone for our trip was set by lunch in Pouilly, four hours out of Paris. Paul had written ahead to Monsieur Pierrat, a well-regarded chef, asking him to fix us "a fine meal." He did. It took us over three hours to work our way through Pierrat's terrines, pâtés, *saucissons*, smoked ham, fish in *sauce américaine, coq-sang, salade verte, fromages, crêpes flambées*—all accompanied by a lovely Pouilly-Fumé 1942. We finished with (and were finished off by) a rich and creamy dessert called *prune*, for which the cheerful chef joined us. It was an extraordinary meal. And by its conclusion we were utterly flooded with a soft, warm, glowing pleasure.

We spent the night in Vienne, and were still so full of Chef Pierrat's lunch that we could only fit a small dinner into our gullets. Our bodies hummed with contentment. Even the Flash seemed to purr.

"*Incroyable! Ravissant!*" we intoned in unison the next day, as vista after gorgeous vista revealed itself. Every field was an explosion of fragrant and colorful bougainvilleas, brooms, mimosas, or daisies. Warm, salty breezes blew off the Mediterranean. There were dramatic rocky cliffs along the coast, snow-topped Alps looming in the background. The air was cool and the sky was brilliant. It was all so beautiful and fragrant that I found my senses were nearly overwhelmed.

Hélène was as gay as a bobolink and an amusing source of art-historical nuggets. Paul—with one large camera, one small camera, and a monocular hung around his body—looked like a veritable American Tourist, as he happily snapped photos left and right. If it wasn't a beautiful castle on a hilltop, then it was bands of sun-filtered mist settling in the peach orchards below. If it wasn't a perfect fourteenth-century stone bridge, then it was a deep valley with a rushing brook bright as quicksilver. We ate *nougat de Montélimar.* We inhaled the smell of sage. We sang "Sur le Pont d'Avignon" as we Flashed under the bridge at Avignon. We sat on a hillside outside of Aix drinking Pouilly. At Miramar, we gathered armfuls of mimosas with the Mowrers, whom we'd met with there. In the evening, we watched the lights of Cannes winking across the darkening water.

This was my first experience of the famous Côte d'Azur, an area that was already close to Paul's heart. It appealed to me deeply, in part because it was reminiscent of southern California, and in part because of its own rugged vitality.

On the return loop to Paris, we crossed over the mountains, and the scenery changed dramatically. Grasse, a hothouse filled with flowers, gave way to great barren limestone ridges, like hardened taffy, and tumbling rivers that were a bright aqua-blue color from the glacial melt. Nestled into hillsides were little towns where every building was made of local stone that had weathered for hundreds of years. After coffee and apéritifs at Castellane, in a deep mountain valley, we climbed up and up into sparkling cold air, the sun beating warm. Crossing Alpine passes, we drove into a world of evergreens and snow, with towns clustered in the mountain cracks like periwinkles. At Grenoble we drove into a dramatic cloud of icy fog, and spent the night in a snug little hotel in Les Abrets.

As we crossed Burgundy the next morning, the Mowrers grew tired of our dawdling and accelerated back to Paris. We were happy to take our time. We passed valley towns whose names sounded like a carillon: Montrachet, Pommard, Vougeot, Volnay, Meursault, Nuits-Saint-Georges, Beaune. The nuns, the wine, the lovely courtyards—there were so many extraordinary things to see, and by the end of the day our cups had filled to the brim. By eight-thirty that night we were back at the Roo de Loo, where we unloaded armloads of mimosas.

SPRING HAD SPRUNG in Paris. In the park on the Île de la Cité, the grass was bright green and alive with new babies, doting grannies, and fussing nannies. Along the river, barges were tied up side-by-side, and their rigging was decorated with drying white sheets and socks. Women sunned and sewed pink underwear. Fishermen dangled their feet in the water and snacked on *moules*. Minette had spring fever. She bolted out the window onto the roof and made gurgling noises, raced up and down the stairs, leapt into my lap then out again, then sat in the middle of the rug gurgling some more. The vet had informed me that she was not a mutt at all, but a rare type of Spanish cat called *le tricolaire*, which pleased me no end. When she started to gobble up our handpicked mimosa, we called her Minette Mimosa McWilliams Child.

In early April, my younger sister, Dorothy, arrived. She stood six foot three to my six-two, and was known in the family as Dort, from our childhood nicknames. She was Dort-the-Wort, or Wortesia, and I was called Julia Pulia, or, in less charitable moments, Juke-the-Puke. (Our brother, John, somehow escaped a nickname.) Dort had just graduated from Bennington, was single, and didn't have any idea of what she wanted to do in life. So I encouraged her to come stay with us in Paris, rent-free. That was an offer that would warm the heart of any red-blooded American girl, and she hopped on the next boat.

Not in the least intimidated by her lack of French, Dort made a big impression on her first day at 81, when, for fun, she picked up the phone and began to call stores: "Bong-joor!" she honked. *"Quelle heure êtes-vous fermé? . . . Mair-ci!"*

Dort was five years younger than me, and fifteen years younger than Paul. She and I weren't all that close, and, to be honest, when she arrived I felt as if I knew Hélène Baltru better than my own flesh and blood. But the longer Dort stayed with us, the closer we became.

Parisians took a shine to "the tall American girl," and my outgoing sister's willingness to do whatever it took to communicate. The results of her efforts were occasionally hilarious. There was, for instance, the day she went to the hairdresser's for a shampoo and a trim and sweetly asked: *"Monsieur, voulez-vous couper mes chevaux avant ou après le champignon?"* The hairdresser looked at her quizzically while the ladies under the hairdryers broke into laughter. What Dort had been trying so earnestly to ask was: "Sir, would you like to cut my hair before or after the shampoo?" But it came out as: "Sir, would you like to cut my horses before or after the mushroom?"

She bought a nifty little Citroën for eleven hundred dollars. It was black, had four seats and a minuscule engine. She loved it, except that on her second day of ownership it got a short circuit at 6:00 p.m., in the middle of the rush hour in the middle of la Place de la Concorde, and tied up traffic in the center of the city. When she finally made it back home that night, poor Dort burst into tears of rage. We calmed her, and assured her that everything would be all right. Our *garagistes* gave the car a once-over, and soon Dorothy was zipping around town, looking for work, and staying out late with the youthful expat crowd.

ON JUNE 25, Bumby Hemingway married Puck Whitlock.

Bumby was twenty-five, short, with a square, muscular body, stiff blond hair, and a clean-cut, outdoorsy look. During the war he had parachuted behind enemy lines for the OSS to form teams of agents, and although the Germans captured him a number of times, he'd always managed to escape. Now he was in Berlin, working for U.S. Army intelligence. The wedding was held in Paris because he didn't have enough

leave-time to fly home. Besides, his mother and stepfather lived there. And it was *Paris.*

Puck was tall, dark, and slim, a strong and attractive Idaho girl, who had once worked for United Airlines. She had been married to Lieutenant Colonel Whitlock, a pilot killed in action over Germany. She and Bumby had met in Sun Valley, Idaho, in 1946, and he had been pursuing her ever since. They hardly knew a soul in Paris, so I acted as her matron of honor, and Paul and Dort escorted people to their seats.

The wedding was held in the American Church, on Rue de Berri, where Paul had made his reputation as Tarzan of the Apse. The officiant was Joseph Wilson Cochran, an American who had married Charlie and Freddie in that very space, in April 1926. It was a perfectly natural and unpompous ceremony, just like the Mowrers themselves. There was quite a crowd at the reception, including the writer Alice B. Toklas—an odd little bird in a muslin dress and a big floppy hat—and Sylvia Beach, owner of the famed Shakespeare & Co. bookstore. (Papa Hemingway did not attend.) The weather was heavenly: clear blue sky with high, wispy clouds, the landscape bright green and yellow, with roses abloom in the Tuileries. By the end of the afternoon, I was thoroughly marinated with strawberries and cherries, champagne, brandy, Monbazillac, Montrachet, and Calvados, and speckled by tidbits of grass.

VI. LE GRAND VÉFOUR

WHEN FRIEDA, our emotional *femme de ménage,* took a job as a concierge in another building, Marie des Quatre Saisons helped us find a replacement. The new girl, Coquette, chased our dust chickens and brightened our giltwork part-time, from eight to eleven every morning. But her real job was with a prince and princess who lived around the corner.

Coquette was very sweet but a little nutty, and in private we referred to her as "Coo-Coo" Coquette. Like Frieda, she was of humble origins, and, not surprisingly, was rather bowled over by the glamorous prince and princess. *La princesse* was no ordinary princess, Coo-Coo breathlessly informed me, but a "double princess," and she was English! The prince, Philippe de B—— (a name pronounced "boy," appropriately), had a château and was the son of a noted scientist. They had four

Pekingese dogs, who were so special and so cute, Coo-Coo said, that they were practically human. "Oh, madame!" she'd sigh, the prince and princess were so noble, so chic, so much a part of the fabulous "*tout Paris*" café set. But the dogs were never walked and made pee-pee all over the apartment. As a result, the apartment smelled like a *poubelle* (garbage bin). And how did the princess react? Well, she would grab anything she could lay her hands on—one of the prince's shirts, a table napkin, a nightgown, or even one of her own silk dresses—to wipe up the mess.

In August, the princess and her dogs left for vacation in Normandy, leaving the prince alone in Paris. This was not a good thing, for he was "*un peu difficile.*" Coo-Coo would prepare him a delicious lunch, but the prince wouldn't appear until 3:00 p.m., after drinking apéritifs at a café all morning with his loutish friends. He complained about the cost of potatoes. He refused to pay the four hundred francs he owed the old woman who sewed up his coat. And when he finally decamped to the château, he neglected to pay Coo-Coo's Social Security and the two thousand francs he owed her in salary. She was mortified. But he was a *prince*. What could she do?

Well, it didn't take long for the neighborhood to get wind of Coo-Coo's dilemma. And then the horrible truth was revealed: the prince and princess owed money all up and down the Rue de Bourgogne. *Alors*, everyone from the vegetable-cart lady to the *tripier* hated them and threw up their hands in horror when their names were mentioned!

When the prince and princess returned from their *vacances*, the situation did not improve. The prince would scrounge up a bit of money, then spend it all on horse races or apéritifs. The princess would "buy" a dress from a leading fashion house, wear it to a big affair, and return it for a refund. It was a *scandale*!

Finally, Coo-Coo had had enough, and rebelled. She suggested to the prince that if he didn't have the money to buy potatoes, or to pay her, he should sell his title, or perhaps the château, to make ends meet. He ignored her. And when the princess treated her with extra insensitivity, Coo-Coo announced she was going to quit. But she didn't. After all, it meant quite a lot to "*les gens*" that she worked for a prince and princess, even if they were cheapskate layabouts. And they owed her quite a lot of back pay, which she was hoping to recoup at least part of. I found it all deeply fascinating.

ONE DAY, Paul and I were exploring the Palais Royal park when we peeked in the windows of a beautiful old-style restaurant tucked into a corner under the arched colonnade at the far end. The dining room was resplendent with gilded decorations, a painted ceiling, cut glass and mirrors, ornate rugs and fine fabrics. It was called Le Grand Véfour. We had unknowingly stumbled onto one of the most famous of the old Parisian restaurants, which had been in business since about 1750. The maître d'hôtel noticed our interest, and waved us in. It was near lunchtime, and though we were hardly used to such elegance, we looked at each other and said, "Why not?"

There weren't many patrons yet, and we were seated in a gorgeous semicircular banquette. The headwaiter laid menus before us, and then the sommelier, an imposing but kindly Bordeaux specialist in his fifties, arrived. He introduced himself with a nod: "Monsieur Hénocq." The restaurant began to fill up, and over the course of the next two hours we had a leisurely and nearly perfect luncheon. The meal began with little shells filled with sea scallops and mushrooms robed in a classically beautiful winy cream sauce. Then we had a wonderful duck dish, and cheeses, and a rich dessert, followed by coffee. As we left in a glow of happiness, we shook hands all around and promised almost tearfully to return.

What remained most vividly with me as we strolled away was the graciousness of our reception and the deep pleasure I'd experienced from sitting in those beautiful surroundings. Here we were, two young people obviously of rather modest circumstances, and we had been treated with the utmost cordiality, as if we were honored guests. The service was deft and understated, and the food was spectacular. It was expensive, but, as Paul said, "you are so hypnotized by everything there that you feel grateful as you pay the bill."

We went back to the Véfour every month or so after that, especially once we'd learned how to get invited there by wealthy and in-the-know friends. Because I was tall and outgoing and Paul was so knowledgeable about wine and food, Monsieur Hénocq and the Véfour's wait staff always gave us the royal treatment. And that is where we first laid eyes on Grande Dame Colette. The famous novelist lived in an apartment in the Palais Royal, and the Véfour kept a special seat reserved in her name in a banquette at the end of the dining room. She was a short woman

Me looking out the window of the Roo de Loo

with a striking, almost fierce visage, and a wild tangle of gray hair. As she paraded regally through the dining room, she avoided our eyes but observed what was on everyone's plate and twitched her mouth.

VII. *LA MORTE-SAISON*

THE NEWSPAPERS CLAIMED that the summer of 1949 was the worst *sécheresse*, or drought, since 1909. Riverbeds were filled with stones, fields were toasted gold, and the grass was crunchy to walk on. Leaves were drying up on trees, crops of vegetables were destroyed, grapes withered on the vine. With almost no water for hydroelectric power, people began to worry about the price of food in the coming winter. Air-conditioning was nonexistent.

On weekends, everyone headed out of town to cool off in a favorite hidden picnic spot. Many couples used tandem bicycles. The men would sit in front and women in back, usually dressed in matching costumes of, say, blue shorts, red shirt, and white hat. They'd furiously pedal along the highways, sometimes with a baby in a box on the handlebars, or a little dog in a box jiggling on the back fender.

On the Fourth of July, a reception for several thousand was held at the U.S. Embassy, and it seemed that every American in Paris was there, all talking at once. We were surprised to run into five people who we didn't know were living in the city, including our old friends Alice and Dick, who were acting very strange. I felt that Alice, in particular, was snubbing us. I didn't understand why. Perhaps she was miserable. But then she suddenly blurted out how much she loathed the Parisians, whom she considered horrid, mean, grasping, chiseling, and unfriendly in every way. She couldn't wait to leave France, she claimed, and would never return.

Alice's words were still ringing in my ears the next morning, when I went marketing and suffered a flat tire, broke a milk bottle, and forgot to bring a basket for my strawberries. Yet every person I met was helpful and sweet, and my nice old fish lady even gave me a free fish-head for Minette.

I was flummoxed and upset by Alice. She was someone I had once considered a good and sympathetic friend, but I just didn't understand her anymore. In contrast to her, I felt a lift of pure happiness every time I looked out the window. I had come to the conclusion that I must really *be* French, only no one had ever informed me of this fact. I loved the people, the food, the lay of the land, the civilized atmosphere, and the generous pace of life.

AUGUST IN PARIS was known as *la morte-saison,* "the dead season," because everybody who could possibly vacate did so as quickly as possible. A great emptying out of the city took place, as hordes migrated toward the mountains and coasts, with attendant traffic jams and accidents. Our favorite restaurants, the creamery, the meat man, the flower lady, the newspaper lady, and the cleaners all disappeared for three weeks. One afternoon I went into Nicolas, the wine shop, to buy some wine and discovered that everyone but the deliveryman had left town. He was minding the store, and in the meantime was studying voice in the hope of landing a role at the opera. Sitting next to him was an old concierge who, twenty-five years earlier, had been a seamstress for one

of the great couturiers on la Place Vendôme. She and the deliveryman reminisced about the golden days of Racine and Molière and the Opéra Comique. I was delighted to stumble in on these two. It seemed that in Paris you could discuss classic literature or architecture or great music with everyone from the garbage collector to the mayor.

On August 15, I turned thirty-seven years old. Paul bought me the *Larousse Gastronomique*, a wonder-book of 1,087 pages of sheer cookery and foodery, with thousands of drawings, sixteen color plates, all sorts of definitions, recipes, information, stories, and gastronomical know-how. I devoured its pages even faster and more furiously than I had Ali-Bab.

By now I knew that French food was *it* for me. I couldn't get over how absolutely delicious it was. Yet my friends, both French and American, considered me some kind of a nut: cooking was far from being a middle-class hobby, and they did not understand how I could possibly enjoy doing all the shopping and cooking and serving by myself. Well, I did! And Paul encouraged me to ignore them and pursue my passion.

I had been cooking in earnest at Roo de Loo, but something was missing. It was no longer enough for me to salivate over recipes in the *Larousse Gastronomique*, or chat with Marie des Quatre Saisons, or sample my way through the menus of wonderful restaurants. I wanted to roll up my sleeves and dive into French cuisine. But how?

Out of curiosity, I dropped by L'École du Cordon Bleu, Paris's famous cooking school. There professional chefs taught traditional French cooking to serious students from all over the world. After attending a demonstration one afternoon, I was hooked.

The next class began in October. I signed myself up for a six-week intensive course, and smacked my lips in anticipation of the great day.

CHAPTER 2

Le Cordon Bleu

1. CHEF BUGNARD

AT 9:00 A.M. on Tuesday, October 4, 1949, I arrived at the École du Cordon Bleu feeling weak in the knees and snozzling from a cold. It was then that I discovered that I'd signed up for a yearlong Année Scolaire instead of a six-week intensive course. The Année cost $450, which was a serious commitment. But after much discussion, Paul and I agreed that the course was essential to my well-being and that I'd plunge ahead with it.

My first cooking class was held in a sunny kitchen on the building's top floor. My classmates were an English girl and a French girl of about my age, neither of whom had done any cooking at all. (To my great surprise, I'd discovered that many Frenchwomen didn't know how to cook any better than I did; quite a lot of them had no interest in the subject whatsoever, though most were expert at eating in restaurants.) This "housewife" course was so elementary that after two days I knew it wasn't what I'd had in mind at all.

I sat down with Madame Élizabeth Brassart, the school's short, thin, rather disagreeable owner (she had taken over from Marthe Distel, who had run the school for fifty years), and explained that I'd had a more rigorous program in mind. We discussed my level of cooking knowledge, and her classes on haute cuisine (high-end, professional cooking) and *moyenne cuisine* (middle-brow cooking). She made it quite clear that she didn't like me, or any Americans: "They can't cook!" she said, as if I weren't sitting right in front of her. In any event, Madame Brassart decreed that I was not advanced enough for haute cuisine—a six-week course for experts—but that I'd be suitable for the yearlong "professional restaurateurs" course that had conveniently just begun. This class was taught by Chef Max Bugnard, a practicing professional with years of experience.

"*Oui!*" I said without a moment's hesitation.

At this point I began to really miss my sister-in-law, Freddie Child. We had grown so close in Washington, D.C., that when people said, "Here come the twins," they meant me and Freddie, not Paul and Charlie. She was an excellent, intuitive cook, and, to scare our husbands, we'd joke about opening a restaurant called "Mrs. Child & Mrs. Child, of the Cordon Bleu."

Secretly, I was somewhat serious about this idea, and was trying to convince her to join me at the Cordon Bleu. But she couldn't tear her-

Learning to cut a chicken with Chef Bugnard

self away from her husband and three children in Pennsylvania. *Eh bien*, so I would be on my own.

It turned out that the restaurateurs' class was made up of eleven former GIs who were studying cooking under the auspices of the GI Bill of Rights. I never knew if Madame Brassart had placed me with them as a form of hazing or merely because she was trying to squeeze out a few more dollars, but when I walked into the classroom the GIs made me feel as if I had invaded their boys' club. Luckily, I had spent most of the war in male-dominated environments and wasn't fazed by them in the least.

The eleven GIs were very "GI" indeed, like genre-movie types: nice, earnest, tough, basic men. Most of them had worked as army cooks during the war, or at hot-dog stands in the States, or they had fathers who were bakers and butchers. They seemed serious about learning to cook, but in a trade-school way. They were full of entrepreneurial ideas about setting up golf driving-ranges with restaurants attached, or roadhouses, or some kind of private trade in a nice spot back home. After a few days in the kitchen together, we became a jolly crew, though in my cold-eyed view there wasn't an artist in the bunch.

In contrast to the housewife's sun-splashed classroom upstairs, the restaurateurs' class met in the Cordon Bleu's basement. The kitchen was medium-sized, and equipped with two long cutting tables, three stoves with four burners each, six small electric ovens at one end, and an icebox at the other end. With twelve pupils and a teacher, it was hot and crowded down there.

The saving grace was our professor, Chef Bugnard. What a gem! Medium-small and plump, with thick round-framed glasses and a waruslike mustache, Bugnard was in his late seventies. He had been *dans le métier* most of his life: starting as a boy at his family's restaurant in the countryside, he had done *stages* at various good restaurants in Paris, worked in the galleys of transatlantic steamers, and refined his technique under the great Escoffier in London for three years. Before the Second World War, he owned a restaurant, Le Petit Vatel, in Brussels. The war cost him Le Petit Vatel, but he had been recruited to the Cordon Bleu by Madame Brassart, and obviously loved his role as *éminence grise* there. And who wouldn't? The job allowed him to keep regular hours and spend his days teaching students who relished his every word and gesture.

Because there was so much new information to take in every day, it was confusing at first. All twelve of us cut vegetables, stirred the pots, and asked questions at once. Most of the GIs struggled to follow Bugnard's rat-a-tat delivery, which made me glad that I had developed my language skills before launching into cooking. Even so, I had to keep my ears open and make sure to ask questions, even if they were dumb questions, when I didn't understand something. I was never the only one confused.

Bugnard set out to teach us the fundamentals. We began making sauce bases—*soubise, fond brun, demi-glace,* and *madère.* Later, to demonstrate a number of techniques in one session, Bugnard would cook a full meal, from appetizer to dessert. So we'd learn about, say, the proper preparation of crudités, a fricassee of veal, glazed onions, *salade verte,* and several types of *crêpes Suzettes.* Everything we cooked was eaten for lunch at the school, or sold.

Despite being overstretched, Bugnard was infinitely kind, a natural if understated showman, and he was tireless in his explanations. He drilled us in his careful standards of doing everything the "right way." He broke down the steps of a recipe and made them simple. And he did so with a quiet authority, insisting that we thoroughly analyze texture and flavor: "But how does it *taste,* Madame Scheeld?"

One morning he asked, "Who will make *oeufs brouillés* today?"

The GIs were silent, so I volunteered for scrambled-egg duty. Bugnard watched intently as I whipped some eggs and cream into a froth, got the frying pan very hot, and slipped in a pat of butter, which hissed and browned in the pan.

"*Non!*" he said in horror, before I could pour the egg mixture into the pan. "That is absolutely wrong!"

The GIs' eyes went wide.

With a smile, Chef Bugnard cracked two eggs and added a dash of salt and pepper. "Like *this,*" he said, gently blending the yolks and whites together with a fork. "Not too much."

He smeared the bottom and sides of a frying pan with butter, then gently poured the eggs in. Keeping the heat low, he stared intently at the pan. Nothing happened. After a long three minutes, the eggs began to thicken into a custard. Stirring rapidly with the fork, sliding the pan on and off the burner, Bugnard gently pulled the egg curds together— "Keep them a little bit loose; this is very important," he instructed.

"*Now* the cream or butter," he said, looking at me with raised eyebrows. "This will stop the cooking, you see?" I nodded, and he turned the scrambled eggs out onto a plate, sprinkled a bit of parsley around, and said, "*Voilà!*"

His eggs were always perfect, and although he must have made this dish several thousand times, he always took great pride and pleasure in this performance. Bugnard insisted that one pay attention, learn the correct technique, and that one enjoy one's cooking—"Yes, Madame Scheeld, *fun!*" he'd say. "Joy!"

It was a remarkable lesson. No dish, not even the humble scrambled egg, was too much trouble for him. "You never forget a beautiful thing that you have made," he said. "Even after you eat it, it stays with you— *always.*"

I was delighted by Bugnard's enthusiasm and thoughtfulness. And I began to internalize it. As the only woman in the basement, I was careful to keep up an appearance of sweet good humor around "the boys," but inside I was cool and intensely focused on absorbing as much information as possible.

As the weeks of cooking classes wore on, I developed a rigid schedule.

Every morning, I'd pop awake at 6:30, splash water across my puffy face, dress quickly in the near dark, and drain a can of tomato juice. By 6:50 I was out the door as Paul was beginning to stir. I'd walk seven blocks to the garage, jump into the Blue Flash, and roar up the street to Faubourg Saint-Honoré. There I'd find a parking spot and buy one French and one U.S. newspaper. I'd find a warm café, and would sip café-au-lait and chew on hot fresh croissants while scanning the papers with one eye and monitoring the street life with the other.

At 7:20 I'd walk two blocks to school and don my "uniform," an ill-fitting white housedress and a blue chef's apron with a clean dish towel tucked into the waist cord. Then I'd select a razor-sharp paring knife and start to peel onions while chitchatting with the GIs.

At 7:30 Chef Bugnard would arrive, and we'd all cook in a great rush until 9:30. Then we'd talk and clean up. School let out at about 9:45, and I would do a quick shop and zip home. There I'd get right back to cooking, trying my hand at relatively simple dishes like cheese tarts, *coquilles Saint-Jacques*, and the like. At 12:30 Paul would come home for lunch, and we'd eat and catch up. He'd sometimes take a quick catnap, but more often would rush back across the Seine to put out the latest brushfire at the embassy.

At 2:30 the Cordon Bleu's demonstration classes began. Typically, a visiting chef, aided by two apprentices, would cook and explain three or four dishes—demonstrating how to make, say, a *soufflé au fromage*, decorate a *galantine de volaille*, prepare *épinards à la crème*, and end with a finale of *charlotte aux pommes*. The demonstration chefs were businesslike and did not waste a lot of time "warming up" the class. They'd start right in at 2:30, giving the ingredients and proportions, and talking us through each step as they went. We'd finish promptly at 5:00.

The demonstrations were held in a big square room with banked seats facing a demonstration kitchen up on a well-lit stage. It was like a teaching hospital, where medical interns sat watching in an amphitheater while the famous surgeon—or, in our case, chef—demonstrated how to amputate a leg—or make a cream sauce—onstage. It was an effective way of delivering a lot of information quickly, and the chefs demonstrated technique and took questions as they went. The afternoon sessions were open to anyone willing to pay three hundred francs. So, aside from the regular Cordon Bleu students, the audience was filled with housewives, young cooks, old men, strays off the street, and the odd gourmet or two.

We learned all sorts of dishes—*perdreaux en chartreuse* (roasted partridges placed in a mold decorated with savory cabbage, beans, and julienned carrots and turnips); *boeuf bourguignon*; little fish *en lorgnette* (a pretty dish in which the fish's backbone is cut out, the body is rolled up to the head, and then the whole is deep-fried in boiling fat); chocolate ice cream (made with egg yolks); and cake icing (made with sugar boiled to a viscous consistency, beaten into egg yolks, then beaten with softened butter and flavorings to make a wonderfully thick icing).

All of the demonstration teachers were good, but two stood out.

Pierre Mangelatte, the chef at Restaurant des Artistes, on la Rue Lepic, gave wonderfully stylish and intense classes on *cuisine traditionnelle*: quiches, *sole meunière*, *pâté en croûte*, trout in aspic, ratatouille, *boeuf en daube*, and so on. His recipes were explicit and easy to understand. I scribbled down copious notes, and found them easy to follow when I tried the recipes later at home.

The other star was Claude Thilmont, the former pastry chef at the Café de Paris, who had trained under Madame Saint-Ange, the author of that seminal work for the French home cook, *La Bonne Cuisine de Madame E. Saint-Ange.* With great authority, and a pastry chef's characteristic attention to detail, Thilmont demonstrated how to make puff pastry, pie dough, brioches, and croissants. But his true forte was special desserts—wonderful fruit tarts, layer cakes, or showstoppers like a *charlotte Malakoff.*

I was in pure, flavorful heaven at the Cordon Bleu. Because I had already established a good basic knowledge of cookery on my own, the classes acted as a catalyst for new ideas, and almost immediately my cooking improved. Before I'd started there, I would often put too many herbs and spices into my dishes. But now I was learning the French tradition of extracting the full, essential flavors from food—to make, say, a roasted chicken taste really *chickeny.*

It was a breakthrough when I learned to glaze carrots and onions at the same time as roasting a pigeon, and how to use the concentrated vegetable juices to fortify the pigeon flavor, and vice versa. And I was so inspired by the afternoon demonstration on *boeuf bourguignon* that I went right home and made the most delicious example of that dish I'd ever eaten, even if I do say so myself.

But not everything was perfect. Madame Brassart had crammed too many of us into the class, and Bugnard wasn't able to give the individual attention I craved. There were times when I had a penetrating question to ask, or a fine point that burned inside of me, and I simply wasn't able to make myself heard. All this had the effect of making me work even harder.

I had always been content to live a butterfly life of fun, with hardly a care in the world. But at the Cordon Bleu, and in the markets and restaurants of Paris, I suddenly discovered that cooking was a rich and layered and endlessly fascinating subject. The best way to describe it is to say that I fell in love with French food—the tastes, the processes, the history, the endless variations, the rigorous discipline, the creativity, the wonderful people, the equipment, the rituals.

I had never taken anything so seriously in my life—husband and cat excepted—and I could hardly bear to be away from the kitchen.

What fun! What a revelation! How terrible it would have been had Roo de Loo come with a good cook! How magnificent to find my life's calling, at long last!

"Julie's cookery is actually improving," Paul wrote Charlie. "I didn't quite believe it would, just between us, but it really *is*. It's simpler, more classical. . . . I envy her this chance. It would be such *fun* to be doing it at the same time with her."

My husband's support was crucial to keeping my enthusiasm high, yet, as a "Cordon Bleu Widower," he was often left to his own devices. Paul joined the American Club of Paris, a group of businessmen and government officers who met once a week for lunch. Here he met a pump engineer who introduced him to another, smaller group of American men who were wine aficionados. Frustrated that most of our countrymen never bother to learn about even a fraction of the good French vintages, the members of this group pooled their resources and enlisted Monsieur Pierre Andrieu—a *commandeur* de la Confrérie des Chevaliers du Tastevin (a leading wine-and-food group) and author of *Chronologie Anecdotique du Vignoble Français*—to explain the wines of each region, answer oenological questions, and advise them on how to pair specific vintages to foods.

Every six weeks or so, the men would meet at a notable restaurant— Lapérouse, Rôtisserie de la Reine Pédauque, La Crémaillère, Prunier— to eat well and drink five or six wines from a given region. Occasionally they went on outings, such as the time they went to the Clos de Vougeot château, in Burgundy, and went through practically all the *caves* of the Côte d'Or. Paul especially liked this group because it had no formal membership, no leader, no name, and no dues. Each meal cost six dollars, which covered food, wine, and tip—and must have been one of the greatest deals in the history of gastronomy.

II. NEVER APOLOGIZE

BY EARLY NOVEMBER 1949, the gutters were full of wet brown leaves, the air had turned cold, and, now that it was too late to benefit the poor parched farmers, we were spattered with rain almost every day. Then it turned really cold. Luckily, Paul had just bought a new gas radiator for 81. We'd turn the gas up to full blast and sit practically on top of the heater to keep warm in our crazy *salon*, like a couple of frozen monarchs.

Paris was exploding with every kind of exhibit, exhibition, and exposition you could think of—the Salon d'Automne, the automobile show, the Ballet Russe, the Arts, Fruits & Fleurs display, and so on and on.

Paris in the cold

Thérèse Asche and I took a trot through the annual art show in the Palais de Chaillot, and after forty minutes on the cement floor in those drafty galleries our lips had turned blue and our teeth were chattering. We ran out of there and downed a couple of hot grogs to act as antifreeze.

Later, Hélène Baltru reinforced our suspicions that the wet Parisian cold was especially bone-chilling. During the German occupation, she said, Parisians rated their miseries as: first, and worst, the Gestapo; second, the cold; third, the constant hunger.

Hélène's war story made me think about the French and their deep hunger—something that seemed to lurk beneath their love of food as an art form and their love of cooking as a "sport." I wondered if the nation's gastronomical lust had its roots not in the sunshine of art but in the deep, dark deprivations France had suffered over the centuries.

Paul and I were not deprived, but we were hoarding our francs for the months ahead. After I'd written two politically provocative letters to my father, he had not replied. Instead, he'd deposited five hundred dollars in the bank so that I could buy some decent winter clothes. This put me in a quandary. I was grateful for his help, of course, but did I really want to accept his money? Well, I did. But when Pop offered to help launch Paul "into the big time," we declined politely but firmly.

November 3, 1949, marked our one-year anniversary in Paris. There was a slashing rainstorm that day, just as there had been a year earlier. Looking back, it had been a year of growth. Paul's personality had enlarged, he'd gained further wisdom, if not salary, and he had continued to expand and refine his artistic vision. I had learned to speak French with some degree of success, though I was not yet fluent, and I was making progress in the kitchen. The sweetness and generosity and politeness and gentleness and humanity of the French had shown me how lovely life can be if one takes time to be friendly.

But I was bothered by my lack of emotional and intellectual development. I was not as quick and confident and verbally adept as I aspired to be. This was obvious the night we had dinner with our American friends Winnie and Ed Riley. Winnie was a naturally warm person; Ed was ruggedly attractive, a successful businessman who held strong conservative opinions. When we got into a discussion about the global economy, I got my foot in my backside and ended up feeling confused and defensive. Under pressure from Ed, my "positions" on important questions—

Is the Marshall Plan effectively reviving France? Should there be a European Union? Will socialism take hold in Britain?—were revealed to be emotions masquerading as ideas. This would not do!

Upon reflection, I decided I had three main weaknesses: I was confused (evidenced by a lack of facts, an inability to coordinate my thoughts, and an inability to verbalize my ideas); I had a lack of confidence, which caused me to back down from forcefully stated positions; and I was overly emotional at the expense of careful, "scientific" thought. I was thirty-seven years old and still discovering who I was.

ONE DAY, my sister and I were practicing how to sound French on the telephone so that no one could tell it was us. Dort held her nose with thumb and forefinger pinched over the nostrils, and in a very high, shrill voice said, "*Oui, oui, J'ÉCOUTE!*," just as Parisiennes always did. Minette, who was sleeping on a flowerpot, suddenly shot up, pounced onto Dort's lap, and gave her hand a little love-bite. We thought this was great, so I gave it a try—"*Oui, oui, J'ÉCOUTE!*"—and it had the same thrilling effect on Mini. This led to more laughter and "*J'ÉCOUTE!*"s and love-bites. Our high notes must have plucked a mysterious feline chord of amorous response.

Dort had quickly made friends in the expat community, and had landed a job in the business office of the American Club Theatre of Paris. It was an amateur troupe, run by a tough woman from New York. They performed at the Théâtre Monceau, which held about 150 people. The actors were a high-strung and emotional lot, and Dort faced a good deal of strain and long, poorly paid hours. Paul did not love the troupe, because its members liked to show up at Roo de Loo late at night, make noise, and drink rivers of our booze.

But Dort continued to amuse and amaze us. One evening, her friend Annie arrived at our apartment looking flustered. "I was on the metro, and a man pinched me on the derrière," she said. "I didn't know how to react. What would *you* do?"

"I'd say, '*PardonNEZ, m'sieur!*'" offered Paul.

"I'd kick him in the balls," cracked Annie's boyfriend, Peter.

Dort chimed in: "I'd say, '*Pardonnez, m'sieur,*' and *then* kick him in the balls!"

One day, my sister was driving through the Place de la Concorde in her Citroën when a Frenchman rammed her bumper. It wasn't much of a bump, and the man sped off without bothering to see if he'd done any damage. Dort was enraged by the man's callous insensitivity. Lights flashing, horn tooting, engine revving, and tires squealing, she gave chase. Finally, about ten blocks later, she managed to corner the man in front of a *flic* (a cop). Standing up through the Citroën's open sunroof, my six-foot-three-inch, red-cheeked sister pointed a long, trembling finger at the perpetrator and with maximum indignation yelled: *"Ce merde-monsieur a justement craché dans ma derrière!"* Her intended meaning is obvious, but what she said was: "This shit-man just spat out into my butt!"

PAUL LOVED WINE, but as a poor artist in the 1920s he had not been able to afford the good stuff. Now he had discovered the wine merchant Nicolas, who had access to an unusually broad and deep selection of vintages, some of which had been buried during the war, hidden from the hated *boches*. Nicolas had posted a sign in his shop that sternly warned: "Because of the rarity of the wines on this list we'll accept orders only for immediate use and *not* for stocking a *cave*. We will reduce orders we think are excessive." Nicolas rated his vintages from "very good" (such as a 1926 bottle of Clos-Haut-Peyraguey, for four hundred francs) to "great" (a 1928 bottle of La Mission Haut-Brion, for six hundred francs) to "very great" (a 1929 bottle of Chambertin Clos de Bèze, for seven hundred francs). I was amused by Nicolas's further notes on "exceptional bottles" (an 1899 Château La Lagune, for eight hundred francs) and *bouteilles prestigieuses* (an 1870 Mouton Rothschild, for fifteen hundred francs). Nicolas himself would deliver the better bottles in a warmed basket one hour before serving time.

Paul admired such attention to detail. An inveterate organizer himself, he used Nicolas's lists as a model to draw up his own elaborate charts of wines, their vintages, and costs, which he and his friends would study for hours.

BY THE END OF November, I was shocked to realize that I'd already been at the Cordon Bleu for seven weeks. I had been having such fun that it had whizzed by in what felt like a matter of days. By this point, I could whip up a pretty good piecrust and was able to make a whole pizza—from a mound of dry flour to hot-out-of-the-oven pie—in thirty minutes flat. But the more you learn the more you realize you don't know, and I felt I had just gotten my foot in the kitchen door. What a tragedy it would have been had I stuck to my original six-week class plan. I'd have learned practically nothing at all.

One of the best lessons I absorbed there was how to do things simply. Take roast veal, for example. Under the tutelage of Chef Bugnard, I simply salt-and-peppered the veal, wrapped it in a thin salt-pork blanket, added julienned carrots and onions to the pan with a tablespoon of butter on top, and basted it as it roasted in the oven. It couldn't have been simpler. When the veal was done, I'd degrease the juices, add a bit of stock, a dollop of butter, and a tiny bit of water, and reduce for a few minutes; then I'd strain the sauce and pour it over the meat. The result: an absolutely sublime meal.

It gave me a great sense of accomplishment to have learned exactly how to cook such a savory dish, and to be able to replicate it exactly the way I liked, every time, without having to consult a book or think too much.

Chef Bugnard was a wonder with sauces, and one of my favorite lessons was his *sole à la normande.* Put a half-pound of sole fillets in a buttered pan, place the fish's bones on top, sprinkle with salt and pepper and minced shallots. Fill the pan with liquid just covering the fillets: half white wine, half water, plus mussel and oyster juices. Poach. When the fillets are done, keep them warm while you make a roux of butter and flour. Add half of the cooking juices and heat. Take the remaining cooking juices and reduce to almost nothing, about a third of a cup. Add the reduced liquid to the roux and stir over heat. Then comes Bugnard's touch of genius: remove the pan from the fire and stir in one cup of cream and three egg yolks; then work in a mere three-quarters of a pound of butter. I had never *heard* of stirring egg yolks into such a common sauce, but what a rich difference they made.

Oh, *crise de foie,* that French sole was so delicious!

ONCE A WEEK, most *quartiers* in Paris lost their power for a few hours. Paul and I were lucky enough to live next to the Chambre des Députés, and so were spared the blackouts by some kind of special political dispensation. But on most Wednesdays, there was no electricity in the Cordon Bleu's quarter. These powerless Wednesdays forced Chef Bugnard to be creative with our classtime. Often he'd take us to the market, an experience that was worthy of a graduate degree unto itself.

Indeed, shopping for food in Paris was a life-changing experience for me. It was through daily excursions to my local marketplace on la Rue de Bourgogne, or to the bigger one on la Rue Cler, or, best of all, into the organized chaos of Les Halles—the famous marketplace in central Paris—that I learned one of the most important lessons of my life: the value of *les human relations*.

The French are very sensitive to personal dynamics, and they believe that you must earn your rewards. If a tourist enters a food stall thinking he's going to be cheated, the salesman will sense this and obligingly cheat him. But if a Frenchman senses that a visitor is delighted to be in his store, and takes a genuine interest in what is for sale, then he'll just open up like a flower. The Parisian grocers insisted that I interact with them personally: if I wasn't willing to *take the time* to get to know them and their wares, then I would not go home with the freshest legumes or cuts of meat in my basket. They certainly made me work for my supper—but, oh, what suppers!

One Wednesday, Chef Bugnard took us to Les Halles in search of provisions for upcoming classes: liver, chickens, beef, vegetables, and candied violets. We made our way through a wonderful hodgepodge of buildings, each filled with food stalls and purveyors of cooking equipment. You could find virtually anything under the sun there. As we dodged around freshly killed rabbits and pig trotters, or large men unpacking crates of glistening blue-black mussels and hearty women shouting about their wonderful *champignons*, I avidly jotted down notes about who carried what and where they were located, worried that I'd never be able to find them again in the raucous maze.

Eventually we arrived at Dehillerin. I was thunderstruck. Dehillerin was *the* kitchen-equipment store of all time, a restaurant-supply house stuffed with an infinite number of wondrous gadgets, tools, implements, and gewgaws—big shiny copper kettles, *turbotières*, fish and chicken poachers, eccentrically shaped frying pans, tiny wooden spoons and enormous mixing paddles, elephant-sized salad baskets, all shapes and sizes of knives, choppers, molds, platters, whisks, basins, butter spreaders, and mastodon mashers.

Seeing the gleam of obsession in my eyes, Chef Bugnard took me aside and introduced me to the owner, Monsieur Dehillerin. I asked him all sorts of questions, and we quickly became friends. He even lent me money once, when I had run out of francs shopping at Les Halles and the banks were all closed. He knew I'd repay him, as I was one of his steadiest customers. I had become a knife freak, a frying-pan freak, a gadget freak—and, especially, a copper freak!

"ALL SORTS OF *délices* are spouting out of [Julia's] finger ends like sparks out of a pinwheel," Paul enthused to Charlie. "The other night, for guests, she tried out a dessert she'd seen demonstrated . . . a sort of French-style brown betty . . . which turned out very well."

In spite of my good notices, I remained a long way from being a maître de cuisine. This was made plain the day I invited my friend Winnie for lunch, and managed to serve her the most vile eggs Florentine one could imagine outside of England. I suppose I had gotten a little too self-confident for my own good: rather than measure out the flour, I had guessed at the proportions, and the result was a goopy *sauce Mornay*. Unable to find spinach at the market, I'd bought chicory instead; it, too, was horrid. We ate the lunch with painful politeness and avoided discussing its taste. I made sure not to apologize for it. This was a rule of mine.

I don't believe in twisting yourself into knots of excuses and explanations over the food you make. When one's hostess starts in with self-deprecations such as "Oh, I don't know how to cook . . . ," or "Poor little me . . . ," or "This may taste awful . . . ," it is so dreadful to have to reassure her that everything is delicious and fine, whether it is or not. Besides, such admissions only draw attention to one's shortcomings (or self-perceived shortcomings), and make the other person think, "Yes, you're right, this really *is* an awful meal!" Maybe the cat has fallen into the stew, or the lettuce has frozen, or the cake has collapsed—*eh bien, tant pis!*

Usually one's cooking is better than one thinks it is. And if the food is truly vile, as my ersatz eggs Florentine surely were, then the cook must simply grit her teeth and bear it with a smile—and learn from her mistakes.

III. THE MAD SCIENTIST

IN LATE 1949, the newspapers informed us that something called "television" was sweeping the States like a hailstorm. People across the country, the papers said, were building "TV rumpus-rooms," complete with built-in bars and plastic stools, in order to sit around for hours watching this magical new box. There were even said to be televisions in buses and on streetcars, and TV advertising in all the subways. It was hard to imagine. There was no TV that we knew of in Paris—we were finding it hard enough to find some decent music on the radio (most of the stations played contemporary stuff, which sounded like music to set the mood on the moors for *The Hound of the Baskervilles*).

When we read an article about the horrifying effects of TV on American home life, we asked Charlie and Freddie if they had bought a television set yet—they hadn't—or if they knew anyone who had—no, again. Did our nieces and nephew feel left out of the gang for not having such a machine? "No . . . for the moment."

IT WAS MID-DECEMBER when Paul wrote his twin:

The sight of Julie in front of her stove full of boiling, frying and sim-mering foods has the same fascination for me as watching a kettle-drummer at the Symphony. (If I don't sit and watch I never see Julie.) . . . Imagine this in your mind's eye: Julie, with a blue denim apron on, a dish towel stuck under her belt, a spoon in each hand, stirring two pots at the same time. Warning bells are sounding off like signals from the podium, and a garlic-flavored steam fills the air with an odoriferous leitmotif. The oven door opens and shuts so fast you hardly notice the deft thrust of a spoon as she dips into a casserole and up to her mouth for a taste-check like a perfectly timed double-beat on the drums. She stands there surrounded by a battery of instruments with an air of authority and confidence. . . .

She's becoming an expert plucker, skinner and boner. It's a wonder-ful sight to see her pulling all the guts out of a chicken through a tiny hole in its neck and then, from the same little orifice, loosening the skin from the flesh in order to put in an array of leopard-spots made of truffles. Or to watch her remove all the bones from a goose without tearing the skin. And you ought to see [her] skin a wild hare—you'd swear she'd just been Comin' Round the Mountain with Her Bowie Knife in Hand.

Paul took to calling the kitchen my "alchemist's aerie," and me "Jackdaw Julie," after the slightly mad bird that collects every kind of stick, trinket, tidbit, and fluff to outfit its nest with. The fact is, I had been making regular raiding trips to Dehillerin to stock up on all manner of culinary tools and machines. Now our kitchen had enough knives to fill a pirate ship. We had copper vessels, terra-cotta vessels, tin vessels, enamel vessels, crockery and porcelain vessels. We had measuring rods, scales, thermometers, timing clocks, openers, bottles, boxes, bags, weights, graters, rolling pins, marble slabs, and fancy extruders. On one side of the kitchen, standing in a row like fat soldiers, were seven Ali Baba–type oil jars filled with basic reductions. On the other side were measurers—for a liter, demiliter, quarter-liter, deciliters, and demideciliters—hanging from hooks. Tucked all round were my specialty tools: a copper sugar-boiler; long needles for larding roasts; an oval tortoise-shelled implement used to scrape a *tamis*; a conical sieve called a *chinois*; little frying pans used only for crêpes; tart rings; stirring paddles carved from maplewood; and numerous heavy copper pot-lids with long iron handles. My kitchen positively gleamed with gadgets. But I never seemed to have quite enough.

One Sunday we went to the Marché aux Puces, the famous flea market on the outer fringes of Paris, in search of something special: a large mortar and pestle used in the preparation of those lovely, light *quenelles de brochet* (a labor-intensive dish made by filleting fish, grinding it up in the big mortar, forcing it through a *tamis* sieve, and then beating in cream over a bowl of ice). The Marché aux Puces was a vast, sprawling market where one could buy just about anything. After several hours of hunting through obscure alleys between packing-box houses in remote corners, I managed by some special *chien-de-cuisine* instinct to run the coveted items to earth. The mortar was made of dark-gray marble, and was about the size and weight of a baptismal font. The pestle looked like a primeval cudgel made from a hacked-off crab-tree limb. One look at it, and I knew there was no question: I just *had* to have that set. Paul looked at me as if I were crazy. But he knew when I was fixated on

something special, and with a shrug and a smile, he pulled out his wallet. Then he took a deep breath, crouched down, and, using every bit of strength and ingenuity, hefted my prize to his shoulder. Staggering back to the Flash with trembling knee and aching lung, he wended his way for miles through the market's narrow, crowded, flea-bitten passageways. As he eased the mega-mortar and pestle into the car, the old Flash positively slumped and wheezed.

Paul was justly proud of his "slave labor," and, a week later, he was rewarded by my first-ever *quenelles de brochet*—delicate, pillowy-light spoonfuls of puréed pike that had been poached in a seasoned broth. Served with a good cream sauce, it was a triumph. In spite of his careful attention to diet, Paul slurped the *quenelles* up hungrily.

I was really getting into the swing of things now. Over a period of six weeks, I made: *terrine de lapin de garenne, quiche Lorraine, galantine de volaille, gnocchi à la Florentine, vol-au-vent financière, choucroute garni à l'Alsacienne, crème Chantilly, charlotte de pommes, soufflé Grand Marnier, risotto aux fruits de mer, coquilles Saint-Jacques, merlan en lorgnette, rouget au safron, poulet sauce Marengo, canard à l'orange,* and *turbot farci braisé au champagne.*

Whew!

Paul's favorite belt was an old leather job that he'd picked up in Asia during the war. In August it was notched at the number-two hole, and he weighed an all-time high of 190 pounds. With great difficulty he forced himself to cut down on his carbohydrates and, most significantly, on his alcohol intake. He also started attending exercise classes, where he'd throw heavy medicine balls around with men half his age. By December, the belt notched right into the number-five hole, indicating a new svelteness of 170 pounds. I admired his self-discipline. Yet, in spite of his robustness, Paul was often plagued by poor health. Some of his problems, such as his sensitive stomach, were the result of amoebic dysentery from the war; others were the result of his jumpy nerves. (His brother never had a physical exam, because he figured Paul would take care of all the worry and ailments; indeed, Charlie hardly ever got sick.)

As boys, Paul and Charlie used to wrestle each other, race, climb steep walls, and generally attempt to outdo one another in feats of derring-do. In quieter moments, the twins invented games with whatever was lying around the house. One of their favorites was the "sewing" game, in which they used a real needle and thread. One day when they were seven years old, Charlie was sewing and Paul leaned over his brother's shoulder to see what he was doing. Just then, the needle came rising up in Charlie's hand and went straight into Paul's left eye. It was a terrible accident. Paul had to wear a black patch for a year, and lost the use of that eye. But he never complained about his handicap, could drive a car perfectly, and learned to paint so well that he taught perspective.

OFF TO ENGLAND for Christmas! We stayed with our friends the Bicknells in Cambridge: Peter was a don of architecture at the university, a mountaineer, and a lovely fellow with a big mustache; Mari was a good cook, had studied ballet with Sadler's Wells, and now taught ballet to children; they had four children, and loved French food. We shared a pre-Christmas feast in the kitchen together, with a menu of *sole bonne femme*, roasted pheasant, *soufflé Grand Marnier*, and great wines—including a Château d'Yquem 1929 with the soufflé.

From there to jolly old London, where we walked and ate all over town, then to Newcastle, and finally to a friend's farm in Hereford. The countryside was poetic, filled with such great trees, cows, hedges, and thatched-roof cottages that I felt compelled to read Wordsworth. But the public food was every bit as awful as our Parisian friends had warned us it would be.

One evening, we stopped at a charming Tudor inn, where we were served boiled chicken, with little feathers sticking out of the skin, partially covered with a typical English white sauce. Aha! At last I would try the infamous sauce that the French were so chauvinistic about. The sauce was composed of flour and water (not even chicken bouillon) and hardly any salt. It was truly horrible to eat, but a wonderful cultural experience.

I admired the English immensely for all that they had endured, and they were certainly honorable, and stopped their cars for pedestrians, and called you "sir" and "madam," and so on. But after a week there, I began to feel wild. It was those ruddy English faces, so held in by duty, the sense of "what is done" and "what is not done," and always swigging tea and chirping, that made me want to scream like a hyena. The Old Sod never laid a haunting melody on me gut strings.

In a way, I felt that I understood England intuitively, because it reminded me of visiting my relatives in Massachusetts, who were much more formal and conformist than I was.

My mother, Caro, with me and John

My mother, Julia Carolyn Weston (Caro), was one of ten children (three of whom died) raised in prosperous surroundings in Dalton, Massachusetts. The Westons could trace their roots back to eleventh-century England, and had lived in Plymouth Colony. Mother's father had founded the Weston Paper Company in Dalton, was a leading citizen in western Massachusetts, and had served as the state's lieutenant governor.

My father's family was of Scottish origin. His father, also called John McWilliams, came from a farming family near Chicago; he left the farm as a sixteen-year-old to pan for gold in California during the covered-wagon days. He invested in California mineral rights and Arkansas rice fields, and retired to Pasadena in the 1890s. He lived to be ninety-three. His wife, Grandmother McWilliams, was a great cook who made delicious broiled chicken and wonderful doughnuts. She was from Illinois farm country, and in the 1880s her family had a French cook—something that was fairly common at the time.

My mother was in the class of 1900 at Smith, where she was captain of the basketball team and was known for her wild red hair, outspoken opinions, and sense of humor. My father—tall, reserved, athletic—graduated in the class of 1901 from Princeton, where he studied history. My parents met in Chicago in 1903 and, after marrying in 1911, settled in Pasadena, where my father took over his father's land-management business. I was born on August 15, 1912; my brother, John McWilliams III, was born in 1914; and Dorothy was born in 1917. As children, we'd occasionally travel east to visit our many aunts, uncles, and cousins in Dalton and Pittsfield, Massachusetts, where I learned about my New England roots.

I was enrolled at Smith College at birth, and eventually graduated from there in 1934, with a degree in history. My upper-middle-brow parents weren't intellectual at all, and I had no exposure to eggheads until the war. At Smith I did some theater, a bit of creative writing, and played basketball. But I was a pure romantic, and only operating with half my burners turned on; I spent most of my time there just growing up. It was during Prohibition and in my senior year a bunch of us piled into my car and drove to a speakeasy in Holyoke. It felt so dangerous and wicked. The speakeasy was on the top floor of a warehouse, and who knew what kind of people would be there? Well, everyone was perfectly nice, and we each drank one of everything, and on the drive home most of us got heartily sick. It was terribly exciting!

My plan after college was to become a famous woman novelist. I moved to New York and shared a tiny apartment with two other girls under the Queensboro Bridge. But when *Time*, *Newsweek*, and *The New Yorker* did not offer me a job, for some reason, I went to work in the advertising department of the W. & J. Sloane furniture store. I enjoyed it, at first, but I was only making twenty-five dollars a week and living in tight, camping-out circumstances. In 1937, I returned to Pasadena, to help my ailing mother; two months later, she died of high blood pressure. She was only sixty.

I kept house for my father, did some volunteer work for the Red Cross, and generally felt like I was drifting. I knew I didn't want to become a standard housewife, or a corporate woman, but I wasn't sure what I *did* want to be. Luckily, Dort had just returned home from Bennington, so, while she watched Pop, I headed east, to Washington, D.C., where I had friends. Then the war broke out, and I wanted to do something to aid my country in a time of crisis. I was too tall for the WACs and WAVES, but eventually joined the OSS, and set out into the world looking for adventure.

I could at times be overly emotional, but was lucky to have the kind of orderly mind that is good at categorizing things. After working on an air-sea rescue unit, where we developed a signal mirror for downed pilots and had a "fish-squeezing" department trying to create a shark repellent, I was posted to Ceylon as the head of the Registry, where I kept files and processed highly secret material from our agents.

As for Paul, he, Charlie, and their sister, Meeda, who was two years older than the twins, were raised in Brookline, Massachusetts, in the countryside outside of Boston. Their father, Charles Tripler Child, was an electrical engineer, who died of typhoid fever in 1902, when the boys were only six months old. Their mother, Bertha Cushing Child, was a concert singer, a theosophist, and a vegetarian. In those days, widows had few opportunities to find decent work, but she was beautiful, had long honey-blond hair and a splendid voice.

There was a tradition of "gentle" entertaining in private homes—poetry readings, lectures, spiritual sessions, and so forth. Paul played the violin and Charlie played the cello; with Meeda on piano, they performed together as "Mrs. Child and the Children." At that time, Brookline swarmed with new Irish, Italian, and Jewish immigrants, and gangs were common. One day, teenage Paul and Charlie, dressed in gray flannel suits (which they loathed) and carrying their instruments, were jumped by a band of thugs as they walked to a recital. But the Child boys had learned judo from the Japanese butler of a friend, and stood their ground. Years later, Charlie wrote: "Swinging our instruments around like clumsy battle-axes and screaming a series of bloodcurdling oaths . . . we went into battle. Twang! went the fiddle on someone's skull. . . . Whomp! went the cello. . . . Like two berserk Samurai . . . we charged into the howling enemy." Paul and Charlie emerged victorious. But when they greeted their mother with ripped suits, bloody noses, and crushed instruments, that was the end of "Mrs. Child and the Children"!

Despite his lack of a college education, I considered Paul an intellectual, in the sense that he had a real thirst for knowledge, was widely

Charlie and Paul

read, wrote poetry, and was always trying to train his mind. We met in Ceylon, in 1944. Paul had come down from Delhi, India, to head the OSS's Visual Presentation group in Kandy, where he created a secret war room and maps of places like the Burma Road, for General Mountbatten.

We were based at a lovely old tea plantation, and I could look out my office window into Paul's office. I was still unformed. He was ten years older than me and worldly; he courted various other women there, but we slowly warmed up to each other. We took trips to places like the Temple of the Tooth, or elephant rides into the bush (one elephant knew how to turn on faucets for a drink of water), and we shared an interest in the local food and customs. Unlike most of the U.S. Army types, our OSS colleagues were a fascinating bunch of anthropologists, geographers, missionaries, psychiatrists, ornithologists, cartographers, bankers, and lawyers. They were genuinely interested in Ceylon and its people. "*Aha!*" I said to myself. "Now, *here's* the kind of person I've been missing my whole life!"

After Ceylon, Paul was assigned to Chungking, then Kunming, China, where he designed war rooms for General Wedemeyer. I was also assigned to Kunming, where I fixed up the OSS files. By this point we were becoming a couple. We loved the earthy Chinese people and their marvelously crowded and noisy restaurants, and we spent a lot of our off-hours exploring different types of regional foods together.

Back in the States after the war, we took a few months to get to know each other in civilian clothes. We visited Pop and his second wife, Phila, in Pasadena, then drove across the country and stayed with Charlie and Freddie in Maine. It was the summer of 1946; I was about to turn thirty-four and Paul was forty-four. After a few days there, we took deep breaths and announced: "We've decided to get married."

"About time!" came the reply from Charlie and Freddie.

In September 1946 we married—extremely happy, but a bit banged up from a car accident the day before.

WHEN PAUL AND I returned to Paris from England to celebrate the new year, 1950, I almost wept with relief and pleasure. Oh, how I *adored* sweet and natural France, with its human warmth, wonderful smells, graciousness, coziness, and freedom of spirit!

Paris was full of specialized things to buy at that time of year. Hermès was one of the best-known shops for "people who have everything." I longed for a few of their famous but frightfully expensive scarves. The store was so chic that I'd only dared to venture inside twice. Even when dressed in my very best clothes and with a lovely hat on, I felt like an old frump in those luxe surroundings.

I *wanted* to look chic and Parisian, but with my big bones and long feet, I did not fit most French clothes. I'd dress in simple, American-made skirts and blouses with a thin sweater and canvas sneakers. Many times, I had to mail-order things from the States, especially if I wanted, say, a smart pair of shoes. One night, my friend Rosie (Rosemary Manell)—another big-boned California girl—and I got dressed up for a fancy party at the U.S. Embassy. We had expensive hairdos, put on our nicest dresses, chicest hats, and best makeup. Then we looked at each other. "Pretty good," we declared, "but not great." We had tried, and this was the very best we'd ever look.

THE CORDON BLEU got back in full swing in the first week of 1950. In thinking about all I had learned since October, I realized that it had taken a full two months of near-total immersion for the teaching to take hold. Or *begin* to take hold, I should say, because the more I learned the more I realized how very much one has to know before one is in-the-know at all.

I could finally see how to cook properly, for the first time in my life. I was learning to take *time*—hours, even—and *care* to present a delicious meal. My teachers were fanatics about detail and would never compromise. Chef Bugnard drilled into me the necessity of proper technique—such as how to "turn" a mushroom correctly—and the importance of practice, practice, practice. "It's *always* worth the effort, Madame Scheeld!" he'd say. "*Goûtez! Goûtez!*" ("Taste! Taste!")

Of course, I made many boo-boos. At first this broke my heart, but then I came to understand that learning how to fix one's mistakes, or live with them, was an important part of becoming a cook. I was beginning to feel *la cuisine bourgeoise* in my hands, my stomach, my soul.

When I wasn't at school, I was experimenting at home, and became a bit of a Mad Scientist. I did hours of research on mayonnaise, for instance, and although no one else seemed to care about it, I thought it was utterly fascinating. When the weather turned cold, the mayo suddenly became a terrible struggle, because the emulsion kept separating, and it wouldn't behave when there was a change in the olive oil or the room temperature. I finally got the upper hand by going back to the beginning of the process, studying each step scientifically, and writing it all down. By the end of my research, I believe, I had written more on the subject of mayonnaise than anyone in history. I made so much mayonnaise that Paul and I could hardly bear to eat it anymore, and I took to dumping my test batches down the toilet. What a shame. But in this way I had finally discovered a foolproof recipe, which was a glory!

I proudly typed it up and sent it off to friends and family in the States, and asked them to test it and send me their comments. All I received in response was a yawning silence. Hm! I had a great many things to say about sauces as well, but if no one cared to hear my insights, then what was the use of throwing perfectly good béarnaise and *gribiche* down a well?

I was miffed, but not deterred. Onward I plunged.

I made the lovely *homard à l'américaine*—a live lobster cut up (it dies immediately), and simmered in wine, tomatoes, garlic, and herbs— twice in four days, and spent almost all of another day getting the recipe for that dish in good shape. I was striving to make my version absolutely exact and clear, which was excellent practice for whatever my future in cooking might be. My immediate plan was to develop enough foolproof recipes so that I could begin to teach classes of my own.

Immersed in cookery, I found that deeply sunk childhood memories had begun to bubble up to the surface. Recollections of the pleasant-but-basic cooking of our hired cooks in Pasadena came back to me—the big hams or gray roast beef served with buttery mashed potatoes. But then, unexpectedly, so did yet deeper memories of more elegant meals prepared in a grand manner by accomplished cooks when I was just a girl—such as wonderfully delicate and sauced fish. As a child I had barely noticed these real cooks, but now their faces and their food suddenly came back to me in vivid detail. Funny how memory works.

IV. FIRST CLASS

THE WALLS ACROSS the street from the Roo de Loo were plastered with screaming yellow posters claiming that the "Imperialistic Americans" were trying to take over the French government: "Strike for Peace!," etc.

So icy was the Cold War now that Paul and I were half convinced that the Russians—"the wily Commies," he called them—would invade Western Europe. He suffered nightmares over the possibility of an all-out nuclear war. He grew snappish at the office, convinced that the busywork that ate up his days was trivial in light of our nation's unpreparedness. I declared that I was ready to man the barricades to defend *la belle France* and her wonderful citizens, like Madame Perrier, Hélène Baltrusaitis, Marie des Quatre Saisons, and Chef Bugnard!

Much of the American press, meanwhile, denounced the French for "just sitting there, doing nothing about the Communists, and looking for appeasement in Indo-China." But this was absurd. France was still in a state of post-war shock: she had lost hundreds of thousands of men during the German occupation, had only minimal industrial production, and had a large and well-organized Communist fifth column to deal with. And now she was mired in a sticky and disheartening war in Indochina. The government of France believed it was "saving the lives of all other non-Communist nations" by fighting for the rice paddies there. But the war was proving expensive and unpopular. In fact, the U.S.A. was furnishing arms to France, which allowed the war to continue and brewed up an anti-American sentiment in the streets. There was a rash of strikes and troubles throughout the country. It was easy for Americans to criticize from afar, but I didn't see what other course of action the French could take: they *had* to muddle through their turmoil, day to day, and hope for the best.

My parents, Big John and Phila, collectively known as "Philapop," were among those who liked to criticize France without any real understanding of the country. Dort and I were determined to change that, and had invited them to visit. Our goal was to show them a bit of the life and

Phila and Pop

people that we found so heartwarming and satisfying. Then we'd tour Italy with them. (Paul didn't want to use his precious vacation time on his in-laws, and I can't say I blamed him.)

When they arrived and settled in at the Ritz, my father looked like *un vieillard*, an old man, which he never used to be. He'd launch into long speeches in English about American business and agriculture, leaving our French friends mystified. He and Phila ate simply so as to avoid any stomach trouble. My sister and I had been prepared for the worst, but Philapop were surprisingly mellow and lovely.

On April 10, the four of us McWilliamses began a slow drive toward Naples. The main French highways were filled with madly driven trucks, and people with their noses buried in their Michelin guides, so we stuck to side roads. As we reached the Mediterranean, we Californians all responded to the colors and palm trees and waves.

But this wasn't real travel, as I saw it. Phila liked to go to all the gay places she'd read about in American magazines, but she didn't really care where we were. Pop was interested in how the French made money, and he preferred the country to cities, but he was stiff in the joints and couldn't walk much, and had zero interest in ruins or culture or food or wine. When we roared past the Roman arch at Orange, he mumbled, "Oh yes, Roman, you say? Hmm."

Dort and I grew restless on those days of driving and driving and eating and driving and eating at the biggest-best restaurants and sleeping at the biggest-best hotels. To hell with it! It seemed like we'd never really *been* anywhere or *done* anything and the whole point of the trip was for Philapop to get back to Pasadena and say, "I've just been through France and Italy." In fact, I didn't like traveling first-class at all. Yes, it was nice to have a bathroom in the hotel and fine service at breakfast, and I'd probably never visit those grand hotels again, but none of it seemed *foreign* enough to me. It was all so pleasantly bland that it felt as if I were back on the SS *America*. I don't like it when everyone speaks perfect English; I'd much rather struggle with my phrase book.

One exception was the Hôtel de Paris, in Monte Carlo. It was an enormous, old-fashioned, ornate building across from the Casino. What a treat! It had a splendid Louis XVI–style dining room, with black-and-white Carrara-marble pillars, gilt molding, Cupids, murals of virginal nudes willowing about forest-glen fountains, splendiferous eighty-foot chandeliers, a string orchestra playing Viennese waltzes, and so on. In detail it sounds insane, but the effect was nostalgic elegance. Our dinner there was superb, and the service—provided by a headwaiter, two sub-headwaiters, two waiters, and a busboy for each table—was faultless. It made us feel as if we had been transported back in time to the Gilded Age.

Italy was nice, with a tremendous shining yacht in the harbor at Portofino, except that the entire coast was still shot up from the war. Even the big Autostrada from Pisa to Florence remained a wreck, with many bridges and overpasses not yet repaired. The country seemed poverty-stricken. The food didn't strike me as anything special, either; it didn't have much finesse. Maybe that's why Italy didn't hit me with the same vibrations that France did. Or maybe it was because I hated being without my husband.

Paul and I liked to travel at the same slow pace. He always knew so much about things, discovered hidden wonders, noticed ancient walls or indigenous smells, and I missed his warm presence. Once upon a time I had been content as a single woman, but now I couldn't stand it!

I really wanted Philapop to enjoy their super-deluxe trip, though, and I was trying my damnedest to be the way they wanted me to be: nice and amenable and dumb, with no thoughts or feelings about anything.

We whizzed through Florence, Rome, Sorrento, Naples, and Lake Como. After thirty minutes at the Pitti Palace, Pop announced he was "educated." The poor man couldn't wait to return to California. "I can't talk to these people, I just poke around the streets," he grumbled. "I'm so happy at home, where I've got my nice house, my friends, and I can talk the language." It struck me how utterly divorced I had become from old Pop and his type—moneyed, materialistic, not at all introspective—and how profoundly, abysmally, stupefyingly apathetic his world-view had rendered me. No wonder I had been so immature at Smith!

When we returned to Paris on May 3, I fell into Paul's arms and squeezed him tight.

BACK AT THE Cordon Bleu, I picked up my routine again, beginning at 6:30 a.m. and ending around midnight every weekday. But I was growing increasingly dissatisfied with the school. The $150 tuition was expensive. Madame Brassart paid little attention to the details of management. Many of the classes were disorganized, and the teachers lacked basic supplies. And after six months of intensive instruction, not one of the eleven GIs in my class knew the proportions for a *béchamel* sauce or how to clean a chicken the right way. They just weren't serious, and that irritated me.

Even Chef Bugnard was beginning to repeat such dishes as *sole normande*, *poulet chaud-froid*, omelettes, and *crêpes Suzettes*. It was useful practice to do these dishes over and over, and at last I could make a decent piecrust without thinking twice. But I wanted to be pushed harder and further. There was so much more to learn!

Bugnard, I suspect, had been quietly monitoring my progress, and had now gained enough confidence in me that he began to take me aside

and show me things that he didn't show "the boys." This time when he took me around Les Halles, he personally introduced me to his favorite meat, vegetable, and wine purveyors.

I decided to give up the Cordon Bleu for the time being. I didn't want to lose my momentum, though, so I continued to attend the afternoon demonstrations (a dollar each), and go to as many of the pâtisserie demonstrations ($1.99 per class) as I could. In the meantime, I was constantly experimenting on the stove at home. On the QT, Chef Bugnard joined me at 81 for an occasional private cooking lesson.

One of the things I loved about French cooking was the way that basic themes could be made in a seemingly infinite number of variations—scalloped potatoes, say, could be done with milk and cheese, with carrots and cream, with beef stock and cheese, with onions and tomatoes, and so on and on. I wanted to try them all, and did. I learned how to do things professionally, like how to fix properly a piece of fish in thirteen different ways, or how to use the specialized vocabulary of the kitchen—"*petits dés*" are vegetables "diced quite finely"; a *douille* is the tin nozzle of a pastry bag that lets you squeeze a cake decoration as the icing blurps out.

There was, in fact, a method to my madness: I was preparing for my final examination. I could take it anytime I felt ready to, Madame Brassart said, and I was determined to do as well as possible. After all, if I were going to open a restaurant or a cooking school, what better credentials could I have than the Cordon Bleu, of Paris, France?

I knew that I'd have to keep honing my skills until I had all of the recipes and techniques down cold and could perform them under pressure. The exam didn't intimidate me. In fact, I looked forward to it.

v. Bastille Day

"*Ça y est! C'est fait! C'est le quator-zuh juillet!*" That revolutionary ditty has a catchy swing to it in French, but is quite meaningless in a literal translation. I render it as something like "Hooray, we did it! The Fourteenth of July!"

Oh, the fury of the French Revolution, where the people of the streets rushed at the hated symbols of the King, especially the Bastille prison, which they tore down, stone by stone, and distributed all over the city. Some of those stones were built into the foundation of 81 Rue de l'Université.

In the summer of 1950, Charlie and Freddie and their three children—Erica, Rachel, and Jon—had finally come to visit us. It was a dream come true to spend time together in Paris. In the meantime, Paul and I had hired a new *femme de ménage*. I had once pictured French maids as chic creatures in starched white aprons—shades of *Vogue* magazine. Coo-Coo had changed that perception, and now our latest, Jeanne, shattered it forever. She was a tiny, slightly wall-eyed, frazzle-haired woman with a childish mind that often wandered astray.

Jeanne was a hard worker and unfailingly faithful; she and Minette became fast friends, and when we hosted parties she became even more excited than we did. But we called her "Jeanne-la-folle" ("crazy Jeanne"), because she looked rather mad, and sometimes acted it, too.

At the height of the summer, all of the toilets in the house suddenly stopped flushing. This being dear old Paris, we couldn't find a *plombier* willing to rush over. Finally, after a few uncomfortable days, help

"Jeanne-la-folle"

arrived. After much sweat and toil over our toilet waste-pipe, the plumber discovered an American beer can lodged deeply inside. When I asked Jeanne-la-folle if she had flushed it down the toilet, she replied, *"Mais oui—je rejete TOUJOURS les choses dans les toilettes! C'est beaucoup plus facile, vous savez."* Hm. Cost of repair: a hundred dollars.

On the evening of Bastille Day, July 14, we planned a special buffet dinner to precede the traditional fireworks. The *pièce de résistance* of our meal would be a *ballottine* of veal: veal that has been stuffed and rolled into the shape of a log and served hot with a luscious sauce. Two days before the feast, Jeanne-la-folle and I prepared a goodly amount of perfect, Escoffier-type veal stock for poaching the *ballottine*. It was the best and most careful stock I had ever made. Next we prepared an elaborate veal forcemeat that included quite a generous bit of *foie gras*, mushroom *duxelles*, Cognac, Madeira, and blanched chard leaves which would be used to make a nice pattern. We then stuffed the veal with the forcemeat, tied it up ever so neatly in its clean poaching cloth, and refrigerated it for the following day. I also used some of the veal stock to simmer up a first-class truffled Madeira sauce. The night of the thirteenth, we readied everything that could be readied, for Jeanne was setting off to celebrate the national holiday with her family in the country. She was so excited about our party that she hardly slept.

The morning of July 14, the seven of us Childs got ourselves up and out to the parade route early. We trooped over the Concorde Bridge and up the Champs-Élysées to stand strategically in the front row, just beyond the Rond-Point. Fortunately, we were there in good time, before too much of a crowd had gathered along the avenue. Eventually we heard the martial music, and the troops began to sweep down the Champs in waves. There were tootling military bands of various sorts, regiments of smartly garbed French foot soldiers, groups of camels, colorful African troops in native costume on handsome horses, and French cavalry officers in elaborate uniforms, their horses prancing high. Now and then a cannon would trundle by, and a gaggle of fighter planes would swoop down and pass right over us with a deafening roar.

The crowd cheered, clapped, and *ooh-la-la*-ed at each passing display. It was a real parade, a lively and seemingly spontaneous outpouring of patriotic glee. Erica and Rachel and Jon were delighted by the spectacle and the foreignness of it all.

That evening we held our party, an informal group of about twenty people, at our apartment. A few were relics of the old days, before my time, when Paul, Charlie, and Freddie had been bohemians in the Paris of the 1920s. One such couple were Samuel and Narcissa Chamberlain. He was an etcher, a food writer, and author of *Clementine in the Kitchen*, the charming memoir of an American family living in a French village with a super *femme de ménage*, Clementine, who was also a great cook. Narcissa collaborated with her husband and acted as his recipe developer. Another visitor that night was a fleeting, wrenlike person in a tan pongee accordion-pleated skirt and wide-brimmed pongee-colored hat. She was so small that the hat hid her face until she looked up and you noticed that it was Alice B. Toklas. She always seemed to be popping up in Paris like that. She stayed only for a glass of wine before dinner.

After a decent amount of champagne and toasts, we dove into the large buffet. The *ballottine*, poached in the spectacular veal stock and then allowed to linger in it a while to enhance the flavor, was an immense success with its truffled sauce. Watching my family and friends happily enjoy the meal, savoring every drop of that poaching stock, which had been further enriched by the complex flavors of the *ballottine*, I secretly bestowed upon myself a French culinary compliment of the highest order: "*impeccable.*"

But the fireworks would soon begin! After dinner, and a dessert of a beautiful meringue-ringed chocolate-mousse cake that I had bought from the very chic pastry shop near us on la Rue du Bac, we rushed through a quick preliminary cleanup. Charlie and Paul insisted that the rest of us stay downstairs in the *salon*, while they took on the piles of dishes in the third-floor kitchen. When they reappeared, red in the face from exertion, we headed up to Montmartre to view the evening's display.

The event started off in a leisurely fashion, one rocket at a time arcing through the sky, giving us time to savor their artistry. The crowd oohed with pleasure at the glittering sparks. The pace gradually quickened, until a bouquet of rapid detonations gave way to the three tremendous cannon booms of the finale. The crowd fell into an awed silence. Then there were sighs of satisfaction, as people began to disperse into the warm night. It felt as if France herself was finally stirring again, and shucking off the nightmares of war.

We joined the throng of celebrants walking down the Montmartre hill. As the young were bedded down at home, I went up to the kitchen for the final cleanup. The boys had done a splendid job of scraping and stacking plates in our vast stoneware sink. But where had they put all the garbage? My eyes darted this way and that. After poaching the *ballottine*, I had set my big stockpot on the floor, to cool off. Eyeing it with a sense of foreboding now, I just *knew:* they had dumped it all in there—into my precious, wonderful, unique, never-to-be-equaled veal stock!

I sighed. There was no undoing what had been done, and I could only sob in my innermost self. I vowed never to mention it—or forget it.

VI. AN AMERICAN STOMACH IN PARIS

BY SEPTEMBER 1950, Paul was suffering from mystery pains in his chest and back, not sleeping well, and feeling nauseated all the time. Generally, he let his afflictions ride themselves out. But this time they wouldn't quit. The embassy doctor diagnosed Paul with some kind of "local condition" of heart and strained nerves, probably the effects of a long-ago judo accident. "Could be," said Paul, with a shrug, sounding unconvinced.

He went to a French doctor, Dr. Wolfram, who happened to be a tropical-disease specialist. Wolfram looked at Paul's medical reports dating back to Ceylon, China, and Washington, D.C., which all said there was no evidence of tropical disease. But after measuring Paul's liver and spleen, Wolfram said that Paul's symptoms matched the amoebic dysentery he'd seen in French colonials. The sharp mystery-pains in the chest and back were probably the result of gas buildup from the bugs in Paul's gut. Paul was skeptical, but after more tests Dr. Wolfram discovered active amoebae in Paul's system. The cure was a set of shots followed by a regimen of pills, and a strict diet. Paul dreamed of *rognons flambés*, but was not allowed wine or alcohol, rich sauces, or cooked fats. It was an exquisite torture to be living in Paris, with a cook, and to be denied any tasteful food at all.

I, too, had had tummy troubles. Ever since our trip to Italy with Philapop, my stomach was no longer a brass-bound, iron-lined, eat-and-drink-any-amount-of-anything-anywhere-anytime machine that it had been. I had suffered bouts of feeling quite queer the entire time we'd been in France. "It must be something in the water," I'd say to myself. But when I continued to feel suddenly sick and gaseous, I declared: "Aha, pregnant at last!"

We had tried. But for some reason our efforts didn't take. It was sad, but we didn't spend too much time thinking about it and never considered adoption. It was just one of those things. We were living very full lives. I was cooking all the time and making plans for a career in gastronomy. Paul—after all his years as a tutor and schoolteacher—said that he'd already spent enough time with adolescents to last him a lifetime. So it was.

A French doctor diagnosed my persistent nausea as nothing more than good old *crise de foie*—a liver attack, also known as "an American stomach in Paris." Evidently, French cuisine was just too much for most American digestive systems. Looking back on the rich gorge of food and drink we'd been enjoying, I don't find the diagnosis surprising. Lunch almost every day had consisted of something like *sole meunière*, *ris de veau à la crème*, and half a bottle of wine. Dinner might be *escargots*, *rognons flambés*, and another half-bottle of wine. Then there was a regular flow of apéritifs and cocktails and Cognacs. No wonder I felt ill! In a good restaurant, even a simple carrot-cream soup has had the carrots and onions *fondus* gently in butter for ten to fifteen minutes before being souped.

Alas, when I lightened my diet and got plenty of rest, my gaseous upset persisted. Upon hearing this, Dr. Wolfram said it was entirely possible that I, too, had picked up something in Asia during the war. He put me on an anti-dysentery treatment and restricted my diet. No fun!

PAUL AND THE American cultural attaché, Lee Brady, were organizing a number of exciting exhibits at the embassy, including shows of Grandma Moses paintings, dance photos from the Museum of Modern Art, and a collection of U.S. engravings and printing books. To mount these shows, he had to be a combination diplomat-hustler-bully, in order to navigate the wildly different styles of the French and American bureaucracies.

The individualistic, artisanal quality of the French baffled the men Paul called the "Marshall Plan hustlers" from the U.S.A. When American experts began making "helpful" suggestions about how the French

Paul with a visitor at one of his exhibits

could "increase productivity and profits," the average Frenchman would shrug, as if to say: "These notions of yours are all very fascinating, no doubt, but we have a nice little business here just as it is. Everybody makes a decent living. Nobody has ulcers. I have time to work on my monograph about Balzac, and my foreman enjoys his espaliered pear trees. I think, as a matter of fact, we do not wish to make these changes that you suggest."

The Americans couldn't even *scare* the French into changing their ancient ways. Why should they wreck a small but satisfying system that everybody liked, only to have the Communists take over? The French were personally patriotic, but too individualistic to create a new system to benefit the nation as a whole, and dubious about the cost of new machinery, the hurry-hurry-hurry, the instability of change, and so on.

This clash of cultures was quite amusing, and though Paul and I were temperamentally more sympathetic to the French than to the American approach, we were also its victims. Once, a French friend took us to a wonderful little café on the Right Bank—the kind of out-of-the-way place one needs a local guide to find—and introduced us to the proprietress. "I've brought you some new customers!" our friend proudly said. With hardly a glance in our direction, Madame waved a hand, saying, "Oh no, I have enough customers already. . . ." Such a response would be unimaginable in the U.S.A.

Near the end of 1950, Lee Brady was suddenly ordered to Saigon as public-affairs officer (PAO) in charge of USIS activities for Indochina— a most difficult and dangerous assignment indeed. He would be forced to work with the Bao Dai regime, which had not been freely chosen by the majority of citizens. Paul grew upset that the U.S.A. often found itself supporting weaklings and stooges—King George in Greece, Chiang Kai-shek in China, Tito in Yugoslavia, and now Bao Dai. What was an emissary of the U.S. government supposed to say when the Communists claimed, correctly, that his government supported a puppet, dictator, or horror?

VII. THE ARTISTES

IT WAS OCTOBER, and cold, but those wonderfully juicy and perfumed Parisian pears were in season, and despite our tender tummies we ate them for breakfast, along with bowls of cornflakes and Grape-Nuts. We would wash it all down with Chinese tea, which had a less poisonous effect on our plumbing than coffee.

Oh, it was so cold now. I hated it. The water hadn't frozen in the gutters yet, although it was twenty-seven degrees and should have. It took real courage to leave our warm(ish) *salon* and venture into the *frigorification* of the house, where our breaths came out as steam. Every year at this time, I found myself thinking about our toasty little house in Washington, D.C.: push a button, and the entire place was warm in literally five minutes. But, I scolded myself, I'd had such a soft life—never known Hunger, never known true Fear, or been forced to live under the boot heel of an Enemy—that it was good for me to have an idea of what so many people in the world were going through.

On November 7, 1950, we celebrated our second anniversary in Paris. On a whim, Paul and I decided to indulge ourselves at one of our places, Restaurant des Artistes, up near Sacré-Coeur. At the Chambre des Députés we jumped on a metro to the Place Pigalle, and walked a couple of blocks toward the Montmartre hill. Along the way, we stopped to look at the pictures of naked girls in front of Les Naturistes. As we stood there gazing at a funny photo of a line of girls, back to the camera, holding their skirts up to show a row of bare buttocks, a young, fast-talking tout was giving us a non-ending pitch on the glories awaiting us within, uttered in about five languages—French, German, Italian, English, and a weird one which might have been Turkish. We laughed and kept moving along the avenue, crowded cheek-to-jowl with shooting galleries, strongman tests, and merry-go-rounds. We paused to shoot ten arrows with an all-metal bow, then, at Rue Lepic, we ducked into the restaurant.

The Artistes was a small, neat place with only ten tables (about forty seats) in its dining room. But stashed away in its *cave* were some fifty thousand bottles of exquisite wine. The dining room was warm and always filled with that wonderful smell of good cooking—a white-wine fish stock reducing, a delectable something being sautéed in the best butter, the refreshing sting of a salad tossed in a vinaigrette.

As we came through the door, Monsieur Caillon, the maître d'hôtel and owner, and his wife, the cashier, greeted us like the prodigal son and daughter. Their young daughter (that lucky girl) was in the kitchen with Chef Mangelatte, one of my favorite teachers at the Cordon Bleu. He was a small, intense man with dark hair and piercing dark eyes. He had started his career as a pastry chef and, like many of that special breed, had evolved into a precise cook. Mangelatte had eloquent hands, and was as skillful as a surgeon. I'd seen him *vider* a full chicken—plucking out the pinfeathers, degutting, and cutting the bird into pieces—in four minutes flat.

At eight-thirty, we began dinner with an apéro of Blanc de Blanc and cassis. Sitting at the next table were a fat Belgian and his plump wife, eating slices of *lièvre à la royale* and imbibing from a dust-covered bottle of 1924 Burgundy. As we chatted with them about wine, our first course arrived: a *loup de mer* (sea bass), its stomach cavity stuffed with fennel, grilled over charcoal. With this we drank a lovely 1947 Château-Chalon, a white from the Jura, which had a deep-topaz color and an interesting taste, almost like Manzanilla. ("It is made from grapes that are picked and hung to dry like raisins for about six months," Monsieur Caillon said.) After that, Paul had two venison cutlets with a wine sauce that was so deep and richly concentrated it looked almost black, accompanied by a chestnut purée. I had roasted *alouettes* (larks) and puffed-up potatoes. We drank a bottle of Saint-Émilion 1937. Finally, a wedge of Brie and coffee. A perfect meal.

By eleven, we were the last customers in the dining room. Chef Mangelatte emerged from his kitchen and joined the Caillons at our table. We discussed French cooking, and Mangelatte said that the French culinary arts were slowly going downhill. In response to this crisis, he'd organized an academy of professional chefs, limited to fifty members, whose goal was to promote classical cuisine. They were jointly writing a cookbook that would set forth the whole gamut of classical dishes. He hoped to find a financial backer, so that the group could issue awards for new dishes, much as the Goncourt Academy does for literature (the Prix Goncourt).

When the conversation drifted, inevitably, to the Cordon Bleu, Mangelatte revealed that he felt the school was doing a great disservice to the *métier*, as the administration was focused on a mad scramble for money rather than on the excellent training of their pupils. The school had lowered its standards, he said, and sometimes didn't even have basic commodities like pepper or vinegar for the chefs to demonstrate with. A boy had to scurry out around the corner to buy what was needed with the chef's own money! His chefs' group saw an opportunity to establish a rival school, a really high-standard establishment to teach the classical *métier*.

I greatly admired Mangelatte's devotion to his craft and the systematic way he was attempting to ensure that the traditions were passed along. But it was sad to see that even such an energetic chef, with such a deep-seated sense of artistry, had to fight so hard to protect a civilized piece of French culture from barbarism. On the way home, Paul lamented that if he'd only known about the chef's cooking academy a year earlier, he probably could have funneled ECA money for tourism into it; but now, with America's focus swinging from butter to guns, it was too late.

"THROWN ANY PIES lately?" These were the first words that Ivan Cousins said to Dort. She burst out laughing, but didn't recognize him.

He was a short, dapper, musical Massachusetts man of Irish stock. Before the war, he had gone to visit friends at Bennington College, in Vermont. Sitting in the dining room there, he noticed a strikingly tall, thin, vivacious woman throw a pie in the face of another girl, then run off cackling. That was my sister.

Ivan recognized Dort at the American Club Theatre in Paris, where she worked in the business office and he had just signed on as an actor. When he wasn't working his day job with the Economic Cooperation Administration (ECA), which administered the Marshall Plan, Ivan starred in such plays as Thornton Wilder's *Happy Journeys*. During the war, he had volunteered for the navy, where he rose to lieutenant commander and captained a PT boat in the Pacific (he was nearly blown sky-high by a floating mine). After the war, his navy friend the poet

Toasting Dort and Ivan

Lawrence Ferlinghetti—who called himself Larry Ferling—convinced Ivan to join him in Paris to "cool out." In Paris, Ivan roomed with Ferlinghetti and joined the expat swirl.

Dort and Ivan began to date and hang around with the theater's young, self-consciously bohemian crowd. After a bit, we oldsters had suggested that it might be a good idea for Dort to find a place of her own. She agreed that it was time, and found a little *garçonnière*—a small apartment, so named because families rent them for their sons (and their girlfriends)—on the Boulevard de la Tour Maubourg. It was on the Left Bank, near the Pont Alexandre III, not far from Roo de Loo.

BY CHRISTMASTIME, which we once again spent with the Bicknells in Cambridge, England, Paul had a renewed appetite, had finally gained a few pounds, and was sleeping like a veritable Yule log. My tummy troubles had also disappeared. And so, during the quiet holiday, we ate a lot of local fare, like Scottish pheasant, and cakes imbued with the concentrated essence of essential concentrates. On Christmas Eve, Mari and I once again made a *soufflé Grand Marnier,* which we accompanied with a bottle of Château d'Yquem 1929. It was still a perfect combination, and now a holiday tradition.

We were back in Paris by New Year's Eve. I took a hot bath at nine-fifteen and retired to bed with a book. Paul wrote letters. At eleven-fifteen we hoisted glasses of Pouilly-Fumé, toasted the future, and went to sleep.

VIII. *SURPRISE*

BY LATE 1950, I felt ready to take my final examination, and earn my *diplôme* from the Cordon Bleu. But when I asked Madame Brassart to schedule the test—politely, at first, and then with an increasing insistence—my requests were met with stony silence. The truth is that Madame Brassart and I got on each other's nerves. She seemed to think that awarding students a diploma was like inducting them into some kind of secret society; as a result, the school's hallways were filled with an air of petty jealousy and distrust. From my perspective, Madame Brassart lacked professional experience, was a terrible administrator, and tangled herself up in picayune details and petty politics. Because of its exalted reputation, the Cordon Bleu's pupils came from all over the globe. But the lack of a qualified and competent head was hurting the school—and could damage the reputation of French cooking, or even France herself, in the eyes of the world.

I was sure that the little question of money had something to do with Madame Brassart's evasiveness. I had taken the "professional" course in the basement rather than the "regular" (more expensive) course upstairs that she had recommended; I never ate at the school; and she didn't make as much money out of me as she would have liked. It seemed to me that the school's director should have paid less attention to centimes and more attention to her *students*, who, after all, were—or could be—her best publicity.

After waiting and waiting for my exam to be scheduled, I sent Madame Brassart a stern letter in March 1951, noting that "all my American friends and even the U.S. ambassador himself" knew I had been slaving away at the Cordon Bleu, "morning, noon and night." I insisted that I take the exam before I left on a long-planned trip to the U.S.A., in April. If there was not enough space at the school, I added, then I would be happy to take the exam in my own well-appointed kitchen.

More time passed, and still no response. I was good and fed up, and finally spoke to Chef Bugnard about the matter. He agreed to make inquiries on my behalf. Lo and behold, Madame Brassart suddenly scheduled my exam for the first week in April. Ha! I continued to hone my technique, memorize proportions, and prepare myself in every way I could think of.

On the Big Day, I arrived at the school and they handed me a little typewritten card that said: "Write out the ingredients for the following dishes, to serve three people: *oeufs mollets avec sauce béarnaise; côtelettes de veau en surprise; crème renversée au caramel.*"

I stared at the card in disbelief.

Did I remember what an *oeuf mollet* was? No. How could I miss *that*? (I later discovered that it was an egg that has been coddled and then peeled.) How about the *veau "en surprise"*? No. (A sautéed veal chop with *duxelles*—hashed mushrooms—on either side, overlayed with ham slices, and all wrapped up in a paper bag—the "surprise"—that is then browned in the oven.) Did I remember the exact proportions for caramel custard? No.

Merde alors, and *flûte!*

Madame Brassart giving out diplomas

I was stuck, and had no choice but to make everything up. I knew I would fail the practical part of the exam. As for the written exam, I was asked how to make *fond brun*, how to cook green vegetables, and how to make *sauce béarnaise*. I answered them fully and correctly. But that didn't take away the sting.

I was furious at myself. There was no excuse for not remembering what a *mollet* was, or, especially, the details of a caramel custard. I could never have guessed at the *veau en surprise*, though, as the paper wrapping was just a lot of tomfoolery—the kind of gimmicky dish a little newly-wed would serve up for her first dinner party to *épater* the boss's wife. Caught up in my own romanticism, I had focused on learning far more challenging fare—*filets de sole Walewska, poularde toulousaine, sauce Véni-tienne*. Woe!

There were no questions about complicated dishes or sauces, no dis-cussion about which techniques and methods I'd use. Instead, they wanted me to memorize basic recipes taken from the little Cordon Bleu booklet, a publication written for beginner cooks that I had hardly both-ered to look at. This exam was far too simple for someone who had devoted six months of hard work to cooking school, not to mention countless hours of her own time in the markets and behind the stove.

My disgruntlement was supreme, my amour-propre enraged, my bile overboiling. Worst of all, it was my own fault!

I despaired that the school would ever deign to grant me a certificate. Me, who could pluck, flame, empty, and cut up a whole chicken in twelve minutes flat! Me, who could stuff a sole with forcemeat of weakfish and serve it with a *sauce au vin blanc* such as Madame Bras-sart could never hope to taste the perfection of! Me, the Supreme Mistress of *mayonnaise, hollandaise, cassoulets, choucroutes, blanquettes de veau, pommes de terre Anna, soufflé Grand Marnier, fonds d'artichauts, oignons glacés, mousse de faisan en gelée, ballottines, galantines, terrines, pâtés* . . . Me, alas!

Later that afternoon, I slipped down to the Cordon Bleu's basement kitchen by myself. I opened the school's booklet, found the recipes from the examination—*oeufs mollets* with *sauce béarnaise, côtelettes de veau en surprise,* and *crème renversée au caramel*—and whipped them all up in a cold, clean fury. Then I ate them.

CHAPTER 3

Three Hearty Eaters

1. *LES GOURMETTES*

ONE FRIDAY IN APRIL 1951, I invited eight members of Le Cercle des Gourmettes for lunch at 81 Rue de l'Université. The Gourmettes was an exclusive women's eating club started back in 1929 by some wives of the all-male Club des Cent (the premier men's gastronomic club, limited to one hundred members) to show that women knew something about food, too. Most of the Gourmettes were in their seventies, of the right sort of family background, and were mostly French—although their leader, Madame Paulette Etlinger, was a spry old American who spoke in a kind of half-English/half-French of her own. They met for lunches or dinners in a model kitchen lent by the EDF (Électricité et Gaz de France) every other Friday for a *cours de cuisine:* while a professional chef did the cooking and teaching, the Gourmettes gabbled and gossiped, and sometimes helped with things like peeling and seeding, then sat down to a stupendous lunch.

I had joined the club a few months earlier, urged on by Madame Etlinger, who wanted more American members. It was terribly amusing, as I met all types of Frenchwomen and learned quite a bit about cooking.

I had instigated the Gourmettes' lunch *chez nous* because I enjoyed the members' dedication and wanted to get to know them better. But my real agenda was to help Chef Bugnard, who was retiring from the

Cordon Bleu and was looking for catering work and private lessons. Although I never mentioned it blatantly, my plan was that Bugnard would cook such an impressive meal that my guests would want to hire him themselves.

The Gourmettes took themselves rather seriously, and as I rushed about, dusting and straightening things, I noticed that my favorite Aubagne pottery suddenly looked a bit *too* rustic, and that there was more than one spot where the ancient wallpaper sagged from the wall. We had a lovely set of wineglasses, but I had to run downstairs to borrow some decent silverware from Madame Perrier. No sooner had I finished spiffing up than the doorbell rang.

My eight guests ranged in age from about forty-five to seventy-three, and were all Frenchwomen who had lived elegantly *"dans le temps."* Each had a discerning and expectant look in her eye.

Chef Bugnard started us off with *tortues* of crab pounded together with shrimp and herbs and mayonnaise, served in pastry shells with toast on the side. Then came a fantastic *poularde Waterzooi:* chicken poached in white wine and white bouillon, on a bed of julienned carrots, leeks, and onions that had been pre-cooked in butter; slathered on top was a sauce made with egg yolks and cream. And for the grand finale, he served *crêpes Suzettes flambées,* which he presented with a theatrical, flaming flourish.

Sitting back with satisfied smiles at the end of the meal, the delighted Gourmettes agreed that my dear old chef had done a fine job indeed.

When the Gourmettes gathered for a meal, their husbands—calling themselves *les Princes Consorts Abandonés*—would often meet on their own for a fabulous restaurant luncheon. Paul was visibly excited by this prospect, and was not disappointed by his first outing with the Princes: "This appears to be the group of civilized, witty, intelligent gourmets I've been looking for all these years," he said. On special occasions, the Gourmettes and Princes would share a meal together. Once, a mob of about thirty of us trooped out into the countryside to eat at a charming farmhouse restaurant, and another time fifty of us were taken on a guided tour of the Chambre des Députés, where we saw the speaking room, the wonderful old library, the murals and statues, and had a splendid lunch at the *députés'* own restaurant. As with *le groupe Foçillon,* we felt lucky to have found such an interesting bunch of like-minded, and very French, friends.

ONE NIGHT we hit the town. Paul and I were joined by Cora du Bois and Jeanne Taylor, friends from the OSS days, for dinner at the Tour d'Argent. The restaurant was excellent in every way, except that it was so pricey that every guest was American. At eleven-thirty, we drove up to the Place du Tertre, where we struggled past the barkers and milling tourists in the narrow streets. At the Lapin Agile we paid two thousand francs and squeezed our way to some stools in back. The air was foggy with tobacco smoke, and a chap played boogie-woogie on an upright piano. We ordered brandied cherries, but they never arrived. Finally, a man with a good baritone voice sang four traditional French folk songs, and then we crammed our way outside again and breathed deeply in the cool night air. We strolled along the terrace in front of Sacré-Coeur to stare down at the city. Paris was serene and quiet in the moonlight, and seemed to stretch away to infinity.

Les Halles at night

Working our way over to Place Pigalle, we dipped into Les Naturistes. Drinking demi-blondes at the bar, we watched about twenty young women wearing rhinestone-encrusted triangles walk across the stage in time to the music. The show lacked sparkle, so we headed off to the Left Bank, where we found a jolly nightclub called Le Club Saint-Yves. The walls were plastered with posters, postcards, and handbills from the theater world of the 1890s. The audience was made up of simple folk, all French, who were obviously having fun. What the singers lacked in voice, they made up for with personality and verve. After the club closed, at 3:00 a.m., we went on to Les Halles and walked around admiring the *forts des Halles*—the barrel-chested market workers—unloading crates of fresh watercress from trucks, stacking freshly cut flowers, and preparing for the day. It was cold and dark, but the vast marketplace was beautiful under splotches of yellow electric light. As dawn lightened the edges of the sky, we found ourselves at Au Pied de Cochon for a traditional bowl of onion soup, glasses of red wine, and cups of coffee. At five-fifteen, we straggled home.

FOR THE FIRST TIME since the war, strikes were legal in France, and now the Communists were having a high old time bollixing everything up—instigating fights in the Chambre des Députés, and starting little strikes here and there. By the spring of 1951, Paris was in the grip of a debilitating general strike led by the Confédération Générale du Travail, or CGT, the biggest holding company for the unions. The CGT was said to be Communist-dominated, and it had cynically prodded gas, electricity, telephone, and dockworkers to strike under the name of "increasing workers' wages" (which was a legitimate need), but really for the CGT's own political gain (which was not).

As a result, there were hardly any buses or metros running, little electricity, and just a whisper of gas for our stove. (To avoid an explosive mixture of air and gas seepage, they continued to feed the tiniest bit of gas into the pipes.) Cooking became a challenge. Even a simple dinner of lamb chops (forty-five minutes), boiled potatoes (over one hour), canned peas (ten minutes), and grapefruit suddenly wasn't so simple. My ten-day supply of cat food came unfrozen in the icebox. And when we gave a dinner party for six, I had to do most of my cooking on the electric stoves in the basement of the Cordon Bleu.

As many streets still relied on gaslit lanterns, the dimming effect was reminiscent of a wartime blackout. Driving at night was hazardous, as pedestrians were invisible, bikes looked like fireflies, and other cars would dazzle you when they flashed on their headlights every few seconds. The few metros that did run were jammed to impossibility, and it took from two to four hours to make a metro trip that usually took forty minutes.

Paul and I initiated the Blue Flash Bus Service, picking up and dropping off embassy staff all over Paris—at Port de Clichy, Gare de Lyon, Nation, and Commerce. We'd never seen such traffic. Half of it was made up of bicycles; the rest was army trucks being used as commuter buses, and any kind of vehicle that could be dragged out of scrap yards and root cellars and made to run on homemade fuel.

During this unsettled period, Paul became preoccupied with two subjects: the fact that most people didn't believe in the possibility of flying saucers, and the fact that the U.S. wasn't doing enough to prepare Western Europe for a Russian invasion. In both cases, he claimed, "people need to see the thing in order to believe it." Paul and Charlie—the sons of an electrical engineer and a bohemian singer—shared a dual nature: they were extremely practical and could build you a house or wire your lamp without batting an eye; but they were also mystical, enjoyed the mumblings of fortune-tellers, and believed in the possibility of ghosts and flying saucers.

I did not share this trait. I was more concerned with the problems in front of me, such as how to get around Paris during the strikes, where to find the best asparagus, and how to further my program of self-education.

I had been trying to read Serious News Articles—a *Harper's* essay about post-war England, a *Fortune* article about free trade—and to remember their facts and lines of argument in order to discuss them intelligently at dinner parties. But it was a struggle. My sievelike mind didn't want to lock away dates and details; it wanted to float and meander. If I mixed all those facts and theses up with a little gelatine and egg white, I wondered, would they stick together better?

11. HOME LEAVE

DORT AND IVAN were engaged, and the wedding would be held in New York, in June 1951. She blossomed like a peony around him, and I was supportive of their union. But it was no secret that Big John was not wildly enthusiastic about it. Just as I had done, Dorothy had chosen someone completely different from our father to be her life-mate.

We hosted a farewell jamboree for them at 81 Roo de Loo. The *pièce de résistance* for the evening was a mammoth *galantine de volaille*, which took me three days to create and had been adopted from a recipe in *Larousse Gastronomique*. First you make a superb bouillon—from veal leg, feet, and bones—for poaching. Then you debone a nice plump four-pound chicken, and marinate the meat with finely ground pork and veal strips in Cognac and truffles. Then you re-form the chicken, stuffing it with a nice row of truffles wrapped in *farce* and a fresh strip of pork fat, which you hope ends up in the center. You tie up this bundle and poach it in the delicious bouillon. Once it is cooked, you let it cool and then decorate it—I used green swirls of blanched leeks, red dots of pimiento, brown-black accents of sliced truffle, and yellow splashes of butter. The whole was then covered with beautiful clarified-bouillon jelly.

This exquisite dish took time, but it was great fun. The hardest part was arranging the decorations on top, which in my color-pencil rendering looked meager and childlike. Luckily, that nice Mr. P. Child came to the rescue with a stylish design. The final result, I must say, was magnificent—a suitably grand send-off for the beaming bride- and groom-to-be.

SINCE 1944, Paul and I had spent four and a half years out of the United States and two and a half years in it. On May 4, we would board *La Liberté*, bound for New York, and excited to see our distant homeland.

Before we left Paris, and with a lump in our throats, we had decided to sell the Blue Flash. The car had served us well—carrying American ham and Burgundy wine and Italian spaghetti and Swiss typewriters and Maine lobsters. But it had a wheeze in every pipe, busted springs, peeling chrome, and a tick in the motor, and was in need of two hundred dollars' worth of repairs. We ordered a new car, which we'd pick up in the States.

In the meantime, Chef Bugnard had told me that, despite my exam debacle, I was well qualified to be chef in a *maison de la haute bourgeoisie*. It was a nice compliment, but I was no longer satisfied with being "just" an accomplished home cook. Cooking was so endlessly interesting that I wanted to make a career of it, though I was sketchy on the details. My plan was to start by teaching a few classes to Americans in Paris. My guiding principle would be to make *cooks* out of people, rather than gobs of money: I wouldn't lose money, but I'd dedicate myself to the teaching of gastronomy in an atmosphere of friendly and encouraging professionalism.

Still, if Freddie and I were ever going to open the Mrs. Child & Mrs. Child restaurant, I'd need a *diplôme* from the Cordon Bleu. This meant retaking the final exam.

When I made inquiries, Madame Brassart once again failed to respond. Fed up, I wrote, "It surprises me to see you take so little interest in your students." Once again, Chef Bugnard spoke to her on my behalf, and once again a date for my test was miraculously set. This time, instead of steeping myself in challenging recipes, I simply memorized the dishes in the Cordon Bleu's little booklet. When the day came, I took the exam in my own kitchen at Roo de Loo. It consisted of a very simple written section followed by the preparation of a basic meal for Bugnard and my friend Helen Kirkpatrick. I passed.

In September, after we had returned from the States, I finally received my diploma. It was signed by Madame Brassart and Chef Max Bugnard, and had been backdated to March 15, 1951! At last, Julia McWilliams Child could say that she was a full-fledged graduate of Le Cordon Bleu, of Paris, France.

MEANWHILE, DORT and Ivan had a lovely wedding at the St. Thomas Church in New York City. After the ceremony, Paul and I jumped aboard the Chief in Pennsylvania Station and crossed the familiar-unfamiliar U.S.A. to California—where the weather, the flowers, and the trees were always wonderful, everybody had a Cadillac, and where, as Candide put it, "everything was for the best in this best of all possible worlds."

In Pasadena, we were absorbed into a seemingly endless stream of cocktail parties, lunches, and dinners. The atmosphere of ease and charm there felt both intimately familiar and strangely foreign. I did my best to remain polite and positive during our two-week stay. So did Paul, who nearly strained a muscle trying to create good feelings while staying true to his own convictions. He had to bite his tongue when my father's friends would casually scorn President Truman, Jews, Negroes, the United Nations, or "all those Phi Beta Kappas" in Washington.

Back in New York we picked up our brand-new car, a gleaming black Chevrolet Styleline Deluxe Sedan, model 2102, which we promptly christened La Tulipe Noire. The Tulipe swept us north along the interstates, to Charlie and Freddie's cabin in Maine, where the car's new tires and fenders were immediately christened with some good old-fashioned sticky brown mud. Over the next week, we managed to sun and swim and work California and its discontents out of our systems. While Paul helped Charlie construct a new road, fell trees, and build a new room for the cabin, I busied myself making bread and bouillabaisse in the makeshift kitchen. It was a little slice of heaven. In mid-July we celebrated my thirty-ninth birthday (a month ahead of the actual date) with a picnic on the stony beach, where my niece Rachel presented me with a gloriously silly hat, decorated with wildflowers, seashells, and Slinkys.

Finally, it was back to New York and onto the *Nieuw Amsterdam*, for an uneventful return trip to France. We arrived in Le Havre on July 27.

After driving to Rouen, we stopped in for lunch at La Couronne, where we ordered exactly the same meal that we'd had on my first day in France, more than two and a half years earlier: *portugaises* (oysters), *sole meunière*, *salade verte*, *fromage blanc*, and *café filtre*. Ah me! The meal was just as sublime the second time around, only now I could identify the smells in the air quicker than Paul, order my own food without help, and truly appreciate the artistry of the kitchen. La Couronne was the same, but I had become a different person.

III. LA CHASSE

IT WAS *la morte-saison*, and an estimated one million Parisians had evacuated the city for their summer *vacances*. All the decent restaurants were boarded up. So were the laundry places. We had intended to have our kitchen repainted, but could not find anyone to do the work for us.

Paul spent an evening on home improvements—patching holes in the Cordova-leather walls in the dining room, hanging a lovely nude painted by Charlie in our bedroom, then using the lumber from the nude's packing case to add a one-foot extension onto the end of our bed. At last, I could fit my size 12 feet comfortably under the covers, rather than have them sticking out like a pair of gargoyles.

The locals were gone, but the streets of Paris were thick with Youth from all over the world. Many of these were Boy Scouts, returning from a worldwide Jamboree in Austria. One of them, a fifteen-year-old cousin of mine named Mac Fiske, had lunch, dinner, and a bath at our place.

"What do Boy Scouts like to eat, anyway?" I asked.

"A lot," Paul quipped. And he was right. Mac had the appetite of a Russian wolf. As he departed, Mac said: "You're such nice people! You're the only people I seen around here who have a lot to eat all the time!"

IN SEPTEMBER, the weather turned rainy and cool and satisfyingly beautiful, with big shadowy thunderclouds alternating with bright shafts of sunlight. The Tulipe Noire still wore its New York license plates, but the rain washed the New England mud and grit out from behind its ears. Paul was madly busy at the USIS, arranging a fall show of Frank Lloyd Wright's work and going to a million and one official functions.

In October, we were at a cocktail party at Averell Harriman's house, where I noticed he'd hung photographs of some of his heroes, like General Sherrill, on the wall. This gave me a thought: if I ever went into the cookery business, it would help to have photos of some of my heroes on display—Carème, Escoffier, and, *naturellement*, Bugnard. One should always prepare for the future!

Autumn was hunting season, "*la chasse*," a serious passion in France, and suddenly wild game of every pelt and feather appeared in the marketplaces. Wild hares and rabbits hung whole; haunches of elk, wild boar, and venison were presented with hoof and fur intact. The shoppers insisted on this, Bugnard explained, for how would you know what you were buying if the game was all skinned and wrapped up?

I was eager to try these delicacies, and was thrilled when Bugnard instructed me on where to buy a proper haunch of venison and how to prepare it. I picked a good-looking piece, then marinated it in red wine, aromatic vegetables, and herbs, and hung the lot for several days in a big bag out the kitchen window. When I judged it ready, by smell, I roasted it for a good long while. The venison made a splendid dinner, with a rich, deep, gamy-tasting sauce, and for days afterward Paul and I feasted on its very special cold meat. When the deer had given us its all, I offered the big leg-bone structure to Minette. "Would you like to try this, *poussiequette?*" I asked her, laying the platter on the floor. She approached tentatively and sniffed. Then the wild-game signals must have hit her central nervous system, for she suddenly arched her back and, with hair standing on end, let out a snarling *groowwwwlllll!* She lunged at the bone and, grabbing it with her sharp teeth, dragged it out onto the living-room rug—luckily a well-worn Oriental—where she chewed at it for a good hour before stalking off. (Even in such intense circumstances, she rarely laid paw on bone, preferring to use her teeth.)

Game birds are especially popular in autumn. You see gaggles of pheasants and grouse, woodcocks with their long thin bills, partridges, and wild duck in the marketplace of every village, hamlet, and town. It seems the French will eat almost any feathered flying creature, from thrushes to swallows to blackbirds and larks (called *alouettes*, as in the song "Alouette, Gentille Alouette"); on several occasions we ate a tiny but delicious avian called *un vanneau*, or lapwing.

Partridge was one of my favorite discoveries. During one early-morning exploration of Les Halles, Chef Bugnard stopped at a friend's stall and, picking up a partridge, said, "Here you see a *perdreau*." The generic name for partridge is *perdrix*, but a young roasting bird is a *perdreau*. He decided to demonstrate how to make the famous *perdreau rôti sur canapé*, a roast partridge on a crouton of its own chopped liver.

Bending the tip end of the bird's breastbone, he said, "Feel that. It bends a little at the end." With some difficulty at first, because of the feathers, I felt the breastbone. It did indeed have about half an inch of flexibility at the tail end. The bird's legs and feet were also subjected to Chef's inspection: if there was a claw above the back of the heel, it was mature; youthful *perdreaux* have but a nubbin where the eventual claw will be, and their legs are not raddled by age. The feathers, too, tell something, since those of the young have a bit of white at the very tips.

Picking up a mature partridge, a *perdrix*, he said, "When you feel a rigid bone from neck to tail, you have maturity." A *perdrix* wants braising in cabbage, he said, and *perdrix en chartreuse* is the classic recipe.

At the Restaurant des Artistes, on Rue Lepic, Chef Mangelatte offered a beautifully roasted *perdreau* nesting on a toasty crouton, surrounded by sprigs of very fresh watercress and a small haystack of just-cooked crisp shoestring potatoes. Its nicely browned head, shorn of feathers but not of neck or beak, would be curled around its shoulder, and its feet, minus claws, folded up at either side of its breast. It's hardly an American presentation, but a game-lover wants to see all those telltale appendages, just to be sure it's really a *perdreau* on the platter.

The patron beautifully and swiftly carved off legs, wings, and breast, and served each person an entire bird, including the back, feet, head, and neck (when eating game, you nibble everything). He had placed the breast upon the *canapé,* an oval-shaped slice of white bread browned in clarified butter, topped with the liver—which had been chopped fine with a little fresh bacon—then mixed with drops of port wine and seasonings before a brief run under the broiler. The sauce? A simple deglazing of the roasting juices with a little port and a swirl of butter. Delicious!

The bird itself is smallish, with a different whiff, a winey brown promise of rosy dark meat that is also tantalizingly yet subtly gamy. You want it hung just long enough so that when you flare the breast feathers you begin to smell game; then you pluck it and roast it at once.

This is the kind of food I had fallen I love with: not trendy, souped-up fantasies, just something very good to eat. It was classic French cooking, where the ingredients have been carefully selected and beautifully and knowingly prepared. Or, in the words of the famous gastronome Curnonsky, "Food that tastes of what it is."

IV. SIMCA AND LOUISETTE

ONE DAY IN NOVEMBER 1951, we had a Gourmette, a Madame Simone Beck Fischbacher, to lunch at Roo de Loo. We talked about food, of course. She was a tall, dashing, vigorous *française* of about forty-two, with shoulder-length blond hair parted on the side, pale milky skin, high cheekbones, dark-rimmed glasses, and firmly held convictions.

Raised in an aristocratic household in Normandy (her grandfather produced Benedictine, a cordial liqueur), she had been brought up partly by English nannies, and could speak decent, if heavily accented, English. She was mad about food, and her specialty was pastry and desserts. She was intensely energetic. Although she never attended college, Simone had channeled her vigor into things like bookbinding, at first, and then into cooking, her true love. She studied at the Cordon Bleu under the famed chef and author Henri-Paul Pellaprat, whom she also hired for private cooking lessons. She had extensive knowledge of the cuisine of her native Normandy, the northern region of France, renowned for its rich butter and cream, beef, and apples.

Simone's second husband, Jean Fischbacher, was a lively Alsatian and a chemical engineer at the L. T. Piver perfume company. (Her first marriage ended in divorce.) For Simca and Jean, the subject of food was a precious and meaningful thing. During the war, they had faced terrible deprivations: Jean had been captured by the Nazis, and Simca sent him messages sewn inside prunes that were delivered to his prison camp. A humorous and cultured man, he had nicknamed his wife Simca after the little Renault model she drove: he thought it was funny that such a big woman (she stood over five feet eight inches tall—lanky for a Frenchwoman) could fit into such a tiny car.

Simca and I had met earlier that year, at a party for French and Americans involved with the Marshall Plan. Knowing we were both food-obsessed, our host, George Artamonoff, the former president of Sears International, introduced us. Simca and I hit it off right away. For the next hour we talked about food, food preparation, food people, wine, and restaurants. We could have kept talking all night, and agreed to meet again.

A few days later, Simca introduced me to another Gourmette, Madame Louisette Bertholle, a slim, pretty woman with cropped dark hair who had spent time in New Orleans, Louisiana, and Grosse Pointe, Michigan. She was married to Paul Bertholle, the European representative of an American chemical company; they had two daughters. Louisette was a dear person, small and neat, with a wonderfully vague temperament. As Paul said, she was "every American's idea of a perfect Frenchwoman."

Simca and Louisette, it turned out, had been working on a cookbook that they hoped to publish in the United States. (Simca had already published a slim brochure of recipes, *Le pruneau devant le fourneau*, about prunes and prune liqueurs, for a group of prune-boosters.) Louisette had contributed a few dishes, but, as Simca told it, it was she who had worked like a madwoman to muster over a hundred recipes for their book—ideas garnered from her own experiments, her mother's note-

Louisette, me, and Simca in the Roo de Loo kitchen, using the famous mortar and pestle and a tamis *to make* quenelles

books, her family's cook, restaurant chefs, the Gourmettes, and so on. She had sent the recipes to a family friend in the U.S.A., Dorothy Canfield Fisher, a successful author from Vermont and a member of the Book-of-the-Month Club's editorial board.

In her reply, Mrs. Canfield Fisher did not mince words: "It won't do," she wrote. "This is just a dry bunch of recipes, with not much background on French food attitudes and ways of doing things." Americans were accustomed to eating lots of meat and processed foods, she said, and French cooking was virtually unknown there. "You've got to preface the recipes and tell little anecdotes—something that explains the whole way the French do things in the kitchen." Mrs. Canfield Fisher ended her letter with a suggestion: "Get an American who is crazy about French cooking to collaborate with you; somebody who both knows French food and can still see and explain things with an American viewpoint in mind."

It was good advice. Through a friend of Louisette's, the would-be authors had placed their collection of recipes with the small New York publisher Ives Washburn. Washburn had agreed to produce and distribute the book, and had given their material to a freelance food editor named Helmut Ripperger, who would get the book into shape for the U.S. market.

It sounded like a wonderful idea, a modest little book filled with tried-and-true French recipes written just for American cooks. I wished them *bonne chance*!

ALL THIS COOKERY talk made me eager to put the finishing touches on my own recipes and to start teaching. My ideal pupils would be just like the kind of person I had been: those who aspired to be accomplished home cooks, capable of making the basic themes and variations of *la cuisine bourgeoise*, but didn't know where to begin. Simca and Louisette and I discussed this idea, and discussed it some more, and before long we had agreed to start up a little cooking school of our own, right there in Paris!

With their knowledge of food and local connections, my recent experience at the Cordon Bleu and access to American students, it seemed a logical step for the three of us to make *en concert*. We unanimously agreed that our fees would be nominal—just enough to cover our expenses—and that our classes would be open to anyone who wanted to join them. Louisette offered the use of the kitchen in her rather grand apartment on Avenue Victor Hugo, on the Right Bank, once she had finished renovating it. I offered to place an ad in the U.S. Embassy newspaper. In a nod to the Gourmettes that had brought us together, we decided to call our venture L'École des Gourmettes.

v. *L'ÉCOLE*

IN DECEMBER 1951, *Life* magazine ran a damning article entitled "First, Peel an Eel," about the Cordon Bleu. In it, the author, an American named Frances Levison, recounted her six-week elementary cooking course with Chef Bugnard in an arch, amusing style. She made much of the school's small rooms, non-working ovens, ancient knives, lack of basic supplies, "cryptic" teachers, and the French "attitude toward hygiene and water, neither of which has much appeal for them." Perhaps she overstated her case for the sake of drama, but her facts were basically correct.

In Paris there was a cry of alarm over what impact the *Life* story would have on the school. But when Simca and Louisette discussed it with Madame Brassart, she waved her hand dismissively and denied the school had any problems whatsoever.

In mid-December, Chef Bugnard told me that, since the article had appeared, "nothing has been done to improve matters" at the school. And when I attended two cooking demonstrations there just before Christmas, I couldn't help noticing that there was no thyme, not enough garlic, a broken basket, and no proper pot for cooking *nids de pommes de terre*. Hm.

ON JANUARY 15, 1952, Paul and Charlie celebrated their half-century birthday on either side of the Atlantic. Paul was alternately vexed by his advancing years, and buoyed by his theory that "old age is a state of mind and a function of mass hypnosis rather than an absolute." He took to quoting the phrase *Illegitemus non carborundum est* ("Don't let the bastards grind you down").

Over in Lumberville, Pennsylvania, our country cousins Charlie and Freddie began their *demi-siècle* celebration with iced champagne and continued on in a sort of free-floating bacchanal all night long.

In Paris, meanwhile, the celebration of Paul's fiftieth birthday was our most impressive party yet. We had six couples for dinner. So that I could avoid hopping in and out of the kitchen all night, we hired Chef Bugnard to cook for us, a maître d'hôtel to serve, and another man to pour wine. Jeanne-la-folle was beside herself with excitement, and she provided enthusiastic help in the kitchen. Paul hand-lettered invitations, and we made spiffy "medals" of colored silk ribbon, enamel pins, and nonsense inscriptions for each guest (mine was labeled "Marquise de la Mousse Manquée"). Paul chose the wines from our *cave* to match an elaborate menu that Chef Bugnard and I composed: *amuse-gueules au fromage* (hot *pâtes feuilletées* topped with cheese, served in the living room with Krug champagne); *rissolettes de foie gras Carisse; filet de boeuf Matignon* (served with a nearly perfect Bordeaux, Château Chauvin 1929); *les fromages* (Camembert, Brie de Melun, Époisses, Roquefort, Chèvre); *fruits rafraîchis; gâteau de demi-siècle;* café, liqueurs, hundred-year-old Cognac; Havana cigars and Turkish cigarettes.

Three days before the party, Paul awoke with a swollen and aching jaw. At breakfast he couldn't even bite into a soft piece of bread without rising three feet out of his chair in pain. Was it a sign of Creeping Decrepitude? Was it a psychological reaction to turning fifty? Or was it just plain bad luck? Furious at himself, he swallowed fistfuls of Empirin tablets to ease the pain, but they had no effect. "What a cynical little twist of the knob on Fate's machine," Paul despaired. The dentist diagnosed Paul with an advanced case of pyorrhea: eventually three of his teeth would have to be pulled. For now, the dentist ground down the surfaces of Paul's afflicted teeth, scraped away calcareous deposits from under the gums, and injected lactic acid into the pocket.

By Monday evening, Paul had a fever and was hardly the Birthday Boy of our dreams. To make things even more interesting, he had bitten his tongue while it was numbed. Nevertheless, the party went off magnificently.

Paul smiled handsomely in a brilliant-green wool waistcoat with brass buttons, a bright-red tie, and bright-red socks. I wore a wreath of tiny roses around my head, to which I added a golden crown given to me by Hélène Baltrusaitis. Chef Bugnard performed magic in the kitchen, and we all agreed it was one of the finest meals we'd ever eaten, anywhere, anytime.

A FEW DAYS after the party, our vague plans for a cooking school were snapped into sharp focus when Martha Gibson, a wealthy, fifty-five-ish Pasadenan, called to say she wanted cooking lessons. The next day, a friend of hers, Mrs. Mary Ward, called to say she'd like to join in, too.

Then a third American, a nifty forty-year-old gal named Gertrude Allison, called with the same request. All three of them had plenty of free time and money in hand.

There was only one problem: we three profs weren't quite ready for them. Louisette's kitchen renovation was not finished, we had not discussed menus or even our teaching format, and we had never cooked together before. But is anyone ever completely ready for a new undertaking, especially in a profession like cooking, where there are at least a hundred ways to cook a potato?

Tant pis, we decided: we have three students and three teachers—*allons-y!*

L'École des Gourmettes convened its first class on January 23, 1952, in our kitchen at 81 Rue de l'Université. We focused on French food, for that's what we all knew, and classical technique, as we felt that once a student has the basic tools they can be adapted to Russian, German, Chinese, or any other cuisine. There was much discussion *parmi les professeurs,* as we all had different methods. Whereas Simca and I tended to take a scientific approach (i.e., we measured quantities), Louisette took a more romantic approach (she'd use a pinch of salt or a splash of water, and worked out her recipes by instinct).

My colleagues had a lifetime of eating and cooking in France, and had been working on a cookbook together. I had learned how to clean and carve all sorts of things, make wonderful sauces, and sharpen a knife; plus, I brought an American practicality to such questions as how to shop, cook, and clean without a staff (something that Simca and Louisette did not have a grasp of at all). It took us a bit of time to get used to working side-by-side, but ultimately the combination of our three personalities meshed very well indeed.

Every Tuesday and Wednesday, we'd begin our class at ten and would end at one, with lunch. A typical menu would include poached fish, beef knuckle, salad, and a banana tart. Beforehand, we'd pool our money and shop for ingredients; then we'd type up detailed notes on the menu, steps to take in preparation, and the techniques we'd be using. The atmosphere of our classes was just what we'd hoped for—homey and fun, informal but passionate. Everyone was free to comment or criticize, and if mistakes were made we discussed what they were and how to avoid them. In one of the early classes, we made a leek, potato, and watercress soup; instead of using cream, we used some old milk, which

L'École des Gourmettes

curdled. It was embarrassing, but we soldiered on. We teachers were learning just as much as, if not more than, our students!

We charged seven thousand francs (about twenty dollars) for the first three lessons, which worked out to six hundred francs apiece per lesson. That included everything, plus about three dollars' worth of wear-and-tear on our kitchen per lesson.

My friends in the markets were fascinated by our *école*. The darling chicken man on la Rue Cler gave us a special price, and was most anxious to give our students a demonstration on how to choose a fine bird. The butcher felt the same way about his meats. Dehillerin, the cook-

Chef Bugnard giving a class at our école

ware store, offered a 10 percent discount on all student purchases. Jeanne-la-folle enjoyed the classes hugely; she'd arrive at one to eat leftovers and help clean up. Minette was interested, too, though she felt she wasn't getting her share of leftovers.

We were lucky in our early students, for they were enthusiastic and hardworking. Martha Gibson and Mary Ward were both widows, and very pleasant, but neither had found a passionate calling in life. Gertrude Allison had spent three years in the cafeteria business, had studied home economics at Columbia University, and had a sound business sense. She ran an inn in Arlington, Virginia, called Allison's Little Tea House, which catered mostly to officers from the Pentagon at lunchtime and to family groups in the evening. Gertrude said she had taken several cooking classes in New York with the English chef Dione Lucas, whom she found adept but not very precise. I quizzed Gertrude about the economics of her restaurant. She charged $1.75 to $3.50 for dinner, she said, adding that studies showed that restaurateurs shouldn't pay more than 6 percent of their gross for rent.

One Wednesday, Paul came home to join us for lunch, and he brought Mary Parsons, the USIS librarian, who lived in the same hotel as Mary Ward. We served *sole meunière*, a mixed salad with chopped hard-boiled eggs, and a dessert of *crêpes Suzettes flambées au Grand Marnier*. As he watched us bustle about the kitchen, Paul was surprised to see how much fun both the students and teachers were having.

Our pupils had not had much exposure to wine, and kept making uninformed statements like "Oh, wine, I don't like it." When Mary Ward said, "I never drink red wine; I like only dry white," Paul took it as a personal insult. "That's like saying, 'I never talk to French people; I only talk to Italians,' " he said. Then he offered her a glass of red wine he considered quite good, a Château Chauvin '29, a flowery, well-rounded Bordeaux. Mary took one sip and said, "Hey, I never realized red wine could taste like that!"

As a result, Paul agreed to give the class a lecture on wines. He explained how to match individual wines to specific food, how to store bottles, cork them properly, and so on. At the end, he served us all a fine bottle of Médoc 1929, and won three new converts.

THE LONGER WE LIVED in Paris, the more the city and its residents got under my skin. We especially enjoyed *le groupe Foçillon*'s evenings *chez* Baltru. It was a memorable bunch. Louis Grodecki, known as "Grod"—the intense, thick-lensed Polish art-historian—was about thirty-nine, and was a medieval stained-glass specialist. He had made an important discovery at the Abbaye de Saint-Denis, which dated the original building back to the sixth century, much earlier than his archaeological rivals had. He reveled in his triumph.

Jean and Thérèse Asche had become dear friends of ours. She taught grammar school, and Jean was a professor of the history of structure at the Conservatoire des Arts et Métiers. He was on a strict dietary regime due to the lingering aftereffects of his time in Buchenwald: forced to carry heavy rocks there, he suffered from compressed disks in his back;

of the sixteen hundred men in his unit, only two hundred survived the camp. The Asches remained hearty, intelligent, and sensitive people, and Paul and I loved their company.

Our luminous hostess, Hélène Baltrusaitis, remained perhaps my closest friend in Paris. Jurgis, however, seemed to grow more sour, prickly, and egocentric every day. Paul took to calling him Yoghurt. He seemed to ignore his son, Jean, a sweet boy who didn't have much direction. Paul made a point of talking to the boy and gave him lessons on how to paint with watercolors. We had even agreed that, if the Baltruses were killed in a plane crash, Paul and I would raise Jean.

But people are constantly surprising. Jurgis, we were shocked to discover, was a genuine war hero. In the early 1940s, Hélène's stepfather, Henri Foçillon, had escaped to the United States, where he broadcast anti-fascist messages back to France on clandestine radio. But in his haste to escape, Foçillon had left behind a mass of incriminating papers in his country house, filled with the names of French Resistance fighters. The house, near Chaumont, was occupied by a group of German engineers, who, as far as anyone knew, had never stumbled on the papers. After a year, the engineers were suddenly transferred elsewhere. Jurgis learned that a new batch of Germans was due to arrive in two days. So he made his way from Paris to Chaumont, broke into the house, found the papers, and destroyed them just before the new contingent arrived. He had undeniably shown selfless bravery.

IN SEPTEMBER 1952, our four-year stint with USIS would automatically terminate. What would happen to us then? No one knew. Despite our best efforts to divine the future, no information of any kind was forthcoming from Washington, D.C. For all we knew, Paul might be offered another post abroad, be recalled to the U.S.A., or be rudely shoved out of government.

I grew depressed at the thought of leaving Paris. Our three-plus years there had been so glorious, had passed so quickly, and had left us with so much more to learn and do, that the very idea of decamping left me cold and disgruntled. Many conversations along the theme of "What Shall We Do Next?" ensued, and the upshot was a fundamental decision: if we were to leave government service, we'd try to find other work in Paris and stay for one more year—at least.

SIMCA, LOUISETTE, AND I had, for diplomatic and psychological reasons, renamed our school L'École des Trois Gourmandes, which I roughly translate as "The School of the Three Hearty Eaters." Anita Littell, wife of Bob Littell, head of *Reader's Digest*'s European office, and a couple of other women had signed up for a class, but before we began this session Simca and I spent hours practicing by ourselves.

We experimented with recipes, tools, and ingredients, and made several useful discoveries. In working on piecrusts, for instance, we had tested French versus American ingredients. To our horror, we discovered that French flour has more body than its U.S. counterpart, and that the French needed a third less fat to make a nice crumbly crust. Why was this? I wanted to know. We supposed that, in order for U.S. flour to last forever on supermarket shelves, it must have been subjected to chemical processes that removed its fats. The French flour, in contrast, was left in its natural state, although it would go "off" more quickly and become maggoty. In order to make our French recipe work for an American audience, we tested different proportions of flour-to-butter, flour-to-margarine (a substance I abhorred and referred to as "that other spread"), and flour-to-Crisco; then we tasted the crusts hot and cold. Based on our experiments, we adjusted our ratios. It was labor-intensive, but a thoroughly satisfying learning process.

Simca was full of inventive ideas for hors d'oeuvres and cakes and pastries, and made delicious things with sugar, egg whites, and powdered almonds. The latter was one of those ingredients I didn't think were widely available in America. To find out, I wrote Freddie and asked what she could find in her local supermarket. She reported back that, although powdered almonds were not available in her rural corner of Pennsylvania, they might be available in cities like Manhattan or Chicago. This sort of on-the-ground reporting from my *belle soeur* in the U.S.A. was extremely helpful. She also sent me pictures of the different cuts of meat from her butcher shop, and a set of American measuring cups. In fits and starts, we were making progress!

In the meantime, I had been working on my "hen scratches"—my collection of recipes. I was amazed to learn, upon close inspection, how inexact many of the recipes in well-regarded books were, and how painfully exact ours must be to be worth anything at all. Each recipe took hours of work, but I was finally getting them into order. Through trial-and-error, for instance, I deduced exactly how much gelatin must go into exactly how much liquid per exactly how much mayonnaise so one can make pretty mayo curlicues on a fish dish.

My friends thought I was insane to be spending so much time on such details. But I found the process of getting recipes into scientific workability absolutely fascinating.

Louisette did not devote as much time as Simca and I did to culinary exactness, but she seemed to know everyone. At one point, she had us over for lunch with Irma Rombauer, author of the *Joy of Cooking*, who was vacationing in Paris. I had always adored "Mrs. Joy's" book, and liked that her personality shone clearly through its pages. In person, she turned out to be a very likable seventy-year-old Midwestern housewife type. She took great interest in our Trois Gourmandes project and told us all about her book. *Joy* was aimed at neither the wealthy nor the poor, she explained, but at the middle masses, who did most of their own cooking. Understanding how important time was around the house, she had concentrated on dishes that were not too fancy and didn't require hours of preparation. She added that she'd had troubles with her publisher: when she wanted to include a detailed index, they refused; plus, she claimed, she'd been weaseled out of the royalties for something like fifty thousand copies of her book. Publishing, it seemed, was a difficult business.

VI. *LE PRINCE*

ONE DAY LOUISETTE took Simca and me to meet the celebrated gastronome Curnonsky. He was about seventy-nine years old, rotund, with twinkling blue eyes, triple chins, and an eagle beak. His ego was enormous, but so were his charm and the breadth of his knowledge. Curnonsky was most famous for his twenty-eight-volume encyclopedia of France's regional foods, but he had also founded the Académie des Gastronomes in 1928, and was editor of the French cooking magazine *Cuisine et Vins de France*.

His real name was Maurice-Edmond Saillant. As a twenty-year-old reporter, Saillant, even then a gourmet, was sent by his newspaper on a routine assignment to cover a feast of Russian royalty in Paris. (All things Russian were very à la mode at the time.) He wrote a magnificent article, but his editor balked at his rather pedestrian byline: "After all, Monsieur Saillant, you are an unknown reporter. If we use your real name, who will ever read this? It's really a pity you aren't a Russian noble."

"That's simple to fix," replied Saillant. "I'll sign it 'Prince Curnonsky.'" And he did. He had cleverly created this vaguely Russian-sounding nom de plume from the Latin words *Cur non* and the English "sky" ("Why not sky?").

The "prince's" article was read by *le tout Paris*. "Who *is* this fabulous Curnonsky who knows so much about our cuisine?" everyone wondered.

By the time the truth leaked out, several months and several more

Les Trois Gourmandes having dinner with Curnonsky

articles later, Curnonsky was established. And he'd written—and eaten and drunk—off his reputation ever since.

The day we met him, Curnonsky greeted us at four in the afternoon in his apartment, dressed in a billowing nightshirt and red bathrobe. He was eating a boiled egg. As usual, he would go out to tea, or for a cocktail, a bit later. Come evening, his biggest decision would be which invitation to accept, as there were always more offers than he could accept. After an enormous meal at one or another of Paris's best restaurants, followed by the theater or music or the latest nightclub (always at someone else's expense), he'd retire by 4:00 a.m.

Simca and I immediately fell for him. He struck me as a character out of a novel, or from another century. I couldn't imagine a person like *le prince* coming from anywhere but France.

DORTIE WROTE TO SAY she was pregnant, and described herself as "fat and helpless." I was so happy for her now that she was a full-fledged *woman*, with a breast-full of milk. Ivan had quit the government, and they had moved to San Francisco, where he was learning the clothing trade at Garfinkel's department store.

Friday, August 15, 1952, was Assumption Day: not only a national holiday but the very nadir of *la morte-saison* in Paris. Paul telephoned nine different restaurants in an attempt to secure a table for my fortieth birthday, but not one of them was open. We finally ate lunch at the Hôtel Ritz, which was fine. That afternoon, we walked over to the Île Saint-Louis, to visit Abe and Rosemary Manell, some friends from the Foreign Service. Abe was a natural politician, loud and quick-minded, and knew all the embassy gossip. Rosie was a large, blonde Californian painter, an Earth Mother type, and we became fast friends. They had wonderful views of Paris from their apartment. Paul was so smitten he'd return to make sketches and take photos of the canted, tiled rooftops in preparation for a series of paintings.

That evening we had a second fancy meal in celebration of my fortieth, at the three-star Lapérouse. We arranged to sit in a back room with seven tables, so as to have some (but not too many) other people to look at. Because of the season, and the prices, every table was occupied by Americans. Paul and I began our meal with *sole aux délices* (sole in a wondrous cream sauce with truffles) and half a bottle of Chablis. Then we had roast duck with a not-too-heavy sauce and a bottle of Chambertin '26. Then cheese, coffee, and raspberry liqueur. It was delicious and expert and pleasant. Despite my advancing age, I still had an appetite!

I gave my first solo cooking lesson, on *pâte feuilletée* (puff pastry), to Solange Reveillon, a Parisienne friend. Though I'd made *pâte feuilletée* many times, I did it again before Solange arrived, in order to think deeply about what I was going to say and do. The lesson went well, and we filled the *pâtes* with mushrooms and cream sauce and ate them for lunch. It was such fun! And I learned so much by teaching. I would have gladly paid Solange for the chance to teach *pâte feuilletée*, rather than vice versa.

Later, I critiqued my teaching technique. When people pay good money for a class they expect skillful professionalism, and I decided that, though the cooking we'd done was fine, my presentation had not been very clear. I lacked experience and self-confidence. Paul, who had taught school for seventeen years, reminded me that when teaching one must be willing to "play God" for a bit—in other words, to be an authority. I knew he was right, but I have never liked dogmatism. I was more inclined to tell my students what I *don't* know, or that there are so many *other* ways of doing things, and admit that I am aware of only a *few* of the possibilities. Ah me, there was still so much to learn, and cooking was only half of it. I felt I'd have to teach at least a hundred classes before I really knew what I was doing.

OUR TENANTS had moved out of our Olive Avenue house in Washington, and the real-estate agent wanted to know if he should rent it again. We didn't have an answer. Nor did anyone else in the U.S. government, apparently. It was maddening. Paul and I didn't want to change our life pattern, nor did we fancy standing in the middle of the prairie with no options at all. So he began to agitate quietly behind the scenes. "I understand how government works," Paul wrote his twin. "To the boys in Washington . . . I am just a body. If there is a slot in Rome, or Singapore, my body could be plunked there—or Zamboanga."

Abe Manell, a bureaucratic operator par excellence, said he'd try to pull strings so that Paul could take over Abe's previous job as public-affairs officer (PAO) in Marseille. "That's the best job in France!" Abe declared. "You should snap it up in a minute." A PAO was a number-two man to the consul general in a place like Marseille. The PAO was a jack-of-all-diplomatic-trades: a public-relations man (who promoted the U.S.A. and French-U.S. relations), a political officer (who sized up Communist influence), a cultural impresario (who acquired American movies and books that local residents might like, worked with educational exchanges, spoke to the press, and arranged sporting events), and diplomatic factotum (who made speeches, laid wreaths, unveiled statues, arranged dances for U.S. Navy sailors, etc.).

"Well," we said to each other, "Marseille is our second-favorite city in France. If we get the PAO offer, why not give it a whirl?"

Feeling a premonitory sadness at leaving Paris, we walked up to the edge of Montmartre to see a movie. Afterward, we wandered over to the Restaurant des Artistes. We arrived late, and as there were no other clients we had a sort of family get-together with Monsieur Caillon, his daughter, and Roger the waiter. We all sat around a big table and chatted in a very familiar way. After that, we walked down the hill and home through streets wet with the rain that had fallen while we were inside. The lamplit city glittered in its puddles, and Notre Dame loomed out of the mist, giving our nerves a twinge. When you know your time in a place is running out, you try to fix such moments in your mind's eye.

VII. OPERATIONAL PROOF

AT NINE O'CLOCK on the night of August 25, 1952, all the bells of Paris began banging and clanging and tintinnabulating at once. It was a remembrance of the Liberation of Paris on that day in 1944. Anyone who had heard the carillon then and heard it now must have had chills running up and down the spine.

A few days later, Simca and Louisette got word that Helmut Ripperger, the freelance editor hired by Ives Washburn to shape their cookbook for the U.S. market, had upped and quit, leaving his work only partly done. My colleagues were distressed, and told me the history of their book. They had started working together in 1948. Once Ives Washburn agreed to take them on, in 1951, the "food adviser" Helmut Ripperger was hired at sixty dollars a week to produce a little booklet, based on their work, as a teaser. Called *What's Cooking in France*, by Bertholle, Beck, and Ripperger, it looked fairly attractive, and the

introduction and bridge passages were charming, but the recipes were not very professional. It was sixty-three pages long, contained fifty recipes, and, priced at $1.25, only sold about two thousand copies. Simca and Louisette were angry that they hadn't even been shown a proof before it was published, and felt embarrassed by it. Now Ripperger had thrown in the towel—or had the towel thrown at him—and disappeared without finishing work on the "big" book.

My disheartened friends now faced the daunting job of finishing their work without a real understanding of how to write for the American market. As we talked it over, they almost shyly asked if I might, perhaps, be willing to help them finish their book.

"I would be delighted to!" I answered, almost before the question was out of their mouths. And so our collaboration began.

I FIRST READ their nearly six-hundred-page manuscript in early September 1952. Its problems and its potential immediately jumped out at me.

Simca and Louisette had created a big jumble of recipes, like any other cookbook. Their language wasn't "American." Most of the directions struck me as needlessly complicated where they should be clear and concise. And the overall conception of the book was not well suited for the American home kitchen. In fact, I didn't like it at all. On the other hand, I wasn't aware of any book that explained *la cuisine bourgeoise* the way this one did.

The more I thought about it, the more this project fired my imagination. After all, the lessons embedded in these recipes were a logical extension of the material we used in our classes. I liked to strip everything down to the bones; with a bit of work, I thought this book could do that, too, only on a much more comprehensive scale. I had come to cooking late in life, and knew from firsthand experience how frustrating it could be to try to learn from badly written recipes. I was determined that our cookbook would be clear and informative and accurate, just as our teaching strove to be.

If my co-authors agreed, not one of the recipes would stand as written. I'd turn this from a rewrite job into an entirely new book. I girded my loins, spit on the old Underwood, and began to type up my suggestions—clickety-clack—like a determined woodpecker.

Part of my problem as a practical American was the deeply ingrained chauvinism and dogmatism in France, where cooking was considered a major art: if Montagne said such-and-such, then it was considered gospel, especially by the men's gastronomical societies, which were made up of amateurs—and, my, how they loved to talk! The history of a dish, who said what about it and when, was terribly important to them. But, as Paul liked to say, "The word is not the thing" (one of his favorite utterances, borrowed from the semanticist Alfred Korzybski). As I worked on the manuscript, I reminded myself not to accept Simca and Louisette's directions at face value. I subjected every recipe to what we called "the operational proof": that is, it's all theory until you see for yourself whether or not something works.

I checked every recipe in the manuscript on the stove and on the page. I also investigated various old wives' tales that weren't in the regular cookbooks but that many people were "certain" were true. This took endless amounts of time.

Working on soups, for instance, I made a soup a day *chez* Child. On the day for *soupe aux choux*, I consulted Simca's recipe, as well as the established recipes of Montagne, *Larousse*, Ali-Bab, and Curnonsky. I read through them all, then made the soup three different ways—following two recipes exactly as written, and making one adaptation for the pressure cooker (the stinking, nasty, bloody pressure cooker— I hated it! It made everything taste nasty! But it was popular in U.S. households). At dinner, my guinea pig, Paul, complimented the three *soupes aux choux*, but I wasn't satisfied. One of the secrets to make this dish work, I felt, was to make a vegetable-and-ham stock before the cabbage was put in; also, not to cook the cabbage too long, which gives it a sour taste. But should the cabbage be blanched? Should I use a different variety of cabbage? Would the pressure-cooked soup taste better if I used the infernal machine a shorter time?

I had to iron out all of these questions of how and why and for what reason; otherwise, we'd end up with just an ordinary recipe—which was not the point of the book. I felt we should strive to show our readers how to make everything top-notch, and explain, if possible, why things work one way but not another. There should be no compromise!

Wiping my hands on my apron, I scribbled my questions and corrections in the manuscript's margins and pressed on. A pile of wrinkled and stained pages grew steadily on the counter next to my stove.

As I went, I made some discoveries in measurement that were every bit as important to me as a *groupe Foçillon* scholar's unearthing of an ancient tomb was to him. In preparing *béchamel* (white sauce), for instance, French cookbooks give the proportions of butter to flour in grams. But American books instruct their readers to use, say, "a tablespoon of butter and a tablespoon of flour," which gives you proportionally much more butter to flour than the French method. This realization forced us to rethink the recipe. In working up our own instructions for *béchamel*, we told our readers to use two tablespoons of butter and three tablespoons of flour for the roux. This may seem rather dry stuff to some, but to me it was a process of discovering an important and overlooked step, and then devising our own rationally thought-out solution. In short, a triumph!

I HAD BEEN WRESTLING with the subject of butter in sauces when Paul took me to a little bistro way over on the Right Bank, off the Avenue Wagram, called Chez la Mère Michel. The house specialty was *beurre blanc nantais*, a wonder-sauce used on fish. It is a regional, not classical, recipe, and the leading French cookbooks, from Carème right up through Ali-Bab, *Larousse Gastronomique*, and Curnonsky, were all extremely vague on the subject. I could find no complete and clear description of how to make *beurre blanc*. So I decided to do a bit of investigative reporting.

Walking into the restaurant, we met La Mère Michel herself: a small, white-haired, capable woman of about sixty-two. She had come to Paris from Nantes, on the Loire River, in 1911, she told us, and had started her restaurant fourteen years later. Her husband's job was to eat, drink wine, and talk to the customers, and he was good at it. The little restaurant could only hold about twenty patrons, but it had survived quite nicely, largely on the strength of its *beurre blanc*—a thick, creamy sauce that is really nothing but warm butter held in suspension by an acidic flavor base of shallots, wine, vinegar, salt, and pepper. It is traditionally a sauce for fish, vegetables, or poached eggs; when served with pike, the dish is known as *brochet au beurre blanc*.

The Michels were extremely friendly and forthcoming, and during a lull, the chef invited us into her kitchen to show us how she made her famous sauce in a brown enameled saucepan on an old household-type stove. I paid careful attention to how she boiled the acidic base down to a syrupy glaze, then creamed tablespoon-sized lumps of cold butter into it over very low heat. When we sat down to eat a carefully poached turbot crowned with a generous dollop of *beurre blanc* we found it stunningly delicious. The whole evening was filled with a sense of glowing satisfaction.

Back in my Roo de Loo laboratory the next day, I whipped up a few batches of *beurre blanc à la Mère Michel,* then wrote up what I believed to be the first clear and comprehensive recipe for the sauce. The final test came one evening when I cloaked a conger eel in *beurre blanc* for a small group of friends. It was of a *perfection historique.*

WE THREE GOURMANDES were a good combination of personalities. Louisette contributed some valuable suggestions of the novelty type—how and where to add flourishes of, say, garlic, shallots, fresh peas, or strips of tomato—which were thoroughly French but in the American spirit. People in the U.S.A. loved food novelties. Simca and I were more straightforward chef-type cooks.

Simca was roaring along on her recipe-testing and note-taking in a very professional way, sometimes for ten hours a day.

As for me, I knew nothing about publishing, other than that it was a cutthroat game, but I had decided that cookbook writing was just the right job for me. I found myself working for entire days on the manuscript with hardly a break. The house was becoming a wreck, but I hardly noticed (and Paul was understanding). Late one afternoon, our friends the Kublers drove up unexpectedly in a big red Jeep. We all trooped out to Chez Marius for supper. It was fun. But as soon as I got back to Roo de Loo, I sat right down at the typewriter and stayed there till 2:00 a.m.

Now that I had started writing, I found cookbookery such fulfilling work that I intended to keep at it for years and years.

VIII. *FRENCH HOME COOKING*

ONE NIGHT, at a dinner *chez* Bertholle, there were a dozen people at the table. The eight women and three of the four men began shouting at each other instead of talking—a French habit. They were having a fine old time arguing about Catholicism versus mysticism, about America's policy in Morocco, car accidents, how to mix a rum sour, and so on. I dove headfirst into the verbal maelstrom. But Paul, the only quiet one at the table, was miserable. He whispered that he wanted to leave. Well, this was one of our differences. On the way home in the car we had a spat. It began as a disagreement over what I saw as Paul's wish to withdraw from Life and go live in an Ivory Tower, and then it somehow devolved into a silly argument over *Time* magazine. Of course, the nub of our argument was probably something else entirely, like the uncertainty of our future.

The U.S. government still hadn't decided what to do with us. Our time in Paris was extended "temporarily."

In October 1952, the cold, gray, wet curtain of winter gradually dropped down around Paris, and word came down from on high that Paul would not get the coveted job as PAO for Marseille after all. The current PAO, who had been on an extended home leave, was returning to work. The news was deflating, but Abe Manell assured us, "You may still have a chance for the job." Two new possibilities had opened up: PAO in Bordeaux, or exhibits officer in Vienna. Paul and I talked it over and decided that we both loved France, spoke the language, had friends and contacts there, and were just not ready to leave yet. So—Bordeaux was our preference.

IN NOVEMBER, I received a letter from Sumner Putnam, head of the Ives Washburn publishing house, about our book, tentatively titled *French Home Cooking*. "After a year of frustration, we are still a long way from a completed book," he wrote. "The big job now rests on your shoulders and you must be the absolute boss of what goes into the book and what stays out." He noted that Ripperger's work on the big book was "by no means polished," and said, "You may want to throw out his efforts entirely."

He continued: "The American woman who buys *French Home Cooking* will probably resent advice on how to arrange her kitchen, set her table, handle a skillet or boil an egg: she learned those things from her mother or Fannie Farmer, don't you think? She expects a book that will show her how she can give her cooking the French touch. . . . If the recipe . . . can't be easily used by the stupidest pupil in your school, then it is too complicated."

Putnam's letter set off a frenzy of discussion amongst us authors, our husbands, and our friends. He seemed serious about publishing *French Home Cooking*, and he had absolutely charmed Louisette when she had visited him in New York a year earlier. But I had learned from friends in the States that Ives Washburn was not a very well-respected house. Mr. Putnam had money, apparently, and had gone into publishing as a hobby; he knew little about cooking, did little advertising for his books, and was said to keep slipshod accounts. We were committed to him morally, but not legally, for we had signed no contract and he had paid us no advance. He wanted to see a polished manuscript by March 1, 1953. How should we respond?

Simca and Louisette argued that we should stay the course with Ives Washburn. We were unknown authors, they pointed out, and Mr. Putnam was a nice man who liked our book. What good would it do to rock the boat?

I was not convinced. Though I quite appreciated that we were unknowns, I saw no reason to crawl about on our bellies. I felt that our revamped book was good enough that, in the right hands, it would sell itself. We were professionals, we had a clear vision, and our book was going to be something new and exciting. I even predicted, without modesty, that it might one day be considered a major work on the principles and practice of French cooking. Therefore, I saw no reason to waste our efforts on a no-account firm.

We talked and talked, and finally agreed to proceed with Ives Washburn—for the moment.

On behalf of the Trois Gourmandes, I wrote Sumner Putnam, explaining that the new version of *French Home Cooking* would not be just another collection of recipes but, rather, an introduction to the methods of French cooking *plus* recipes. Our approach would build off the Bugnard/Cordon Bleu system of teaching "theme and variation," as well as the methods we three had developed in our École des Trois Gourmandes classes. We'd write in an informal and humane tone that would make cooking approachable and fun. But the book would also be a serious, well-researched reference work. Our objective was to reduce the seemingly complex rules of French cooking to their logical sequences, something never before attempted either in English or in French.

"It is not enough that the 'how' [of making hollandaise or mayonnaise] be explained. One should know the 'why,' the pitfalls, the remedies, the keeping, the serving, etc.," I wrote. "This is a new type of cookbook." I concluded: "Competition in this field is stiff, but we feel this may well be a major work on French cooking . . . and could continue to sell for years."

Mr. Putnam did not reply to my letter. Nor did he respond to our chapter on sauces, which I had sent him by diplomatic pouch. It was very odd.

In the meantime, I sent three top-secret sauce recipes—for hollandaise, mayonnaise, and *beurre blanc*—to four trusted confidantes, for them to test in real American kitchens with real American ingredients. We referred to these ladies—Dort, Freddie Child, Dorothy Canfield Fisher, and Mrs. Freeman Gates (a friend of mine)—as our "guinea pigs," and asked them to try making each sauce just as we had described it and to give us honest feedback. "Our object is to explain 'how to cook French' for beginner and expert cooks," I wrote in a cover letter. "Do you like our vocabulary? Do you *care* about such a book?"

IX. AVIS

IN THE SPRING of 1952, Bernard De Voto had written an eloquent complaint about the quality of American-made cutlery in his "Easy Chair" column in *Harper's Magazine*. He was incensed about stainless steel, which may have been rust-resistant but was also resistant to keeping a good edge. This happened to be a favorite complaint of mine, too. So I wrote De Voto a fan note and enclosed two non-stainless French carbon-steel paring knives.

I got a lengthy, stylish letter back—from Mrs. De Voto, writing from their home in Cambridge, Massachusetts. Her name was Avis. She was the one who used the kitchen knives in their household, it turned out, and had suggested the subject to Bernard. Not only was Avis a stylish writer, she was a devoted cook. So began a regular correspondence back and forth, mostly about food.

Avis's letters gushed for five, six, seven pages at a clip. In one she wrote about a wonderful *pipérade*—an omelette with peppers, tomatoes, bacon, and onions—she'd had at a restaurant in Paris. The sense memory of that dish had lingered with her ever since, and she wondered how they made it. So Paul and I tracked the place down to have a look. It was unremarkable-looking and crowded inside, with people shouting and a radio blaring. I wouldn't go back there, but the *pipérade* was indeed excellent, and I took mental notes.

I sent Avis a copy of our sauce chapter, and explained about the troubles we'd had with Ives Washburn. She wrote right back, saying she thought our manuscript had the potential to be made into a splendid book, and asked permission to show it to Houghton Mifflin, her husband's publisher. Avis pointed out that Houghton Mifflin was well established, had plenty of mazuma, and had a cooking expert on staff, a Mrs. Dorothy de Santillana, who would know how to evaluate the manuscript from a culinary standpoint—a skill that Ives Washburn clearly lacked. Avis vouched that Houghton Mifflin were honest, generous, and wonderful to work with.

I was thrilled. But when I brought this idea up with my colleagues, Louisette balked: she felt we had an obligation to keep working with Sumner Putnam. I disagreed, saying that, in light of no advance, no contract, and, lately, no communication from him whatsoever, we had no obligation to the publisher. After some hedging, Simca sided with me. Louisette, feeling guilty, relented.

With a sigh of relief, I dashed off a note granting Avis permission to show our sauce chapter to Houghton Mifflin. Then we Trois Gourmandes crossed our fingers and got back to work.

ON TUESDAY, OCTOBER 28, all of France's best-known eaters, drinkers, food-sellers, preparers, and writers gathered for a fabulous banquet in Paris. These evenings were costly and could be taxing on the digestive system, and up until now we had always declined to go. But this one was special: it was in honor of Curnonsky's eightieth birthday.

There were 387 guests, each of whom was a member of one of the eighteen gastronomic societies of Paris. I belonged to Les Gourmettes, and Paul belonged to Le Club Gastronomique Prosper Montagne (named after the legendary chef, whom many club members had worked with). We couldn't help noticing a few cold stares from the Gourmettes when we sat at the Prosper Montagne table. But we had decided the Montagnes would be a more interesting lot, because they were all food professionals, whereas the ladies were enthusiastic amateurs.

The crowd was hearty and festively dressed. The women wore fancy

hats, and the men wore brightly colored ribbons around their necks, medals, gold chains, badges, and rosettes (based on medieval guild symbols) signifying that they were important. It was snazzy and fun, and those in the know could point out to us Ignorants the difference between *un chevalier du Tastevin, un chaîneur des rôtisseurs,* and *un compagnon de la belle table.*

On my left sat an *aubergiste*-chef who owned a two-star restaurant in the countryside. On my right was a big-shot butcher from Les Halles. Paul was bracketed by the men's wives, and we made a jolly sextet. Each place had nine glasses, and over the course of the meal we were ushered through a wonderful array of juices from a Pineau des Charentes to an 1872 Armagnac. The foods were superb, too: oysters, turbot, tournedos, sherbet, partridge, salad, cheeses, and ice cream. (The turbot and partridge were special "creations" to honor Curnonsky.) It had required sixteen chefs, no doubt working themselves to exhaustion, to prepare this magnificent feast.

The birthday cake was a massive ziggurat, eight layers high, decorated with eighty candles and florid fondant-sugar outbursts by a Parisian pastrymaster.

After coffee, an aged member of Le Cercle des Écrivains Gastronomes with flowing Einstein-like hair stood and gave a lengthy tribute to Curnonsky. After fifteen minutes of ponderous oration, the audience grew restless. After twenty minutes, there was a noticeable babble of talk around the edges of the room. After half an hour, the venerable *homme de lettres* began to pause every few minutes to glare and scold the crowd: "If the art of eating is the only art you are capable of appreciating, and the literary art means nothing to you, then I suggest you go home!"

Each of his asides was met with genial cheers and whistles.

When he finally lumbered to the end, there was loud applause and all sixteen of the chefs trooped out from the kitchen. Curnonsky beamed with pleasure, and kissed the top three chefs on both cheeks. It was now 12:45 a.m., and as more speeches began we drifted out homeward.

As a final salute to the great gastronome, twenty-seven of Paris's leading restaurants had little brass plates made with Curnonsky's name engraved on each. They were fixed to the best seats in every establishment. Anytime he felt like it, Curnonsky could call up, say, Le Grand

Véfour, and his place would be automatically reserved and he'd be served a meal free of charge.

MY STEPMOTHER, Phila, had an operation to remove a polyp from her intestines. I arranged a three-minute call to Pop, in Pasadena. Once he'd told me the polyp was benign, we had another two minutes and forty-five seconds left on the call. With the urgent news taken care of, you never know quite what to talk about in those situations. I said: "Well, I guess you Pasadenans are pretty glad about Ike's election results."

"Glad? I should say we are!" Big John thundered. "Why, who wouldn't be? Everybody's glad! But of course you people over there, you wouldn't know how the country feels—all your news is slanted."

This was hard to take, especially from the man who read only the right-leaning *L.A. Times*. For the record, Paul and I were avid devourers of the *New York Times*, the *Herald Tribune*, *Le Figaro*, *Time*, *Fortune*, *The Reporter*, *Harper's*, *The New Yorker*, even *L'Humanité*, not to mention the flood of embassy cables, intelligence briefs, and twenty-four-hour wire-service and ticker sheets pouring in from around the world. So—whose news was slanted?

A few days later, I received a note from my dear stepmother, Phila, telling me that her health was fine and asking me to please stop riling Pop up about politics, as it was too upsetting. Then my brother, John, chimed in, and told me to keep my liberal views to myself. Ye gads!

I wrote Pop religiously every week, but now that I couldn't mention politics, or my general philosophy of life, it would be pretty dull going. He was a darling man, a generous father, a real do-gooder in his community. In fact, he had everything it would take to be a real world-beater—except that he grew violently emotional over politics (so did I, but I was training myself to be more intellectually objective). He'd gone to Princeton, but was not intellectual, and was intolerant and incurious. He absolutely dismissed Paul as an "artist" and "New Dealer," which meant that there could be no real affection between my father and me. He was an example of how not to be. It was too bad.

IN THE FIRST WEEK of January 1953, we received a letter from Avis De Voto, which I read aloud to Simca and Louisette:

I've just finished reading your manuscript. I must say I am in a state of stupefaction. I am so keen about this proposed book that I am also feeling that it can't possibly be as good as I think it is. . . . I want to take the manuscript to Dorothy de Santillana's house right away. I know she will take fire as I have. . . . If this book makes out as I believe and hope it will it is going to be a classic, a basic and profound book. . . . I like the style enormously. It is just right—informal, warm, occasionally amusing. . . . If it gets the right publisher it wont matter how long it takes to test and try out and edit. If the publisher is inter-ested he will wait until you have finished your book. Alright. I just got D. Santillana on the phone and I'm going to her house tomorrow with the manuscript, which I hate to let out of my clutches. She is excited. . . . We will now join in a moment of silent prayer. . . .

x. A Curry of a Life

On January 15, 1953, Paul turned fifty-one, and was informed that it was "98 percent sure" that he would be named public-affairs officer for Marseille after all. We'd have to start the new job almost immedi-ately, probably in March, our embassy sources said. But as we hadn't gotten official orders yet, it was all very hush-hush.

My first thought was: *What wonderful luck! We could have been sent to Reykjavík or Addis Ababa, but instead we are staying in France!* My second thought was: *A sudden move to the other end of the country will be tough on our cookery-bookery, not to mention the Trois Gourmandes classes. We'll man-age, somehow.*

The impending shift got the old beehive buzzing. We romantically hoped that Paul's salary would double (after four-plus years in Paris, he had yet to receive a single raise or promotion), or that the ambassador would request that we do nothing but travel slowly around France, learning new recipes, taking pictures, and making friends. We'd be sip-ping tea and reading the morning paper when Paul would suddenly say, "I think it would be a smart idea to have calling cards printed before we go down to Marseille, don't you?" Or we'd be walking along the Seine and I'd blurt out, "I simply won't take a house that hasn't got a wine cel-lar. I don't care what they say!"

But then the horrors of moving would creep up on us. "Honestly, I groan when I think of starting over in a new place," Paul grumbled. "No wonder newborn babies cry so much. . . . If variety is the spice of life, then my life must be one of the spiciest you ever heard of. A curry of a life."

He'd heard that when you're a PAO the weekends are sometimes your most concentrated forty-eight hours of work in a week. "I don't think I'm going to like this job," he wrote Charlie. "When do you pause? When do you paint or pant? When write family, loll on moss, hear Mozart and watch the glitter of the sea? . . . Clearly, I am softened by the luxurious style of our Parisian life: comes Friday night in Paris and down comes that iron curtain between job and what I *really* like doing. Wham!, and I'm off with Julie on the flying carpet. . . . No backing-out now . . . Slide's all greased, and they're almost ready to give me the Old One-Two. . . . Hold yer hats, boys—here we go again!"

ON FRIDAY THE SIXTEENTH, we received a magnificent six-page gusher from Avis. Bernard was a meat-and-potatoes man, she wrote; he loved spicy food (especially Mexican and Indian), and wines, but was essentially wedded to the martini. Avis had secondary anemia, but was able to control it through diet; her tastes in food and drink were much like ours. As for our manuscript and Houghton Mifflin? Cautious optimism. Avis's impression was that our sauce chapter had been well received and there was a good chance they'd want to publish our book. But it was too soon to break out the champagne.

We still hadn't received so much as a postcard from Sumner Putnam.

I wrote to my fellow Gourmandes: "If HM [Houghton Mifflin] does happen to like our book and want it, we shall have some delicate dealings with Putnam if he also wants it. My great inclination would be to have ourselves with the HM Company, as they are one of the best. . . . I'm sure [Putnam] is a terribly nice man, but I don't feel he is able to bring up our baby the way the other chaps could."

A FEW DAYS LATER, Simca arrived in my kitchen with Chef Claude Thilmont, one of the great *pâtissiers-en-chef de Paris*, and a fine, honest, salty technician with a ripe accent. He came to teach, not to eat. We pupils showed that we could bake a cake and decorate it, too. But old Thilmont was tough, just as he ought to be, with high standards and a thorough teaching method.

"Good," he judged our first efforts at cake, "but not nearly good enough!"

Soon we had Chef Thilmont making a guest appearance at L'École des Trois Gourmandes. He had a magical touch with piecrusts. And when you saw him squeeze decorations onto a cake, you came to appreciate the famous saying "There are only four great arts: music, painting, sculpture, and ornamental pastry—architecture being perhaps the least banal derivative of the latter."

That January, when I made Paul a fifty-first-birthday cake using my new skills, my husband lauded it as "a mistresspiece." Thilmont himself described it as "not bad," which was just about his highest form of praise. I puffed out my (modest) chest in pride.

THE MISTRAL was a luxurious and speedy Paris-to-Marseille special train, and in mid-February 1953 it rocketed us down the length of France—a rainy, half-flooded, snow-speckled, khaki-colored landscape—in seven hours. We arrived in Marseille at 11:00 p.m. for a preliminary scouting trip.

The venerable port city spread out and slanted down to the Mediterranean under a clear, star-spangled sky. We were met at the station by Dave Harrington, the man Paul would replace as public-affairs officer. He took us on a long hike around town that ended at a bar, where we drank beer and learned about the consulate and the many duties of a PAO. Then we went to another bar, for more beer and talk. Harrington was charming and easygoing and had made wide-ranging local contacts. But something, evidently, had poisoned his relationship with Consul General Heywood Hill. This gave us pause. Harrington didn't seem like the type to make enemies. As we walked back to the hotel, Paul and I reassured each other that CG Hill would turn out to be a nice guy.

The next morning, we awoke to a bright, sunny day filled with noise. "I always forget between visits what a raucous, colorful city this is," Paul wrote. "There seems to be 10 times as much horn-blowing, gear-clashing, shouting, whistling, door-banging, dropping of lumber, breaking of glass, blaring of radios, boat-whistling, gong-clanging, brake-screeching, and angry shouting as anywhere else."

I didn't agree that the locals' shouting was "angry." It seemed to me that the Marseillais were having a wonderful time communicating, and they liked to do it at the top of their lungs. The people were extremely

friendly, the food was highly seasoned, and the wines were young and strong. In other words, Marseille was everything you'd expect in an ancient Mediterranean port city.

While I stayed in the hotel feverishly typing our culinary research, Paul went to the consulate to meet people, ask questions, and go over papers, reports, and figures. In his brief meeting with Heywood Hill, the consul general did not ask Paul a single question and hardly let him get a word in edgewise. Instead, he treated his new PAO to a treacly monologue, along the lines of: "Our little consular family is probably one of the most cooperative and smoothly working teams in the whole Foreign Service . . ." etc. Paul described his new boss as a twitchy fuss-budget who had survived twenty-five years in the Foreign Service by being careful and mediocre. But this was based on only a seven-minute meeting, he admitted, and perhaps Hill would turn out to be an excellent boss after all.

On Friday the 13th, we woke to find the tropical palm trees, red-tiled roofs, and stony Mediterranean beaches covered with snow! It was beautiful but barmy. Paul drove off on the slushy road for a whirlwind of meetings with local mayors, university presidents, music-festival directors, newspapermen, real-estate agents, and other muckety-mucks in Aix, Avignon, Nîmes, and Montpellier. In subsequent days I'd join him for trips to meet another slew of mayors and editors and academics all over the hill and dale of his new *terroir*. We ranged as far west as Perpignan, near the Spanish border, and as far east as Monte Carlo, and along the way I was falling in love with the Côte d'Azur.

The people were hearty and idiosyncratic, the Mediterranean lent its salty-sparkly charm, the mountains were rough and rocky, and there were kilometer after kilometer of vineyards. (The French government subsidized wine-growers. Result: too many people grew grapes, and not enough of them made money, thus requiring more subsidies. A crazy system.) The weather was constantly changing. One day, the skies were piercingly blue and the wind was chilly. The next day, we'd be baking in the hot sun as we ate lunch under an orange tree and basked in the glow of a field of mimosas. And the day after that, a freezing wind called a *tramontane* whistled and buffeted the bony landscape, ferociously whipping the trees and bushes and grasses and grapevines this way and that.

"God, what a pile of stuff!" Paul exclaimed, as we began to pack up at 81 Roo de Loo. Sorting through our accumulated this and that, I wanted to keep everything while Paul wanted to toss it all out. (In one of our throw-away moods some years back, we threw out our marriage license, which was going a bit far.) We cursed and sweated and eventually compromised, with only a few misgivings. We were a good team.

My biggest challenge was to pack up The Book—pounds and pounds of manuscript pages, reference books, file boxes, and loose notes. It filled two wretchedly heavy steamer trunks, and then there was my typewriter and kitchen equipment. There was no room for all of this inside the Tulipe Noire, so Paul had to use a sort of weightlifter's technique to hoist the trunks onto the roof rack: ground to knees, breathe; knees to shoulder, breathe; shoulder to rack, gasp.

To get Madame Perrier's apartment looking the way it had when we moved in, we had to remove from storage every stick of moldy furniture and rehang every gewgaw and gilt-edged mirror in the *salon*, reinstall the fifty-seven *objets d'art* in our bedroom, neaten and clean, label every packing box, and fill every little scratch on the parquet floor with brown shoe polish. Every key had to be returned, and every clause of the lease gone over once more. Looking at the old apartment now, with its red velvet chairs, rickety tables, cracked china, torn rugs, and rusted or dull kitchenware, I wondered how we ever found it so "charming" in the first place.

The Perrier/du Couédics were an adorable family, with honor, principles, and lots of mutual affection. But we worried about them. Madame Perrier owned the building, and since the general's death had made all of the decisions about it. She was eighty-two, and growing vague and forgetful. To make matters worse, her son-in-law, Hervé du Couédic, had suffered a bizarre accident the previous summer, when, at their house in Normandy, a tree fell on his head and badly injured him. Now his speech remained thick, his walk halting, and his mind cloudy. He was fifty-five, too young for retirement. Although he continued to go to the office three days a week, the poor chap knew it was useless and had basically given up.

What this meant was that the brunt of the family's weight fell on poor Madame du Couédic. She had to support the family and keep up the building, but for the sake of family pride had to pretend it was her mother and husband who were in charge. It was awfully tough. She had lots of character, but could be oddly shy and insecure at times. To add further worry, Michel, her youngest son, a naval officer, was about to ship out for the war in Indochina. It was common knowledge that

France was losing as many officers there every year as were graduating from military academies.

From what we could tell, our landlords had little outside income, and would be subsisting largely on the rental of our apartment. We had been trying like crazy to find someone to take the place, but without luck. When a young American couple dropped by, they spent four horrified minutes gawking at the decor and said, "We could never stand it!"

Paul and I sat down with Madame Perrier and Madame du Couédic and said, in effect, "Look, kids, if you're going to raise the rent and want to get foreigners in here, then you've got to clear out some of this floozy stuff, put in some new lights, and get a telephone."

"But those red velvet chairs are from the Belle Époque," Madame Perrier protested, "and the velour, *tout cela va ensemble!*" She simply couldn't fathom why we young American whippersnappers didn't see the quality of the dark-green moth-eaten velvet-on-mahogany that, back in 1875, had been the chicest thing in all of Paris. And General Perrier, she added, *he* never wanted more light than what a twenty-five-watt bulb gave off. And this "need" for a telephone was utter nonsense—"*Mon grand-père n'en a même pas eu un, vous savez*"—and if renters wanted one, they could just go get it themselves.

"Well," we said to each other, "we tried."

What to do with Minette Mimosa McWilliams Child was our last bit of business. I hated to leave her behind, but we simply didn't have room to take her to Marseille, where we didn't yet have an apartment. In search of a good home for her, I went to la Rue de Bourgogne to consult Marie des Quatre Saisons, who knew everyone and everything and was one of my most favorite women in Paris or anywhere. She knew exactly what to do, of course. She took me to see Madame la Charcutière, who had just lost her cat to old age. Madame took a look at Mini and smiled. I felt good about the arrangement, because Madame lived right above the *charcuterie*, along with a nice old dog, and Mini would be treated to all sorts of heavenly meat scraps.

When we were finally ready to move, *les emballeurs* arrived at Roo de Loo at 7:30 Monday morning, and inside of an hour the place looked like Ali Baba's cave after an explosion. We were knee-deep in excelsior, crates, paper, trunks, furniture, art materials, wine bottles, paintings, photographs, bed linens, Venetian glass, Asolo silks, and cookware. Twelve hours later, the movers and I called it quits. I was exhausted. Paul had spent the day wrapped in red tape—filling out things like Form

FS-446, "Advice to the Department of Initiation of Travel," turning in our gas and PX cards, arranging for the shipment of household effects, the disbursement of paychecks, etc.

All of this frantic activity drove home the sensation that we were truly severing our umbilical ties to Paris. Woe!

Simca and Louisette threw a farewell dinner party for us, *chez* Bertholle. There were a dozen guests, including a special surprise: Curnonsky! When the old buzzard and I spotted each other, we hugged fondly. Simca and Louisette had begged Paul to bring his camera that night, but wouldn't tell him why. Now it was clear: they wanted him to take photographs of Les Trois Gourmandes with *le prince*. So he snapped off a few, using a new gizmo called a "flash gun."

The tone that night was celebratory rather than melancholy, for Paul and I had convinced ourselves that, rather than focus on the fact that we were leaving our beloved Paris, we were embarking on a grand new French adventure. Most important, Dorothy de Santillana had written to say she was "thrilled" with our manuscript and that Houghton Mifflin was prepared to offer us a publishing contract—whoopee!

In the nearly two months since we'd sent Ives Washburn the manuscript, we hadn't received a single word of any kind from anyone there, which was highly unprofessional. At the end of January, we sent them a letter-of-dismissal by registered mail. A few days later, I received a blustery letter from Mr. Putnam, although he ended it with a gracious note: "I wish you luck."

Houghton Mifflin would pay us an advance of $750, against a royalty of 10 percent, to be paid in three $250 installments.

"Don't worry about Ives Washburn," I told my nervous colleagues. "This isn't a loss, it's a gain. Houghton Mifflin is a much better publisher." Simca and Louisette nodded warily.

THE NEXT DAY, the air was warm, the sky was a moonstone-blue, and we drove south against a constant stream of traffic—mostly cars with ski racks returning from Switzerland. Patches of snow lay along the shady north sides of ditches and forests, but the fields were sunny and already dotted with peasants seeding the ground.

CHAPTER 4

*Bouillabaisse
à la Marseillaise*

1. Terra Incognita

WE ARRIVED IN MARSEILLE with our minds open, hope in our hearts, and with our taste buds poised for new flavors. It was just turning 5:00 p.m. on March 2, 1953, when the heavily loaded Tulipe Noire rolled to a stop in front of our little hotel. People at the U.S. Consulate had been aghast to learn that we were staying—by choice—in such a tiny, unfancy hotel. But we hated the big swish luxury palaces that have no local flavor at all. Working together like two steam engines, we managed to unpack the car, haul all of our gear inside, and have everything stowed away by six-thirty. Whew!

I looked around. The dim light showed wallpaper busy with flowers, a bidet, and a modest bed. It was all we needed. Sitting on the room's only table, surveying the mound of boxes and bags and suitcases, was our little household god, Shao Pan-Tzu, wearing a serene expression. If only I felt as calm and relaxed as he looked.

BEFORE DINNER, we took a walk along the cobblestoned edge of the Vieux Port. The air was brisk and breezy, and the harbor was redolent of sewage and decaying fish. There were mobs of sailors, soldiers, Arabs, gamins, whores, pickpockets, shopkeepers, tourists, and citizens of every shape and size, all moiling and shouting. About half the men

looked like they'd modeled themselves on Hollywood movie gangsters, and their gals looked like gun molls. The honking cars, bellowing trucks, and whining motorbikes created bedlam. The streets and gutters were cluttered with garbage. Masses of it. We decided this must be a legacy of the medieval habit of tossing refuse out the window. Along the quay, dozens of wooden fishing boats were parked, stern in, and wizened old men and enormous fishwives sold the day's catch from little stalls or sometimes right from the back of their boats. Moving deliberately, the dark-skinned crew of a two-masted schooner from Palma de Mallorca were unloading crates of bright-orange tangerines.

Marseille's hot noise was so different from Paris's cool sophistication. To many of our northern-French friends it was terra incognita: they had never been here, and considered it a rough, rude, "southern" place. But it struck me as a rich broth of vigorous, emotional, uninhibited Life—a veritable "bouillabaisse of a city," as Paul put it.

The USIS was based at the American consulate, a five-story, villa-like building with a garden at 5 Place de Rome, a large, open square near the center of town. Paul's title there was "consul," a dignity he wasn't especially impressed with, given some of the other consuls he'd met; he preferred his previous title, the more mysterious *directeur régional.* When we dropped by, the people at the consulate were welcoming and full of suggestions about where to buy things, how to rent an apartment, and how to negotiate the city's curvy streets and special Mediterranean habits. This was a pleasant change from the impersonal atmosphere of the U.S. Embassy in Paris. The feeling we got here was: we are in a small outpost, and must look out for each other.

Quickly, the new PAO's days became jammed full of decisions, nonsense, and triumphs. Paul complained of "paper poisoning"—an indigestion of the memory and cross-reference collywobbles. My natural inclination was to go out and explore while Paul was at work. But in order to get anything done, I forced myself to keep regular office hours

at the hotel. There, my Royal portable typewriter was my steady companion. With no household or marketing work to distract me, I began to catch up on my correspondence and continued to research our cookbook.

The weather in Marseille was extraordinary. At first, we'd had day upon day of California-bright skies and cool air. But one afternoon the sun was hidden behind thick, dark clouds, which made me feel gloomy and restless. With no sun, there was no point in riding a boat out to visit the famous Château d'If, or in exploring the *villages-perchés* (hill towns) in the *arrière-pays* (back country) we'd heard so much about. The movie houses were packed full. I couldn't go home to bake a cake, as we had no kitchen. Paul couldn't go into his studio to paint a picture, as he had no studio or paint. We couldn't go out and see people, as we had no friends. I had written all I could write. I had read all I could read. I had slept all I could sleep. I found myself feeling . . . bored. To add to my mood, both of us suddenly had bilious tummies again. I knew that drowning my sorrows in wine and bouillabaisse would only make things worse. What to do?

I paced around our little hotel room. It was cute, but we needed more space. To get rid of my restless energy, I decided to look at rental apartments. The first one I saw struck me as a fake Art Nouveau gnome's-hut type of place. Then I saw a tasteless circa-1900 stinker. Then I saw a small apartment on the fifth floor of a building on the Vieux Port, overlooking the fishing fleet. It was owned by a Swedish diplomat who had gone home to recuperate from tuberculosis; the caveat was that once his health improved he could return to Marseille at any time. That didn't appeal. But after a few more days of living out of a suitcase in that dim, cramped hotel room, we decided to take the tubercular Swede's apartment while we looked for a more permanent roost.

I was beginning to learn my way around Marseille's labyrinth. I had stumbled into an exciting street devoted entirely to brothels. I had learned that the wide avenue leading from the train station down to the harbor called La Canebière was known to American GIs as the "Can o' Beer." And I had discovered two nice little restaurants that specialized in fish.

One of them, Chez Guido, was the very good restaurant on Rue de la Paix of the eponymous and charming Chef Guido. He had been *dans le*

métier since he was ten years old. He was a real gentleman, an absolute perfectionist, and he deserved at least two stars from the *Guide Miche*, though he hadn't been open long enough to earn any at all.

Guido was proud and delighted to tell us all about the local cuisine. He gave me the name of his butcher, and when Paul noted that some of the local wine tasted like vinegar, Guido put us on to an excellent *vin-fournisseur*. One of the most charming things about Guido was his eight-year-old boy, Jean-Jacques, who was crazy about the cowboys and Indians of "Le Veeld Vest." This got us thinking. Guido had been very kind to us, and we wanted to pay him back, but indirectly. So Paul asked Charlie to send us either a Sioux war bonnet or a ten-gallon cowboy hat for little Jean-Jacques.

IN OUR FIRST MAIL delivery in Marseille came a letter from Avis De Voto. In responding to some photos we'd sent of ourselves, she wrote: "I am very pleased with your looks, so warm and vigorous and handsome. I am rather astonished that you are such a big girl. Six feet, whoops. I adore height in women. . . . I think you both look absolutely wonderful."

Then she addressed our sauce chapter: "I have now got *beurre blanc* licked to a frazzle and I am getting bilious. Also have put on 5 lb. which on a figure like mine aint good. It looks all right, but I like to be able to wiggle freely in my clothes instead of bursting out the seams. Also I have made yr top secret mayonnaise with great success in spite of the fact that both my electric beaters broke down and I had to shift to the whisk. It's delicious and lovely and I am pleased. But I do so hate to diet. Blast you."

We had grown really fond of Avis. Odd, to feel as though you knew someone quite well whom you had never met.

II. TOP SECRET CONFIDENTIAL

ALTHOUGH OUR MOVE to Marseille was wildly disruptive to my book-work, it also opened up new avenues of research that I wouldn't have been exposed to in Paris. In addition to soups, Simca and I were now plunging into fish, a subject I didn't know much about, but was quickly becoming passionate on, especially since one ate it constantly in Marseille.

I devoted myself to piscatory research, as we tried to systematize the nomenclature and cookability of French-English-American fish for our readers. The translation wasn't always obvious. What we call a "catfish" the Brits called "dogfish." Or take *le carrelet*, which in British English is plaice, but in American English can be sand dab or lemon dab or lemon sole. If you look up "dab" in an English-French dictionary, it gives you not only *carrelet* but also *limande, calimande,* and *plie.* I found that even Latin names, which were theoretically universal, could vary between the three nations. It was a great help when Paul bought me a two-volume 1,488-page English-French, French-English dictionary with sources from both England and America.

There were also cultural translations to be worked out. Creatures that were considered positively delectable in both France and England were sometimes regarded as poisonous in the U.S.A. Many types of European fish did not exist in the States, and vice versa. Our problem was to find equivalent ingredients in the U.S. for, say, the little fish like *rascasse* that the French used in their fish soups.

I loved this kind of research, and it led to all kinds of interesting discoveries. Writing to the French and American fisheries experts, I learned that both governments were working on solving these very problems themselves. (I also discovered that the U.S. government employed a "deputy fish coordinator," a marvelous title.) Apparently, the fisheries people were receiving hundreds of letters a year from chefs, fish hatcheries, cannery operators, and so on, who were confused by the lack of international standards. Perhaps UNESCO would make sense of this Tower of Babblery; in the meantime, we Gourmandes were on the case.

I WAS DISAPPOINTED when our new editor, Dorothy de Santillana, allowed a friend of hers, a Mrs. Fairbanks, to try a recipe from our sauce chapter without first asking our permission. We had worked so hard to develop those recipes, and I considered a number of them to be real innovations, not to mention our intellectual property. Given Irma Rombauer's stories, and my colleagues' experience with Mr. Ripperger, I felt we had every reason to worry that our hard work could be stolen.

Perhaps it was my old OSS training kicking in, or just my natural protectiveness, but when I sent Dort recipes to try out in her San Francisco kitchen, I wrote:

> *Enclosed is a part of our cook book, a section of the chapter on sauces. We are so much bemused by our own petard, that we are unable to look at things objectively. And, besides, we very much need some intelligent American comments, from people like your own self, as to how it appeals to YOU.*
>
> *Naturally, it must be shown to practically nobody, or it will become old stuff. The form, we think, is new, and certainly some of our explanations, such as that on our beloved mayonnaise, are personal discoveries, etc. You might show it to one or two of your very closest friends, in whom you have absolute confidence, and know beyond the shadow of a doubt that they are not, never have been and won't never have anything to do with the publishing business, or who are not sullied by any publishing connections of any sort whatsoever. . . . Please never let it out of your hands, or leave it lying around, or lend it to no one.*
>
> *This may sound overly cautious, but I don't want to take no chances, after all the work we've put in.*
>
> *And please be brutally frank, perhaps it will not appeal to you at all, in which case we want to know.*

With that letter I included a number of "regular" recipes, but also a special batch of three recipes that were hidden between pink cover sheets and labeled "DOROTHY COUSINS—EYES ALONE—CONFIDENTIAL—to be kept under lock and key and never mentioned."

These were the Top Secret Confidential Censored pages: our revolutionary recipes for hollandaise, mayonnaise, and *beurre blanc*. We'd never seen these recipes published before, and the methods for making the first two were revolutionary. We were curious to know if their directions were clear, and if a typical American home cook could follow them successfully. As for the third sauce, the *beurre blanc* that I'd based on my visit to Mère Michel's, it was perfectly delicious and had never been decently explained in a book.

I sent the package off with a bit of anxiety in my gut, but knew I could trust my sister. And just to be sure there were no leaks, I reminded Simca and Louisette to treat the pink-sheeted recipes as "top secret—like a war plan."

Dorothy Cousins

Eyes Alone.

Confidential

to be kept under lock
& key & never mentioned.

Some miscellaneous pages from our work in progress follow

Nov. 1, 1952
FRENCH HOME COOKING   *Top Secret*   SAUCES:
       The Hollandaise Family.   2.   Pg. 36

SAUCE HOLLANDAISE, Continued.

For: Vegetables, fish, eggs, where a delicately-flavored sauce is desired

    THE BOILING BUTTER METHOD. This is the easy "off the stove" method,
      which flares the nostrils and raises the eyebrows of the classi-
      cist, but is certainly "Hollandaise without tears". It is used
      for ordinary standard butters, takes about 5 minutes or less to
      make, and, if served within a few minutes, presents no heating up
      problems at all.

      Ingredients for about 3/4 to 1 cup, or 6 to 8 servings.
         2 tsp. lemon juice (or, for a more strongly flavored sauce:
                        2 TB wine vinegar, 2 TB water or dry
                        white wine, 1 tsp. minced shallot,
                        reduced to 2 tsp.)
         2 egg yolks (2 TB, or 1 ounce)
         8 to 12 TB butter (4 to 6 ounces)
         1/8 tsp. salt; ground pepper.

      Method: Lay a damp dish cloth on a flat surface and place on it
         a small bowl or enamelled saucepan. (Cloth keeps recipient
         from sliding about.)

         Place the egg yolks in the recipient and beat until yolks
         become thick and sticky (about 1 minute). Beat in the
         lemon juice, salt and pepper (1/2 minute).

         Place butter over moderate heat to melt, then raise heat and
         bring to the boil. Boil is reached just when butter begins to
         crackle loudly, indicating its water-content has started to
         evaporate. Immediately remove from heat at this moment, (on
         no account let it brown.) Holding butter-pan in left hand,
         wire whip in right hand, pour the boiling butter in a thin
         stream of droplets onto the egg yolks, beating so all butter
         is being continuously absorbed. The hot butter cooks and
         thickens the yolks as they absorb it. For most purposes,
         sauce should have enough body to hold its shape as a mass in
         a spoon. Taste for seasoning. Add more lemon juice if ne-
         cessary.

    Serving: Serve in a warm sauce-bowl, not a hot one, as a too hot
       recipient can make the sauce turn. If food is to be presen-
       ted, napped with HOLLANDAISE, and food is very hot, it is
       wisest to beat a TB of VELOUTE or BÉCHAMEL into the sauce,
       which will help to bind it.

Top Secret

8

Mayonnaise Legère:

Method II. (for about 1 cup of sauce)

In a clean dry bowl over hot water, beat until light and foamy (about 5 minutes):	1 whole egg pinch of salt
Remove from heat and immediately beat in:	1/2 tsp. prepared mustard or wine vinegar
Immediately beat in, drop by drop and continue as for MAYONNAISE:	2/3 cup oil
Add seasonings to taste:	salt, pepper, mustard, vinegar, minced herbs, etc.

Top Secret

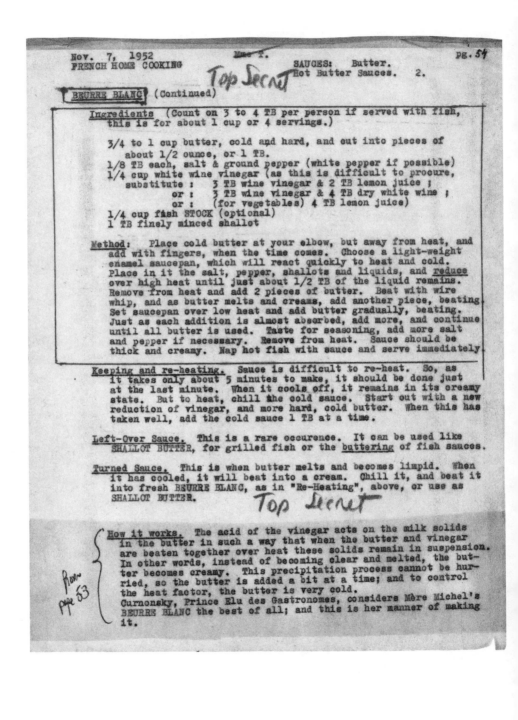

BEURRE BLANC (Continued)

Ingredients (Count on 3 to 4 TB per person if served with fish,
　　this is for about 1 cup or 4 servings.)

　　3/4 to 1 cup butter, cold and hard, and cut into pieces of
　　　　about 1/2 ounce, or 1 TB.
　　1/8 TB each, salt & ground pepper (white pepper if possible)
　　1/4 cup white wine vinegar (as this is difficult to procure,
　　　　substitute :　　3 TB wine vinegar & 2 TB lemon juice ;
　　　　　　or :　　3 TB wine vinegar & 4 TB dry white wine ;
　　　　　　or :　　(for vegetables) 4 TB lemon juice)
　　1/4 cup fish STOCK (optional)
　　1 TB finely minced shallot

Method:　Place cold butter at your elbow, but away from heat, and
　　add with fingers, when the time comes. Choose a light-weight
　　enamel saucepan, which will react quickly to heat and cold.
　　Place in it the salt, pepper, shallots and liquids, and reduce
　　over high heat until just about 1/2 TB of the liquid remains.
　　Remove from heat and add 2 pieces of butter. Beat with wire
　　whip, and as butter melts and creams, add another piece, beating.
　　Set saucepan over low heat and add butter gradually, beating.
　　Just as each addition is almost absorbed, add more, and continue
　　until all butter is used. Taste for seasoning, add more salt
　　and pepper if necessary. Remove from heat. Sauce should be
　　thick and creamy. Nap hot fish with sauce and serve immediately.

Keeping and re-heating. Sauce is difficult to re-heat. So, as
　　it takes only about 5 minutes to make, it should be done just
　　at the last minute. When it cools off, it remains in its creamy
　　state. But to heat, chill the cold sauce. Start out with a new
　　reduction of vinegar, and more hard, cold butter. When this has
　　taken well, add the cold sauce 1 TB at a time.

Left-Over Sauce. This is a rare occurence. It can be used like
　　SHALLOT BUTTER, for grilled fish or the buttering of fish sauces.

Turned Sauce. This is when butter melts and becomes limpid. When
　　it has cooled, it will beat into a cream. Chill it, and beat it
　　into fresh BEURRE BLANC, as in "Re-Heating", above, or use as
　　SHALLOT BUTTER.　　　Top Secret

How it works. The acid of the vinegar acts on the milk solids
　　in the butter in such a way that when the butter and vinegar
　　are beaten together over heat these solids remain in suspension.
　　In other words, instead of becoming clear and melted, the but-
　　ter becomes creamy. This precipitation process cannot be hur-
　　ried, so the butter is added a bit at a time; and to control
　　the heat factor, the butter is very cold.
　　Curnonsky, Prince Elu des Gastronomes, considers Mère Michel's
　　BEURRE BLANC the best of all; and this is her manner of making
　　it.

From
page 53

ONE DAY I JOINED Paul for a business trip to Cannes, which was about four hours east of Marseille by car. We took six hours, in order to explore the windy side roads. What a beautiful countryside. The hills rising from the coast were all golden with flowering mimosa. In a little beach town called La Ciotat, where Charlie and Paul had visited in the 1920s, we stopped for a picnic lunch on the edge of the sea. We sat in the hot sun on flat rocks in a strong breeze. Not far away stood two large casements built of reinforced concrete by the Italians or Germans as defenses against an Allied landing. Rusting rolls of cruel wartime barbed wire lay in the grass behind the beach. Nearby lay the rubble of destroyed houses. Everywhere around these war relics, almond trees were in lovely pink bloom.

The next day, after a visit to the American consul at Nice, hearing a lecture by an American diplomat, and having our picture taken for *Le Nice-Matin*, we drove back to Marseille through the *arrière-pays* of scraggle-topped crags—their tops powder-sugared with snow—and forests of pine and cork oak.

Driving in France was always a competitive sport, but driving in the south was positively death-defying. The roads were steep, built against sheer cliffs, and just barely wide enough for one monster truck and one small car to pass. There were no speed laws, no road police, and few road signs. Trucks took up the middle of the road and refused to budge. Cars would roar around them on blind, uphill curves at seventy miles per hour, blaring their horns and missing death by a hair. Nobody bothered to signal. There were sharp hairpin turns without guardrails, and it was *de rigueur* for aged pedestrians, women with baby carriages, bicycles, and peasants on horse-drawn wagons to launch themselves into traffic. The locals seemed deaf to the incessant horn-blowing and hardened to the brutal driving style, but poor Paul's nerves were stretched thin by the ordeal. We proceeded in our cautious way, just hoping to get back to Marseille in one piece.

III. HILL THE PILL

OUR NEW RENTAL APARTMENT was located at 28-A Quai de Rive Neuve, on the fifth floor of a pale-beige Art Deco building with distinctive wave-patterned metal railings. It was a small space, but charming, and it had marvelously expansive views over the Vieux Port and its fishing fleet.

Paul removed all the ghastly Swedish paintings from the walls and put up a dozen of his own photographs, and it began to take on the aspect of a real home. I was so relieved to have a kitchen, albeit one the size of a sailboat's galley, that I whipped up a wizard *soupe de poisson* for lunch on our first day in residence. That afternoon I bought a fine, sturdy old oaken bucket in the marketplace; I just liked the way it looked, and we used it as a wastebasket.

That night we stayed up past midnight writing letters while just below our window a tugboat went *choopa-choopa-choopa-choopa*.

With time, we learned the building's quirks. The heat didn't work. The water pressure came and went. Paul got stuck in the elevator between floors. But that was okay: we finally had a space to call our own.

Paul was working twelve-hour days, dashing this way and that—to meet with Consul General Hill, to interview a local physics teacher wanting to study at MIT, to assist a veterans'-affairs investigator checking up on six GIs taking classes at local universities (turns out that, as the investigator suspected, two of them were illegally using U.S.-government money to establish their wives in businesses; the GIs were unrepentant). Indeed, he was spending so much time outside now that the pale Parisian skin on Paul's bald head was bronzed and parchmentized from the wind and sun.

Consul General Heywood Hill—whom Abe Manell called "Hill the Pill"—took Paul to meet the local *préfet*, Monsieur Paira. Wreathed in a cloud of cigarette smoke behind a rococo desk outfitted with three important-looking telephones, Paira, a jowly Corsican, opened the meeting by attacking the USIS for attacking the Communists instead of informing French people about the U.S.A. Paul grew angrier and angrier at this misinformed monologue, but when he tried to speak up Paira simply raised the decibel level and rolled on. Hill sat there mutely, fiddling with his watch, gloves, and hat, "nervous as a virgin in a whore-house," Paul said. After Paira, they met the mayor, Monsieur Carlini, another tough guy, who surrounded himself with large-bellied flunkies wearing gold chains. Carlini rattled through the formalities in about four minutes flat. So much for America's great diplomatic initiatives in Marseille!

Old Hill was certainly proving to be a pill. He was a type we recognized from years of government work: feeble but perceptive, and extremely sensitive to criticism. Paul, drawing on his experience as a bureaucrat and teacher of moody adolescents, worked out a strategy to deal with him: take Hill seriously, even when he was being petulant, and back him up when he got himself stuck in a corner (which was often). So far, this approach was working. But Paul awaited the day when Hill would suddenly turn and squirt him with poison.

Another undercurrent of anxiety was due to the congressional budget-cutters who were hacking their way through the Foreign Service system, lopping off good wood along with the deadwood without noticing the difference. Friends in Paris said that morale at the embassy had spiraled down since we'd left. As we heard more and more of these reports, we grew increasingly worried that the bean-counters were chopping their way toward our little Marseille outpost and would lop off our lovely flower.

OVER THE EASTER WEEKEND, we drove La Tulipe Noire way up into the hills of the *arrière-pays*. Off the beaten tourist track, there wasn't much traffic, and we moseyed along. There were dark gorges and bright cliffs, fields of almond trees in delicate pale-pink blossom against serge-dark mountains, purple-gray lavender bushes, tangled olive groves rising on walled terraces, beehives nestled everywhere, and silk-worm farms tucked into barns. High up in the little *village-perché* of Gassin, we had a picnic lunch in a cork forest. Afterward, Paul took photographs of two black-and-white pussycats playing in a fig tree. The air was perfumed by the smell of resin. It was utterly peaceful and remote, and for a few hours we forgot all of our stresses and strains.

In the slightly larger village of Moustier, we delivered—on behalf of the consulate—a stack of books to an elderly, self-taught librarian who had been patiently requesting printed matter for years. He kept all of the volumes in his musty, dark, one-room operation "protected" by wrapping them in plain brown paper (thus obscuring the titles). The books were shelved on rough, hand-hewn planks, which reached to the ceiling and were accessible only by a rickety ladder that not even he dared to climb. Lacking a card catalogue, he had devised his own system: "I organize the books by size!" he proudly announced. From what we could tell, he hadn't had many—or perhaps *any*—visitors in a very long time. In the car afterward, we couldn't help compare this sad little library with what you'd find in most American towns, where everything was bright, well organized, and bustling.

As we descended toward the coast, a fog lifted to reveal Saint-Tropez, with row upon row of pink, yellow, white, and rust-colored stucco villas strung along the sea. It must have been a beautiful, simple fishermen's port fifty years earlier. But now every beach and café was filled with city slickers, faux fishermen, artistes, movie types, and the leisure class trying to see and be seen. Two large buses disgorged tourists from Germany and Denmark. Gleaming automobiles with license plates from a dozen countries inched along the narrow streets. The harbor was clogged with yachts. Man had crushed Nature along the coast. We were both drawn to the simpler, more rustic interior of Provence.

By now I had seen just about all the Mediterranean coast to the right of Marseille, and I had yet to find a spot by the water where I'd like to build my château. It had rarely been my displeasure to see such a spate of plaster-splashed neo-Med box houses and pleasure domes crowded next to an unending row of tourist traps, cheap knickknackeries, Coca-Cola signs, and sleazy bouillabaisse parlors. Phooey! I don't think I'd have liked *la belle France* at all if this were all I knew of it.

IV. THE "INVESTIGATORS"

BACK AT THE CONSULATE, Paul waded through a pile of mail and discovered a note from one of our embassy friends, Charlie Moffley, which said, "Call me at once." When Paul finally tracked Moff down in Paris, he breathlessly explained that all hell was breaking loose up there: two of Senator McCarthy's investigators were poking and prying everywhere for "Reds." Anyone, apparently, was fair game; the embassy's halls reeked with fear and anger. That evening, we boarded Le Mistral to Paris, to finish some last-minute business.

The next morning, Paris was shivering in a fifty-degree downpour as we bustled about preparing for a Trois Gourmandes photo session at the still-unrented Roo de Loo apartment. At nine-thirty, Simca and Louisette arrived with sacks full of fish, eggs, and vegetables. We got to work in the kitchen while Paul shot a series of publicity photographs for us. We three posed while he popped off twelve flashbulbs. We thought we might use these shots as illustrations for The Book.

For lunch we all trooped over to Le Grand Comptoir, where Paul sat in the corner as isolated as a Tibetan hermit and we authors discussed cookery-bookery, our new contract, sauces, fish, and who was doing what. It made me realize just how much I missed such lively company.

At dinner with Abe Manell, we heard more about the McCarthy investigators. They were two lawyers no older than twenty-six, named Cohn and Schine. They were typical bully boys who reminded a French friend of Hitler's Gestapo agents. They weren't really investigating anything, but had come to Paris to show they were "busy" collecting on-the-spot "facts." It was a sham and a disgrace. As Abe recounted, Cohn and Schine had given no decent warning of their arrival: on Friday, a telephone call from New York said, "Stand by—they're on their way." They landed on Saturday, and at the airport held a press conference, in which they flung all sorts of vague, dirty, unsubstantiated charges, such as: (1) USIS was following a pro-Communist line, as proved by the kinds of books in our libraries; (2) USIS was wasting taxpayers' money by featherbedding and empire-building; (3) the personnel of USIS was riddled by security risks, Communists, and/or sex perverts.

On Easter Sunday, Cohn and Schine said, they wanted to interview our Ambassador Draper and the top USIS officers about the books in the embassy library. Everyone canceled their Easter plans. Lo and behold, on Sunday neither Cohn nor Schine appeared. Finally, at four-thirty in the afternoon, they were located in their suite at the Hôtel de Crillon (paid for, no doubt, by American taxpayers) eating breakfast! The young geniuses granted the ambassador fifteen minutes, and the senior USIS staff ten minutes each, and spent most of the time eating scrambled eggs and discussing whether they should go to London or Vienna next. Finally, they flew off to Bonn without alerting anybody there that they were coming. The insolence of this "investigation," and unfair charges about what they'd "found," was enraging.

"As nearly as I can make out, the only 'research' they did was during most of Holy Saturday night among the naked showgirls of Montmartre," Paul snapped.

But there was no mistaking the fear these young thugs had sown in the diplomatic corps. This prompted us to have the "What If" conversation again: *if* Paul were to lose his job, *then* what would we do? We'd quit government and set ourselves up in the world of cookery-bookery-teachery, we decided. It would be so much more congenial.

v. MISTRAL

WHOOOOSH! As we detrained in Marseille, we were almost swept off our feet by a piercingly cold, dusty, savage wind that howled out of Siberia, across the Alps, along the Rhône Valley and down our necks. Boxes, barrels, crates, garbage, and newspapers sailed through the air and banged up against houses. The incessant wind tore away roof tiles, blew down chimneys, and ripped shutters off their hinges. The sea in the Old Port was sloshing and foaming, as hundred-foot-high walls of spume writhed across the harbor. Boats were huddled together like sheep; the masts of the fishing fleet leaned way over, and the rigging moaned like a train whistle. Paul and I had to squint and hunch our shoulders against the blast, and we barely made our way along the quay. When we finally reached home, we found that the windows of our apartment, six floors above the street, were completely frosted over with salt from the sea spray.

This was our first true mistral, the notorious windstorm, and it was so exhilarating it was hard to think straight. It was as if we were under bombardment.

The next day there was no wind at all. It was unbelievable. Our necks and ears were still black from the sideways-flying dirt. At the end of the harbor, guys with big rakes skimmed the water to clear away great mounds of seaweed, planks, oranges, and other flotsam piled up there. We kept bracing ourselves for a new onslaught—the way, after a picnic full of ants, you feel them crawling up your leg even when they aren't there.

In mid-April, Paul was named one of the consulate's delegates to the Cannes Film Festival. When we went for the opening, we arranged to stay with Simca at her mother's house, a villa called La Brise, in Mandelieu, in the foothills about five miles outside of Cannes. Like her daughter, Madame Beck was tall, with pale Norman skin, and a stern face. The two of them were energetic, kind, extremely verbal, opinionated, and generous. They talked twice as fast and twice as loud as most American women did, which I didn't mind but which wore Paul out.

La Brise was large and rambling and stuffed with little bibelots. Sitting in the window of our bedroom, thrown wide open to the delicious cold air, stood a bottle of Air Wick with the wick pulled all the way up. I was surprised, as I considered Air Wick a typically American consumer product. And so our first evening in that wonderful old French villa began with the sound of spring's peeping frogs and the inescapable odor of Air Wick.

Paul didn't really give a hoot about the glitter surrounding the film festival, but as an official representative of the U.S. government he was required to show his face at the big functions. The faces that counted along the Croisette, of course, were the movie stars'. There were clumps of them from France, Spain, Brazil, Mexico, Sweden, Finland, and Hollywood. While Simca and I stayed at La Brise to work on The Book, Paul sipped champagne in the sun on a hotel terrace and watched them drift by: Olivia de Havilland (she had a beautiful, open, "real" face, he noted), Lana Turner (a carefully composed, totally artificial façade), Edward G. Robinson (a Little Caesar type), the latest Tarzan (tall, thick neck, wavy dark hair, a blank Narcissus face), and Jean Cocteau (elderly, distinguished, ravaged, and dressed in a fringed wool shawl and sky-blue pants).

In the evening, Simca and I joined Paul and fifteen hundred other people for a cocktail party, followed by dinner with a large consulate group, and then to see two U.S. films—a Disney documentary short called *Water Birds* that we loved, and *I Confess*, a Hitchcock thriller starring Montgomery Clift that fell flat. We stumbled to bed at 2:00 a.m.

The next day, we enjoyed a late breakfast and a languorous morning around La Brise. It was the first time in days that any of us had taken a break. In the afternoon we drove along cliffs, chasms, gorges, and up to tiny *villages-perchés* balanced on mountaintops—including Gourdon, the highest village in all of the coastal Alps. The swooping heights terrified poor Paul, but I absolutely loved it, and so did Simca and her mother. But when Madame Beck started barking orders at Paul as to *how* and *where* he should take photographs, he seethed at "that Napoleonic general." Later, we had a good laugh when he admitted that her needling had helped to distract him from his vertigo.

Back in Marseille, I declared that I was putting myself on "an absolutely *rigid* schedule": mornings were for marketing and house-work, afternoons were reserved for cookbooking, evenings for reading and recuperation. This schedule was very productive, at first. But Paul was off at the film festival, and I, a movie-lover, kept thinking of him having fun on the Croisette. Finally, I couldn't take it any longer, and asked: "Now, when are *we* going back to Cannes for that final cocktail party?" And so, at eight o'clock the next morning, I rode the train with him to Cannes. It was a double-blue-sky day, and we traveled for three hours through a landscape of rock and pine forests. In Cannes the sun was hot and the champagne was cold, and it was extremely pleasant just to sit and look around. At a black-tie cocktail party thrown by the U.S. delegation that evening, Paul was rather taken with the Spanish and Brazilian starlets sprinkled about, while I was smitten with the relaxed and charming Gary Cooper. When we slipped away, sometime after midnight, the party was still roaring along.

OUR PACKING CRATES from Paris had arrived in Marseille, but we only had room in our apartment for a quarter of our belongings. I spent days sorting, hanging, stuffing-into-closets, shifting, and arranging our household into some semblance of order. Finally, my *batterie de cuisine* and cookbooks were arrayed in the kitchen. Paul hung some of his paintings in the *salon*. We each had a worktable. The rest of our stuff went off to storage. And now the good ship Child was launched!

We had come to love our aerie apartment, despite its lack of space, especially because the living theater of the Vieux Port was literally right outside. One evening in May, we heard a lot of excited shouting from the street below. The fishing fleet had gotten into a big run of tuna. Boats kept pulling up to the quay just outside, and until midnight there was continuous shouting and the wet *Smack! Smack! Smack!* of heavy fish being heaved off the boats onto the stones below, then reheaved into trucks packed with ice. While the run was on, the fishermen just kept going all day and night. It was a beautiful scene to look down on from our balcony at night—thousands of flashing silver tuna, all about the same size, slithering this way and that in blood-pinkened water under the arc lights, while big bow-legged guys in sou'wester pants and bare feet lifted and pushed with a sort of primal urgency.

I couldn't resist, and bought a big slice of tuna, its flesh bright red. The market ladies said to soak it in vinegar and water, to avoid an overly fishy taste, which I did for five hours. The flesh turned almost white. Then I braised it with a *purée de tomates, oignons étuvés à l'huile, champignons, vin blanc,* and *quelques herbes.* Marvelous!

View from our apartment on the Old Port

VI. SOUP

NOW THAT I had taken all of my copper pots out of storage, I made the hard decision to stay home and work rather than to explore afield with Paul. He had six PAO trips lined up, and although we loved to drive and look and compare things with each other, it would just take up too much time. The Book was my top priority now.

Simca stayed *chez nous* for a few days so that she and I could talk, experiment, and write about eggs and more eggs. We got into eggs *soubise*, eggs with puréed mushrooms, eggs *en cocotte à la crème*, eggs *moulés*, and eggs with *sauce périgueux*, to name a few. It was a wonderful creative burst.

Simca was a strong girl with a good work ethic. I began to call her La Super-Française, because she so typified a dynamic, self-reliant, bull-headed kind of Frenchwoman that I admired. Even when sick, she'd equip her bed like an office, with a telephone, typewriter, piles of books, and stacks of papers. She'd sit there like a queen, calling out to her visitors, planning meals, and correcting manuscript pages.

Louisette, on the other hand, was another sort of classic French-woman—short and pretty and much softer. Although she and Simca continued to teach École des Trois Gourmandes classes in her newly renovated Paris kitchen, Louisette's role in our bookwork was minimal. But we showed her everything we were working on, and her suggestions were given due consideration.

The three of us had been invited to join the Confrérie des Chevaliers du Tastevin, the most famous of the old wine-tasting societies. It was headquartered in Burgundy, and entailed elaborate decorations and ceremonies. We were made *chevaliers*, or members, with signed certificates to prove it. It was an honor, and we hoped it would help us establish credentials for our cookbook. (Later, we found out that anybody who could arrange a sponsor and was willing to plunk down sixty thousand francs could join, a fact that few, even the culinary French, were aware of.)

The night we brought Simca to dine Chez Guido, the chef was glad to see us, especially when Paul presented little Jean-Jacques with our gift: a leather cowboy belt with two gleaming six-shooter capguns in the holsters. (Paul liked the getup so much he'd threatened not to give it away!) The present was ceremoniously unveiled, and for the rest of the evening, little Jean-Jacques marched around from table to table, twirling his weapons, snapping the guns at guests, and generally having the time of his life. Papa Guido beamed with delight. With that simple and heartfelt gesture, we felt we had gone a long way toward repaying his kindness.

IN THE MEDITERRANEAN climate I fell very easily into using the local flavor-base of tomatoes, onions, garlic, and *herbes-de-Provence*. Now deep into the soup chapter, I first turned my attention to figuring out *soupe de poisson*, a simple soup—a fish bouillon, really—made from fresh fish trimmings or fish frames (the head, tail, and skeleton), or lots of little "junk" fish, like rockfish, which are boiled up with the flavor-base and then strained. The resulting brew is marvelously fragrant, and served with a garlic-and-pepper *rouille* spread on toasted bread rounds.

This research got me fussing around the fish markets—I especially loved the open-air market near the Rue de Rome, and the Criée aux Poissons, the wholesale market on the Vieux Port. There must have been ten million brilliantly colored little swimmers there, many of them native only to these waters. My challenge was to find American (and English) equivalents.

I learned about *rascasse, galinette, mustèle, murène, merlan, baudroie, saint-pierre, galéna,* and *lotte*—although, when I looked up the latter two fish in my books, they had different names. In fact, the more I studied the subject, the more I got the feeling that cookbook authors were tossing into their recipes lists of fish that they hadn't really investigated. Why on earth would they call a small conger eel a *fielas* without explanation? Perhaps the fishwives could straighten me out.

I loved the fishwives. They were a breed apart: big, loud, and territorial, they screamed at each other in nasal accents. "When one of them dies, there's always another one just like her, ready to take her place," an old *pêcheur* told me. The fishwives were a great resource for me, even though they didn't always agree with each other. A large *rascasse* (an ugly thing, like a sculpin) was called a *chapon*, according to some of the ladies. But other ladies pointed to another fish—flat and red and big, with a watery eye, and identified *that* as a *rascasse*. Hm.

"Is that rigor mortis?" I asked a fish lady, pointing to a stiff silver-and-green fish.

"No," she replied with a blank face. "It's a mackerel."

After I'd gotten the hang of *soupe de poisson*, the next logical leap was into that hometown classic *bouillabaisse à la marseillaise*. It is a fish chowder; a local fisherman would make it with whatever he had at hand, but it can be quite fancy, and an ideal bouillabaisse has a special flavor and texture that come from using a large variety of the freshest fish one can find. Paul and I sampled many versions of bouillabaisse all over town, and found that some were made with a water base and flavored with nothing but saffron, whereas others were quite elaborate, based on a fish stock (*bouillabaisse riche*) and were chock-full of mussels and scallops and fennel and such.

So what was the Real McCoy bouillabaisse recipe? There was a lot of bushwah expounded over this question. Clearly, there were as many "real" recipes for bouillabaisse as there were bouillabaisse makers. I had fun asking people about "*la vraie recette,*" just to hear French dogmatism at its worst.

It was assumed that because I was a foreigner I didn't know anything about anything—not even where a fish comes from. "Well," said one woman, pointing her finger into the air, "*nous, nous de la vraie Méditerranée, nous ne mettons jamais les tomates dans la bouillabaisse—nous, jamais!*" Balls. I checked the "real" recipe from the "real" *cuisinier provençal,* Reboul (author of *Cuisinier Provençal*), and he included tomatoes in his bouillabaisse. So there! Such dogmatism, founded on ignorance and expressed with a blast of hot air, irked me. (This was my only real criticism of the French people.) Indeed, because I had studied up on everything, I usually knew more about a dish than the French did, which is so often the case with a foreigner.

To me, the telling flavor of bouillabaisse comes from two things: the Provençal soup base—garlic, onions, tomatoes, olive oil, fennel, saffron, thyme, bay, and usually a bit of dried orange peel—and, of course, the fish—lean (non-oily), firm-fleshed, soft-fleshed, gelatinous, and shellfish.

A soup made for ten people usually tasted better than one made for four, because one could include a larger number and variety of fish. But should one include potatoes, or just potato flour, or no potatoes at all? Should one drop the crabs into the broth alive, or kill them first? Should one strain the broth a lot or a little, or not at all? The disputes were endless, and people took great pleasure in hashing them out—one reason that bouillabaisse was a perfect reflection of Marseille itself.

ONE DAY the city was suddenly sprinkled with six-foot-two nineteen-year-old American sailors dressed in summer whites. The aircraft carrier USS *Coral Sea* had arrived, and now the bars and brothels were doing a land-office business. The local Communists, meanwhile, had painted the town with anti-American posters and were running fearful headlines in their newspapers warning about "*Bombes Atomiques.*"

Paul ran himself ragged trying to maintain cross-cultural goodwill, arranging basketball games, dances, church services, photographs, press junkets, and a visit by forty French orphans to the carrier.

A few days later, the scene was replayed, only this time it was the carrier USS *Tarawa*. On the *Tarawa's* second day in port, a mistral roared up. The sky was brilliantly clear, but the temperature suddenly dropped from about a hundred degrees to the mid-sixties, and a crazy howling wind buffeted the city all day and night. Yaaaah! Whoooeeeeoooowh! The air was filled with whirling dust and sea spray again, and the wind ripped and smashed and flattened things with an insane force. The poor navy sailors couldn't get off the *Tarawa* to their diversions ashore.

One afternoon, Paul and I fought our way through the gale to a rugged point of land to watch the mistral beat the sea into foamy white-caps. It was exhilarating but exhausting. The wind ripped open the hem of my skirt; then it untied Paul's necktie, flipped his trouser cuffs inside out, and turned his hair absolutely white with sea salt.

A few days later, the French government collapsed again. This time it was over the issue of constitutional reform. The French capacity for muddling and combining into factions against each other seemed to be unlimited. The spectacle of this lovely nation, with its great agricultural wealth and its cultural riches, continually stepping on its own toes, made me wonder if France suffered a kind of national neurosis.

But we Americans had nothing to be proud of, for back home Senator McCarthy continued to hack away at the USIS. The rumor was that the whole operation might be dead by year's end. Our colleagues had been dropping like rotten fruit. Some were fired; others—mostly senior, very experienced, good people—quit in disgust. The agency's book-buying had been cut from twenty thousand volumes a month to 1,592. It seemed that even President Eisenhower had been intimidated, and I couldn't understand why my countrymen didn't cut McCarthy down to size.

Caught in le mistral

In spite of this horror, I found myself missing America. We knew plenty of nice people in Marseille, but had no bosom buddies there. And my feelings only intensified on those rare occasions when we did see our "in-mates," the old friends and family whom we could really let our hair down with.

In June, we took a ten-day vacation to Portugal to visit George and Betsy Kubler, our art-historian pals from New Haven. It was a wonderfully restful break, and we enjoyed the curiously gruff Portuguese and their whitewashed buildings. But one never really gets away. Halfway through our vacation, Hill the Pill recalled us to Marseille (for some sort of emergency), and Paul's very good secretary and librarian were sent home to the States (for budget reasons).

Simca and I had never much cared for Sumner Putnam's title, *French Home Cooking*, and simply called our magnum opus The Book. By now, Paul noted, The Book was growing "with the sloth, but I think the strength, too, of an oak tree."

Our pattern was that we'd work on separate recipes at home (Simca in Paris, I in Marseille), and then we'd trade notes furiously through the mail, with the occasional in-person visit. Although Simca's specialty was pastries, she had much to offer from her vast stores of culinary knowledge. I tested everything, and as the resident Yank was in charge of the actual writing. With all of this collaborative back-and-forth, our manuscripple had grown rather substantial.

I did a quick calculation, and figured that—depending on font, page size, number of illustrations, and so on—the actual book might run as long as seven hundred pages. This worried us a bit: Would Houghton Mifflin want a book that long and detailed? Would America?

We didn't see any way around it. It was very difficult to tighten an explanation of a recipe while giving every step necessary for its successful making. We tried to pack our directions full of useful information, yet not make them so dense that the reader would have to keep turning back to notes on other pages. And we tried to present enough interesting themes and variations without any boring repetition.

Writing is hard work. It did not always come easily for me, but once I got going on a subject, it flowed. Like teaching, writing has to be lively, especially for things as technical and potentially dullsville as recipes. I tried to keep my style amusing and non-pedantic, but also clear and correct. I remained my own best audience: I wanted to know why things happened on the stove, and when, and what I could do to shape the outcome. And I assumed that our ideal reader—the servantless American cook who enjoyed producing something wonderful to eat—would feel the same way.

Houghton Mifflin hoped to publish our book by June 1954, but I didn't honestly think it would happen until June of '55 at the earliest.

AUGUST 15, 1953, the day I turned forty-one, was as hot as a Turkish bath at La Brise. I inspected myself in the mirror for signs of decrepitude: my elbows looked as if they were withering away, but at least I didn't have any gray hairs. My biggest problem was my continuing lack of worldliness. *Maybe if you concentrate on the fact that you are forty-one years old*, I scolded my reflection, *you'd remember to be more worldly!*

While Paul was dragged away from his reading by friends for a "short hike" through the hot, prickly underbrush, Simca and I wrestled with our manuscript. We had gone over the first draft of the soup chapter at least twenty times by now, and I felt as though I were drowning in soup.

Taking a break from the text, we decided to spend some time on the reality of soup. We made a marvelous *aigo bouido*, or garlic soup, which used sixteen whole cloves of garlic, sage, thyme, and cheese-covered croutons. The garlic flavor wasn't harsh: it was indescribably exquisite and aromatic. That evening we all feasted on it with lip-smacking gusto. *Aigo bouido* was said to be good for the liver, circulation, physical tone, and even one's spiritual health. After getting lost during their all-day trek, Paul and his friends had finally made it back to the house feeling famished. The garlic soup was a wonderful restorative, they said. With that, we added *aigo bouido* to The Book.

VII. BOULEVARD DE LA CORDERIE

WE HAD TRIED without success to inspire our tubercular Swedish landlord to tell us whether or not he would be returning to Marseille. We loved his apartment, and you'd be hard put to find *any* place with the drama and intensity of the Vieux Port out your window. But it was so small that half of our household goods still remained in storage. Plus, it was cold, and I had taken to wrapping a big red bathrobe around my normal street clothes while working there.

I'd heard about a bigger apartment for rent up on the hill, and decided to take a look. It was on the seventh floor of a newish building on the leafy Boulevard de la Corderie. It had a wide-spreading view over all the old city, a slummy area, the port, the sea, and the Vauban fortress. There were little balconies on the north and south sides, and sunlight flooded into the back all afternoon. It had six rooms, red-tiled floors, a big kitchen, enough room in the cellar for a wine *cave*; everything was bright, clean, workable, tasteful. But the rent was at the very top of our government allowance. We took it anyway.

On our first day at 113 Boulevard de la Corderie, we sat on the sunny back balcony with our shirts off and ate lunch. It was such a nice feeling that we planned to do it every chance we got. That afternoon, I hoisted up a big empty crate, tottered a few steps, tripped on a pile of books, and fell with the box against one of the tall French windows leading to the front balcony: *Wham! Crash!... Tinkle ... winkle ... inkle.* Ah me, $21.50 worth of glass gone in a blink. To add insult to injury, we were startled awake at five o'clock the next morning by a series of wretched bugle calls squawking from the nearby fortress through the glassless door. The reveille came again at five-fifteen, six, six-fifteen, and at seven, when we finally rousted ourselves.

Here we were again, establishing new patterns about where to hang clothes or turn on the heat, where to store food, and how to decorate the walls. The settling in would take time, but one thing that could not wait was the kitchen. Most French kitchens were designed on the assumption that a household domestic would be working in there—ergo, the place wasn't attractive, convenient, or well lit. But my kitchen was my office. I liked to have my pots and pans hanging within easy reach, my cookbooks *in* the kitchen, and my counter layout to make sense (my kind of sense). So Paul and I designed a new layout of lights, shelves, countertops, and drawers to make it a useful space. After so many moves, we were becoming rather expert kitchen-designers by now.

The first dinner guests to have the honor of an invitation to our new apartment were Clifford and Leonie Wharton, the new American consul general and his wife. They were a warm, honest, comfortable pair. They had a look that was hard for us to place at first. Then we learned that they were both mulatto: Cliff was said to be "the first Negro consul general" in the Foreign Service; he was a big, voluble, energetic lawyer who tended to bull his way through situations without bothering with nuances—"Ya! Ya! I get it!" he'd say, charging ahead. But he was smart and dynamic, and quickly befriended everyone. Leonie was smaller, quieter, and more instinctual. We served four kinds of wines that night—the first as an apéritif, the second with oysters, the third with chicken, and the last with cheese. Conversation was lively, especially once we got into the whole FBO mess.

Thanks to a typical bureaucratic snafu, the Whartons were living in a hotel. This arrangement was the responsibility of the U.S. government's Foreign Buildings Office (FBO), a group of architects, interior

View from our apartment on Boulevard de la Corderie

decorators, engineers, and real-estate agents whose job was to buy, sell, and equip buildings for U.S. diplomatic operations all over the world. Sometime in 1947, the FBO had bought two pieces of land in Marseille: one to build a consulate on (the current building was a rented, temporary space), the other to build the consul general's residence on. For the former, the FBO bought a parcel of nice cheap land right smack in the center of Marseille's stinkingest, most bar-and-whorehouse-infested red-light district. For the latter, they bought a plot at the very top of the most inaccessible, roadless, waterless, granite Annapurna for miles around ("But it has such splendid views!"). Now the U.S. government was stuck with these two white elephants, which had become the joke, and curse, of the entire Foreign Service.

One day an FBO type showed up from Paris, theoretically to help settle the Whartons' housing problem. When this chap started to go on about the value of the FBO's white elephants, Wharton let him have it with a couple of wonderfully earthy zingers, including: "You can't fertilize a five-acre field by farting through the fence!," which stunned the man into silence. Later, after the FBOer had left, Wharton cracked: "Listen, I can stand it if a man pees on my foot, but, by God, when he tries to tell me it's *raining*, that's too much!"

OUR NEW APARTMENT was wonderful in many ways, but rarely had I known a place that suffered so many leaks, loose wires, smoke in the elevator, and other strange problems. There was a period when turning on the stove made the lights go out. We got an electrician over to investigate, and he fooled around with it for a bit. Somehow he fixed the problem, but even he didn't know what he'd done. As he put on his beret and lit up his cigarette, he said, "*Mais, il y a des mystères dans la vie.*"

One day, our downstairs neighbor trotted up in her brown bedroom slippers and said, "*Madame, nous ne savons plus que faites-vous toute la nuit, c'est comme un tambour chez vous!*" ("Madame, we don't know what you are doing all night, but it sounds like a drum in your place!")

So I went downstairs to her apartment to see what the noise sounded like. When I gave the signal, our nice *bonne à tout faire*, Paulette, clattered about a bit up there, and, indeed, the noise sounded quite drumlike indeed. I apologized to the neighbor, and bought little rubber caps for the legs of our chairs, stools, and tables, plus some real French house-slippers so that Paul and I could shuffle about like an old bourgeois couple. Now we would be so quiet that no one would even know we were home.

At about ten-forty-three one evening, while I was ever so quietly rinsing the dishes, a piece of the stove suddenly fell off. Trying to catch it, I knocked over the iron garbage can and screamed. Paul, who thought I had fallen out the window, came charging in to rescue me and knocked over two kitchen stools. Ha! So much for the New Quietude.

VIII. ADIEU

ON JANUARY 15, 1954, I surprised Paul at his office with a cute little cake that had a single candle stuck in the middle. It was his fifty-second birthday, and he was trying to ignore it. But when his staff all joined in singing, he was thrilled. I gave him a book about Brueghel, which so stimulated him that he declared he wanted to quit his job and just paint for the rest of his days.

On February 1, a four-inch-thick blanket of snow covered the ground, and Marseille now looked strangely like Prague. It was twenty degrees outside, and everything that could freeze did, including water pipes, the oysters in front of the fish shops, and a few of the *clochards* huddled in alleyways. The trams couldn't get up the hills. The taxis had no chains, so they stopped running. Buses skidded, so they stopped. Disconsolate householders were out huffing and puffing in the arctic chill, trying to clear the snow away from the cobblestoned streets and drooping palm trees.

We were getting depressed about McCarthy again. From what I had read in *Look*, *The Reporter*, and other magazines, it seemed that this desperate power-monger was supported by Texas oil millionaires and that everyone in Washington was scared to death of him. It was beyond me how anybody with any sense of what our country was supposed to stand for could have anything to do with him, no matter how many votes he brought in. When I expressed my shock to Pop, he wrote:

You are all steamed up about what Europe thinks of America. . . . You are falling right into the plan the Reds are developing—that of creating dissension and distrust among their enemies—ridiculing all efforts to break up their underground machines operating under cover all through every government body. . . . These people carrying the red badge have to be exposed. It's a hard dirty job that has to be done and it takes a rough and ready person like McCarthy to do it. In his zeal he gets out of bounds now and then but that's our business. It's safe to say that a large majority of people here at home believe as I do. I think it's time you two had a vacation at home and got the American idea and forget what the Socialistic element of Europe are trying to sell you.

Pop was a congenital Republican; he and Phila simply didn't know any Democrats other than us, nor did they want to. To Pop, the New Deal was a kind of New Death. He absolutely boiled and seethed with hatred for socialism. He considered "that man Roosevelt!" a socialist. And Ike had gone over to the enemy, too. In fact, everything was going to the dogs, and it was all the fault of the eggheads and left-wingers who liked foreigners. If the U.S.A. somehow got back to the "sound footing" of our isolationism of 1925, Pop felt, then everything would be all right.

This was a primitive way of thinking, which didn't take into account the ways in which the world had changed. To me, this battle of ideologies in America was the most fateful of all the wars under way around the world.

Even my alma mater, Smith College, had gotten itself gummed up by the McCarthy witch-hunters. A Mrs. Aloise B. Heath, who headed the college's Committee for Discrimination in Giving, issued a letter that, without any proof, accused five faculty members of being associated with organizations that were "Communist dominated," or "Communist fronts." Not only did Mrs. Heath's committee accuse these five of being "traitors," and the college of "knowingly harboring" turncoats, but she released her accusations to the public without first presenting them to Smith's president or board for investigation, as the school's rules require.

I was so incensed that I doubled my annual contribution to Smith and wrote Mrs. Aloise B. Heath a scathing letter—which, in a way, was also a bitter denunciation of my father:

In Russia today, as a method for getting rid of opposition, an unsubstantiated implication of treason, such as yours, is often used. But it should never be used in the United States. . . . I respectfully suggest

that you are doing both your college and your country a disservice. . . .
In the blood-heat of pursuing the enemy, many people are forgetting
what we are fighting for. *We are fighting* for *our hard-won liberty*
and freedom; for *our Constitution and the due processes of our laws;*
and for *the right to differ in ideas, religion and politics. I am convinced*
that in your zeal to fight against *our enemies, you, too, have forgotten*
what you are fighting for.

IN THE COURSE of devoting so many hours to The Book, Paul and I came up with a new way to illustrate the making of recipes: rather than the standard depiction of a cook working away at a table, we thought, why not illustrate, say, the trussing of a chicken *from the cook's standpoint?* Paul pointed out that an artist would practically have to sit in the cook's lap to achieve the right combination of technical exactitude and ideal point-of-view; the answer, clearly, was to use photographs. It would be too expensive to print hundreds of step-by-step photos in the book. But the photos could be the basis for simple line drawings that showed the cook's hands and whatever food and tools were required. Besides, a drawing can actually be simpler and clearer, not to mention more aesthetically pleasing with type, than a photograph.

As we talked, a plan evolved: I would cook something, Paul would photograph over my shoulder, and we'd send the resulting prints to an artist who would make drawings for the book. We spent a very enjoyable two hours experimenting on this in the kitchen. We discussed light angles, camera angles, proper backgrounds, how to position my hands to show a technique properly, exposure times, and all the other variables we'd have to bring into harmony. Then Paul hoisted his Graflex and flicked on his new bright floodlights, and we shot eight exposures as a trial run. (He would have loved to do the drawings himself, but simply didn't have the time.)

A few days later, we spent an entire afternoon shooting photographs of the various steps in cleaning and cutting up a chicken. The *salon* was tangled with light-wires, chicken gizzards, rolls of film, notebooks, knives, and a big tarpaulin. The camera was high up on a tripod. Paul stood behind it on a stool, attempting to focus without toppling over. Far below, a chicken was splayed on a cutting board on the floor, and I was lying on my stomach with my arms outstretched as I strained to demonstrate proper knifework.

We were impatient to see the results of all this. But when Paul took his film to the local photo lab, we discovered it was run by a bunch of nincompoop amateurs. Upon seeing his negatives ruined by clipmarks, the photos besmirched with thumbprints and printed on yellow paper, Paul grew so upset he momentarily lost his French.

"That does it!" he sputtered. "The next batch is going to Paris!"— where Paul's favorite printer, Pierre Gassman, would work his magic. (Gassman was world-renowned, and did much of the printing for famous photographers like Capa, Cartier-Bresson, and the like.)

The USIS was now called USIA (U.S. Information Agency), and its RIF (reduction in force) had trimmed Paul's staff from twelve to four— two of whom were out sick while the other two were away on business. That left Paul alone on the consulate's second floor, with five telephones to answer and no one to help with a torrent of letters, wires, aerograms, operations memos, and special requests.

One of the "sick" ones was Henri Pousset, the press assistant, who was *non compos mentis* because his father had disappeared. The old man was a former merchant seaman with a temper. It seems he had envied and/or hated Henri's older brother, who couldn't or wouldn't get a job. When the mother protected the older brother, the father grew jealous. That, plus a lack of money and who knows what else, built up tension for two years, until the father just walked out the door and vanished.

Henri was a sweet bourgeois man, and hated to admit all of this to Paul, who immediately forced him to go to the police. "What if your father is considering suicide, Henri?" Paul asked.

"No, that's not possible," Henri replied. But in the next morning's post, he intercepted a letter to his mother from his father containing all of his identification papers and a note on which was printed one word: ADIEU.

Henri phoned the police.

Later that day, the consulate received a call from the police in Menton, a town five hours away. They had just nabbed the old man on a cliff as he was about to throw himself into the sea! Henri leapt onto a train to retrieve his father. When they returned to Marseille, the whole family had an emotional reconciliation. A few days later, Henri said to Paul: "You have no idea how it is vonderfool at my home.

My favver now is shacking hends wiv my bruvver for first time since two year!"

AT THE END of February, we realized that we'd been in Marseille for a whole year, and were just getting our footing. It had gone by so fast. We consoled ourselves with the thought that we had another year to go, at least. Paul requested our home leave for August, so that we could visit Charlie and Freddie in Maine. It came as a shock when Paul was reminded that we'd been transferred to Foreign Service staff on "a limited appointment," which would expire in September. Given the budget battles, Paul could lose his job if we happened to be on home leave then. It felt like a dirty trick. "*Merde alors!*" Paul said, canceling our plans.

This feeling of impermanence and the lack of say in how our lives were to be lived were getting tiresome, even for us adventurers.

It was only a few weeks later when Charlie Moffley, now the deputy assistant director of USIA for Europe, gave us the news we had been dreading: we would have to leave Marseille soon, maybe even by the end of June, to make way for a new PAO.

It wasn't possible! We had been in France for nearly five and a half years, but it seemed as if we'd just settled in Marseille. How could they tell us to leave *now*? It made no sense! Paul had finally met all the local bigwigs, was working with a consul general he liked, and was just getting the hang of running the office smoothly. It wasn't fair! We'd finally gotten our adorable little apartment in shape, at quite some expense. I was used to the kitchen and was making progress on The Book. But now it was *away with us*! I suppose we should have seen this coming. Our colleagues had said, "You watch out, it always happens that as soon as you fix a place up you get moved."

Where would we be sent? The leading prospect was Germany, which didn't strike us as much fun. We suggested Spain or Italy would make more logical postings, "because they use Romance languages." (In reality, we just liked Spain and Italy better than Germany.) But we had no say in the matter, and even Abe Manell couldn't help this time.

One should ideally have the attitude that "I am my country's creature" and be willing to go anywhere, anytime, to serve. But after the travails of the last few years, I had lost that noble esprit de corps. I felt that at any moment we might be accused of being Communists and traitors, and that no one at the head office would lift a finger to support us.

My new attitude was: We must look out for number one, as no one else was going to do it for us. I was shocked at the depth of my feelings, and dared to reveal my true thoughts only to Paul and Dort.

On April Fool's Day, the word came in from Washington: "Steps Taken Here to Effectuate Transfer of Child to Bonn as Exhibits Officer."

We were being sent to Germany.

The transfer was a real feather in Paul's cap: Bonn was ten times more important than Marseille, and the exhibits department there was far more important than the one in Paris. Yet we'd much rather have stayed in our lovely little backwater!

We fretted about learning German, about living in one of those all-American military compounds, about the lingering stench of the concentration camps. We discussed, again, the idea of quitting the Foreign Service and just staying in *la belle France*. I had The Book to work on, but what would Paul do? He had flirted with the idea of becoming a freelance photographer, had sold his prints to the big New York agencies, and knew people who could help him gain entrée. But he also knew about the ulcers and deadlines that those glamorous photojournalists faced in places like Greenland and Dien Bien Phu, and had decided it was a hell of a life. So the decision was made: we'd stick with government work and see where it took us.

THE REALIZATION that we were really and truly leaving France was painful. Paul had lived here for a total of eleven years. I had been here over five years. I was fluent in the language. I could shop like a Frenchman, and cook like one, too. I could even drive like one, if I had to. We felt nostalgic just sitting there in Marseille.

Perhaps someday, we dreamed, we'd buy an apartment in Paris or a house in Provence, and would spend part of every year here.

In the meantime, we'd be going back to the U.S. for a couple of months of home leave. Charlie and Freddie would meet us on the dock in New York. I couldn't wait to see them and get my feet on U.S. soil. But what I really looked forward to was eating an honest-to-goodness American steak!

PART II

CHAPTER 5

French Recipes
for American Cooks

1. Situation Confused

It was early October 1954, and the sky was gray and the air chilly as we approached the German border. The thought of living in that land of monsters caused me to suffer *le cafard* (the blues). But cross we did, with me trembling like a leaf. We drove straight into Bonn and had lunch at a small restaurant. Having taken eight language lessons before leaving Washington, I could say, "Hello, how are you? My name is Child. How much does that cost? I want meat and potatoes. I am learning German." I used all of these phrases immediately when we ordered beer, meat, and potatoes. The waitress understood me perfectly and smiled nicely as she placed two enormous foaming steins in front of us. My, that beer tasted good.

In the afternoon we made our way to Plittersdorf, in the suburbs of Bad Godesberg, to our new home at 3 Steubenring. Our hearts sank at the sight of it. I felt that if we were going to be in Germany then we should live amongst the Germans. But this wasn't German *at all.* We could have been in Anytown, U.S.A.: there was a movie theater, a department store, a colonial church, and a set of modern beige three-story concrete apartment buildings with red trim, brown tile roofs, and radio antennas. Hmm.

We were shown nine apartments, every one of which was small, charmless, and dark. We chose Number 5, the one with the lightest-colored furniture. The kitchen was adequate, but came with an electric stove, which I didn't like because it was difficult to control the heat. Worst of all, when you walked in our front door, you looked right into the bathroom. Still, we were right near the Rhine River, which was full of barges and looked like the Seine if you squinted. Across the way was a pretty green hill with some kind of Wagnerian ruins perched near the top.

Oh, how I missed our Marseille balconies, with their sweeping views and blazing sunlight!

I wished we lived in Munich or Berlin, somewhere where there was a bit of civilization, rather than sad old Plittersdorf on the Rhine. I found German to be a difficult and bristly language. But I was determined to learn how to communicate so that I could do some proper marketing—an activity I enjoyed no matter where I was. I began by taking language classes from the U.S. Army; Paul wanted to join me, but was immediately swept into work, and had no time for it.

HIS TITLE WAS exhibits officer for all of Germany, which meant he was America's top visual-program man for the entire country. His job was to inform the German people about the U.S.A., and once again he was organizing exhibits, tours, and cross-cultural exchanges. Because of the geopolitical/propaganda importance of Germany, which was right smack up against the Iron Curtain, his department had a budget of ten million dollars a year, more than the combined budgets for all of the USIA's other information programs around the world. It was a big job, a huge professional step up, and I was proud of him.

Paul's office was in a vast structure, seven stories high, and almost half the bulk of the Pentagon. He had a large and very able staff, and since we were living and working in an almost entirely American enclave, they were the only Germans we really got to know. As he was wont to do, Paul treated his staff as individuals rather than as underlings to be bossed around. "They seem more aware of my worth than the Americans do," he noted.

Morale was not great. Paul's boss was a selfish, immature fellow we called Woodenhead, and his assistant was known as Woodenhead the Second. Foreign Service and army types never got along especially well, and the divide was especially noticeable in Plittersdorf. The army families showed almost no interest in Germany or the Germans, which I found depressing. Hardly any of them spoke the language, even after having lived there for several years. The wives were perfectly nice, but conventional, incurious, and conservative; the men spoke in Southern accents, usually about sex and drink.

They drank beer, but only the lighter, American-style beers. What a shame! They were surrounded by some of the most wonderful beers in the world—and, with a 13.5 percent alcohol content, some of the strongest, too—but they deemed the traditional German ales "too heavy." We quite liked German beers. Our favorite was a flavorful local beer called Nüremberger Lederbrau.

On the weekends, Paul and I would drive into Bonn to do our shopping, each with a pocket dictionary in hand. We bought chickens, beans, apples, lightbulbs, an extension cord, olive oil, vinegar, and a rubber stamp that said "Greetings from Old Downtown Plittersdorf on the Rhine." I have always been a nut for rubber stamps, and I couldn't wait to use this one on our letters. Stamp, stamp, stamp! At lunch, we took half an hour to decipher the menu, then ordered smoked sausage, sauerkraut, and beer. It was delicious, and, again, we were struck by how nice the Germans were. I struggled to reconcile the images of Hitler and the concentration camps with these friendly citizens. Could they really be the same people who had allowed Hitler to terrorize the world just a few years earlier?

As my German improved, I began to explore my new surroundings.

The local stores were good for meats. Aside from the usual sausages and chops and steaks, you'd see quite a bit of venison and game for sale. You could buy a hare all cut up and sitting in a tub of hare's blood, which was perfect for making *civet de lièvre*. Krämers was the swish market in Bad Godesberg, and it was there that I picked out a fresh young turkey to roast. By gum if the whole back of the store wasn't turned over to row upon row of fat geese, ducks, turkeys, roasting chickens, and pheasants. They were arranged in neat tiers, each fowl marked with the customer's name. It was a really beautiful sight.

But, to my palate, German cooking didn't hold a match to the French. The Germans didn't hang their meats long enough to develop that light gamy taste I adored, and they didn't marinate. But I discovered that if you bought the meat, hung it, and marinated it yourself, you could make as pretty a dish as you could hope to find.

Soon I was back to woodpeckering on The Book, which we were now calling *French Cooking for the American Kitchen*. Simca and I had finished the chapters on soups and sauces, and we thought the chapters on eggs and fish were nearly done. While I began to focus on poultry, Simca began to work on meats.

She was a terrifically inventive cook. Wildly energetic, Simca was always tinkering with something in the kitchen at 6:30 a.m. or tapping on her typewriter until midnight. Her intensity bothered Paul ("Living with her would send me screaming into the woods," he declared), but was a wonderful asset to me. We agreed that she would be the expert on all things French—spellings, ingredients, attitudes, etc.—while I would be the expert on the U.S.A. Together, we worked like a couple of *vaches enragées!*

Although I resented the distance between us at first, I came to believe that it was a blessing in disguise. It allowed us to work on things independently without getting in each other's hair. We conferred constantly by mail, and visited each other on a regular basis.

Both willful and stubborn, we had by now grown used to each other's idiosyncrasies: I liked finely ground salt, whereas she preferred the coarser style; I liked white pepper, she preferred black; she loathed turnips, but I loved them; she favored tomato sauce on meats, and I did not. But none of these personal preferences made any difference at all, because we were both so enthusiastic about food.

In January 1955, I began to experiment with chicken cookery. It was a subject that encompassed almost all the fundamentals of French cuisine, some of its best sauces, and a few of its true glories. *Larousse Gastronomique* listed over two hundred different chicken recipes, and I tried most of them, along with many others we had collected along the way. But my favorite remained the basic roast chicken. What a deceptively simple dish. I had come to believe that one can judge the quality of a cook by his or her roast chicken. Above all, it should taste like *chicken:* it should be so good that even a perfectly simple, buttery roast should be a delight.

The German birds didn't taste as good as their French cousins, nor did the frozen Dutch chickens we bought in the local supermarkets. The American poultry industry had made it possible to grow a fine-looking fryer in record time and sell it at a reasonable price, but no one mentioned that the result usually tasted like the stuffing inside of a teddy bear.

Simca and I spent a great deal of time analyzing the different types of American chickens versus French chickens, and what the most suitable method of preparing each would be—roasted, poached, sautéed, fricas-seed, grilled, in casseroles, *coq au vin*, *à la diabolique*, and *poulet farci au gros sel*, and so on and on. We had to choose with great care which of these recipes to use in our book. Not only should a dish be of the tradi-tional *cuisine française*, but it should also be composed of ingredients available to the average American cook. And, as always, it was important to develop a theme and several variations. For sautéed chicken, then, we wanted to include a crisp, a fricasseed, and a simmered version, yet we didn't want to do an entire book's worth of chicken dishes.

Even though Simca and I were both putting in forty hours a week on The Book, it went very slowly. Each recipe took so long, so long, so long to research, test, and write that I could see no end in sight. Nor could I see any other method of working. *Ach!*

Louisette, alas, wasn't contributing very much. She had a difficult husband, two children, and a household to run; the most she could offer was three hours a week teaching at L'École des Trois Gourmandes (which Simca continued to run) and six hours a week for book research. I was sympathetic, but our intense effort on a serious, lengthy magnum opus did not really fit Louisette's style. She would have been better suited to a quick book on chic little dishes for parties. The hard truth, which I dared not voice to anyone other than Paul and Simca, was that Louisette was simply not a good enough cook to present herself as an equal author. This fact stuck in my craw.

We had at least another year's worth of work ahead of us, and I felt it important that we formally acknowledge who was actually doing what. It was too late to change the wording on the Houghton Mifflin contract, our lawyer said, but we all agreed that henceforth Simca and I would legally be known as "Co-Authors" and Louisette would be called a "Consultant." We agreed to work out the financial details when, or if, the book was published. This was a difficult subject to discuss, but I was relieved to see our responsibilities clearly laid out on paper.

In matters of business, I felt we had to be as clearheaded and profes-sional as possible, even at the risk of offending our friend. When Simca wavered a bit, I wrote: "We must be cold-blooded."

ONE THURSDAY IN April 1955, Paul received orders to return to Washington, D.C., by the following Monday. No reason was given, but we suspected that someone at headquarters had finally woken up and realized it was time to give my husband a promotion. Would he be made head of the department? Would he finally get a raise? Would we be recalled to the States for important work in Washington? Off he flew, to find out.

I was about to leave for a trip to Paris, but as I was packing I received a telegram from Paul in Washington: "Situation confused."

No one could, or would, tell him why he was there. He had been made to sit and wait in anonymous offices for various VIPs who were MIA. He suggested that I delay my Paris visit, which I did.

"Situation here like Kafka story," he telegrammed.

By Wednesday, the bizarre truth had dawned on me: Paul wasn't being promoted, he was being *investigated*. For what? By whom? Would he be arrested?

I couldn't reach him, and began frantically calling our extensive network of friends in the Foreign Service to find out what was happening. I stayed up until four o'clock in the morning talking on the phone. What I eventually pieced together was that Paul had spent all day and into the evening being interrogated by agents from the USIA's Office of Security, an outfit run by one R. W. McLeod, who was said to be a J. Edgar Hoover protégé.

When they finally appeared, the investigators had a fat dossier on Paul Cushing Child. They attacked him with questions about his patriotism, his liberal friends, the books he read, and his association with Communists. When they asked if he was a homosexual, Paul laughed. When they asked him to "drop his pants," he refused on principle. He had nothing to hide, and said so. The investigators eventually gave up on him.

But, clearly, someone had implicated Paul as a treasonous homosexual. Who would do such a thing, and why? The whole episode was shockingly weird, amateurish, and unfair. Paul felt he had acquitted himself well under the circumstances, and had proved himself "a monument of innocence." Later, at his insistence, the USIA gave him a written exoneration. Still, this shameful episode left the taste of ashes in our mouths, and we would never forget it.

What was happening to America? Several of our friends and colleagues were tormented by McCarthy's terrible witch-hunt. It ruined careers, and in some cases lives. Even President Eisenhower seemed unwilling to stand up to him, which made me angry. When Eisenhower announced that he'd run for a second term, after having a heart attack, I had no doubt that Adlai Stevenson would make the better (and more resilient) president. Ike was just not inspiring: I got nothing but a hollow feeling from his utterances, as if Pluto the dog were suddenly making human noises. Just about anyone from the GOP had, for me, a fake soap-selling ring to him, with the exception of Herbert Hoover, who had impressed everyone on a recent swing through Europe. Stevenson, on the other hand, had a nobility of ideals that appealed to me. I just liked eggheads, damnit!

While Paul was in the States, he decided to zip up to New York, where he met with Edward Steichen at the Museum of Modern Art, to arrange to bring the photographer's wonderful "Family of Man" exhibit to Berlin. He had befriended Steichen while we were stationed in Paris, and Steichen had bought six of Paul's photos for the MoMA collection. That was a real coup, but one that modest Paul played down.

I, in the meantime, had finally packed myself off to Paris for three weeks. I cooked with Bugnard, taught classes with Les Trois Gourmandes, ate with the Baltrus, and immersed myself in cookery-bookery with Simca. What a tonic!

OVER THE SUMMER and into the fall of 1955, I finished my chicken research and began madly fussing about with geese and duck. One weekend I overdid it a bit, when, in a fit of experimental zeal, I consumed most of two boned stuffed ducks (one hot and braised, one cold *en croûte*) in a sitting. I was a pig, frankly, and bilious for days, which served me right. I was also running a continual set of experiments on risotto (finding just the right water-to-rice ratio), how to make stocks in the pressure cooker (determining proper timing, testing poultry carcasses versus beef bones), and various desserts. This sort of research was a challenge to our ongoing Battle of the Belly.

"No man shall lose weight who eats paella topped with *Apfel Strudel*," Paul noted, after doing exactly that.

We had been horrified to notice that baby blubber seemed to bounce on so many people in the States. In Germany, meanwhile, a large figure denoted social status. Our goal was to eat well, but sensibly, as the French did. This meant keeping our helpings small, eating a great variety of foods, and avoiding snacks. But the best diet tip of all was Paul's fully patented Belly Control System: "Just don't eat so damn much!"

At Christmastime, Paul was felled by a nasty infectious hepatitis.

After a recuperative stay in Rome in the early days of 1956 (where I discovered fennel salad and the toothsome little Roman peas), we had decided to eat carefully, exercise rigorously, and eschew alcohol. As a result, he had dropped ten pounds and tipped the scales at 173. I had lost eleven pounds and weighed 158, which made me feel less middle-aged than I had in the U.S.A.

Come February, all of our off time was spent composing letters for the hundreds of valentines we sent out around the globe. Valentine cards had become a tradition of ours, born of the fact that we could never get ourselves organized in time to send out Christmas cards. With our ever-enlarging network of family, friends, and Foreign Service colleagues, we found that Paul's hand-designed valentine cards—usually a woodcut or drawing, sometimes a photograph—were a nice way to keep in touch. But they could be labor-intensive. One year's design was a faux stained-glass window, with five colors in it, each of which had to be hand-painted in watercolors—which took hours. For 1956, we decided to lighten up by doing something different: we posed ourselves for a self-timed valentine photo in the bathtub, wearing nothing but artfully placed soap bubbles.

BY THE SPRING OF 1956, we decided it was high time to start entertaining again. But our first dinner party revealed that our once-crack team of hostess/cook and host/sommelier was woefully out of practice. We had no salad forks, we forgot to clear the cocktail clutter unobtrusively, and we spent the evening rushing about in a breathless rush. This was not up to our usual standard. We liked to treat our guests as if they were royalty, so as to be fully prepared for those occasions when we would be called upon to entertain actual royalty!

For our second dinner party, I served *les barquettes de champignons glacées au fromage, canard à l'orange*, and *glace maison aux marrons glacés*. A week later, I tried *boeuf à la mode, endives braisées*, and a dessert of *désirés du roi* for friends. And now the old "Pulia" entertainment engine was humming along beautifully.

I got a note from *le prince*, Curnonsky, who had broken several ribs in a fall. The doctors, he wrote, had put him on "*un régime terrible*" that did not allow for cream, salt, sauces, or wine. Such a bland diet must have been a torture for the old gastronome.

Health was much on our minds that season. Over the Easter weekend, I had to go into a private *Klinik* in Bad Godesberg for an operation. Two years earlier, I had undergone surgery in Washington to remove uterine polyps, but it had not, apparently, gotten to the root of the matter. "I feel just fine," I said, but the German doctor insisted that an operation was best for me. His *Klinik* was in a grand Victorian mansion painted all white. The surgery was routine. I was not concerned, but poor Paul half convinced himself that "polyps" equaled "Julia is dying of cancer." This was not true, of course, and he knew it, yet he was so worried he hardly slept a wink and even developed a slight fever that night.

Paul thought about death much more than I ever did. In part, this must have come from the early demise of his father, his mother, and his older sister. Paul had also been traumatized by the death of Edith "Slingsby" Kennedy, his serious girlfriend before the war. She was a sophisticated older woman, and they had lived together (unmarried!) in Paris and in Cambridge, Massachusetts. She had died of cancer just before the war, and he remained haunted by her death. Also, our friends were aging now, and some, like Bernard De Voto (whom we didn't know very well), had recently died.

After Benny's death, Avis De Voto, who had two sons to care for, had spent months rearranging her life. Once things had settled, she took a recuperative vacation to Europe in the spring of 1956. Luckily, we had arranged a vacation at just the same time, so we met up with her in London. We had a fine time there, walking and shopping and socializing.

Avis was small, dark-haired, and full of opinions. The better we got to know her the more we liked her. One night she introduced us to a six-foot-seven-inch-tall moose of a Harvard economist named John Kenneth Galbraith. We had quite a lot in common with him, and as we all sat in a loud basement restaurant, we compared notes on time spent in India, art, and global politics. It clearly did Avis good to be out amongst lively friends. And after the dolors of Plittersdorf, it did us good, too.

Avis, Paul, and I crossed the Channel on a beautiful day and met up with Simca and Jean Fischbacher in Rouen, where the war-damaged cathedral was finally being repaired. Ever energetic, Simca had phoned ahead to arrange a special lunch for us at the Hôtel de Dieppe, where the chef, Michel Guéret, specialized in *canard à la rouennaise*, a celebrated pressed-duck dish seldom used anymore. What an experience!

Now comes that season of delight
When Paul and Julia's hearts take wing
So through this migratory flight
A dual warmth of love we bring.

1959

WISH YOU WERE HERE

HAPPY
VALENTINE'S DAY
FROM THE HEART OF
OLD DOWNTOWN PLITTERSDORF
ON THE RHINE

1956

-Valentin, saison des coeurs réunis,
le nôtre, mangez-le chers amis.

...us coeurs en casserole, farcis
d'amour

...our vous. R. & J. 1964

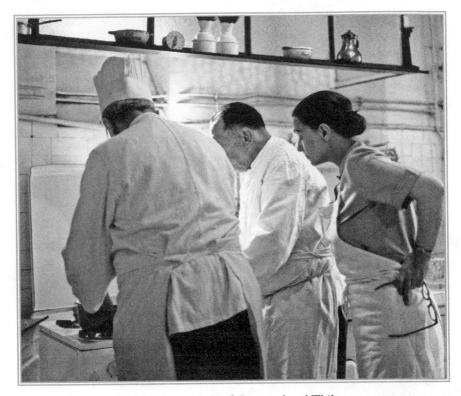

Avis De Voto with Chefs Bugnard and Thilmont

We began with trout stuffed with minnows and a wonder-sauce made of herbs, white wine, and butter. Then on to the famous, ritual-ized *canard*. The duck itself is a special strain bred from a domestic female "covered" by a wild male, which produces handsome dark-feathered birds that are full-breasted and toothsome. They are killed by being smothered, so as to keep the blood inside the body (an example of the lengths the French will go to for a special meal). Chef Guéret roasted two of these ducks on a spit for us, all the while basting them with a wonderful duck-blood sauce he'd prepared at a side table. The birds became mouth-wateringly brown on the outside and roasted very rare on the inside. When they were done, he deftly carved off the ducks' legs and wings, rolled them in mustard and crumbs, and sent them back to the kitchen to be grilled.

He very carefully peeled the skin away from the breast, and carved the meat into thin slices, which he sprinkled with finely minced shallots.

These would be poached in their juices, a little wine, and delicate seasoning, in order to point up the natural flavor. Next the chef wheeled a great silver duck press up to our table. It looked a bit like a silver fire extinguisher with a round crank-handle on top. He cut up the carcass, put it into the canister of the press, and turned the big handle on top. As the pressing plate descended slowly inside the canister, we could hear the cracking of bones, and a stream of red juices dribbled out of the spout into a saucepan. Adding a dollop of red Burgundy wine to the press, the chef turned the crank again, to squeeze some more. He continued like this until the carcass had finally rendered its all. It was a fabulous ritual to watch, and we marveled over Guéret's every move with rapt attention.

Finally, it was time to eat. We began with the tender slices of breast slathered in sauce, and then the nicely crisped and crumbly grilled legs and wings. We washed these delicacies down with a splendid Pommerol. Then we had an assortment of cheeses, glasses of very old apple brandy, and cups of coffee. It was a tour de force.

Normandy was filled with apple blossoms, flowering chestnut trees, and the warm earthy smells of early spring. We drove slowly toward Paris, savoring the landscape, exploring the ruins of a Cistercian monastery, and wandering around old villages where the houses had thatched roofs.

Paris was gorgeous and packed with people. We took Avis for a drink at the Deux Magots, and dined in tremendous style at L'Escargot, where we were surrounded by rich Americans in blue mink and ended our meal with perfectly ripe strawberries and champagne. From there we wandered over to Notre Dame, now illuminated at night by big banks of searchlights, making for a rather dramatic effect. Finally, we ended up at Le Caveau des Oubliettes Rouges, where we sang old French folk songs until one o'clock in the morning. We left with a feeling of pure happiness.

After packing Paul off on the train to Germany, Avis and I dropped by Mère Michel's to see if her famous *beurre blanc* had withstood the test of time. The answer: yes, though it tasted no better than ours.

While I reconnected with Bugnard, the Baltrus, and the Asches, Avis spent a wonderful day in La Forêt de Rambouillet with Simca and Jean Fischbacher, returning to the hotel that night with a great armload of lilies-of-the-valley and a beaming face.

Germany was a frigid, wet fifty-two degrees when I returned. Paul and I had to don our English tweeds to keep warm. We looked at each other and sighed. After the glories of *la belle France*, where all of our impressions were heightened and magnified by the companionship of our friends, it was hard to avoid the conclusion that Plittersdorf was a miserable dump.

IN JULY 1956, we read in the *Paris Herald* that dear old Curnonsky had died. The *prince élu des gastronomes* had fallen off his balcony to his death. Was it an accident, or suicide?

I had seen him in Paris, briefly. He had not looked well, and complained bitterly about the strict diet his doctors had prescribed. At one point he muttered, "If only I had the courage to slit my wrists." What a tragic and bitter end. One couldn't help feeling that he was happier now than in his final days, and that his passing marked the end of an era.

BY THE TIME my forty-fourth birthday rolled around in August, Paul was immersed in an enormous show in Berlin called "Space Unlimited," about the U.S. space program. It drew capacity crowds and was deemed a "phenomenal success." For weeks I hardly saw my husband, and found myself to be an unhappy "widow." *Well*, I reminded myself, *Avis is a* real *widow, so imagine how* she *must feel.*

Paul's success with "Space Unlimited" had been noted in the halls of power, and by the fall of 1956 "they" had decided they needed Mr. P. Child back in Washington, D.C. The main USIA exhibits department there had become a shambles, and he was the man to fix it. So we'd be moving back to the States again, which came as welcome news. I was itching to say *auf Wiedersehen* to Woodenhead (who had given Paul poor marks for administration) and the Plittersdorf way of life.

Once again we were packing up and preparing to move on, like nomads. And, once again, we felt the tingle of excited apprehension about returning to our native soil—now the land of "Elvis the Pelvis," Nixon-lovers, and other strange phenomena. But this time, something was bothering us: ever since Paul had been investigated, we had grown slowly but surely more disenchanted with working for the U.S. government. Paul felt he was doing important work but was not being recognized for it, and I was getting good and sick of uprooting our lives every few years.

"Maybe," we confided to each other, "there is more to life than this." But what else might we do? And where might we do it?

11. The Dream

We arrived back in Washington, D.C., in November 1956, and almost immediately dove into the task of renovating our little jewel of a house at 2706 Olive Avenue. It was a 150-year-old, three-story wooden house, on the outskirts of Georgetown. We'd bought it in 1948. Over the last eight years, we had rented it out, and now it was showing the wear and tear. Luckily, we had banked enough rent money to spiff up an office/guest bedroom for me and a studio for Paul on the top floor, rework the wiring, plug a ceiling leak, and expand the kitchen. What fun to feather our own little nest, the only nest we actually owned.

Using a small inheritance from my mother, I bought a new dishwasher and a sink equipped with an "electric pig," a waste-disposal grinder. (No maids for me!) Then I decided I needed a new stove. One day we were visiting a gourmand friend, Sherman Kent, whom we called Old Buffalo; with a ceremonial sweep of the hand, he showed me the stove in his kitchen. It was a professional gas range, and as soon as I laid eyes on it I knew I must have one. In fact, Old Buffalo sold me his. It was a low, wide, squat black number with with six burners on the left and a little flat-steel griddle on the right. I paid him something like $412 for the stove, and I loved it so much I vowed to take it to my grave!

Paul, meanwhile, had finally been promoted from FSS-4 (Foreign Service rank four) to FSS-3. He now earned a whopping $9,660 a year doing exhibition work.

Our neighborhood was technically in the city but had a nice small-town feel, because everyone marketed at the same place, or met at the post office or in the barbershop. Though I would have preferred to live in Paris while working on *French Cooking for the American Kitchen*, one huge advantage to living in the States was that I could do on-the-ground research about what kinds of produce and equipment were available to our audience.

"It is great fun being back here to live. I never could get the feel of it when we just passed through," I reported to Simca. "One thing I do adore is to be shopping in these great serve-yourself markets, where . . . you pick up a wire push cart as you come in and just trundle about looking and fingering everything. . . . It is fine to be able to pick out each separate mushroom yourself. . . . Seems to me there is everything here that is necessary to allow a good French cook to operate."

But American supermarkets were also full of products labeled "gourmet" that were not: instant cake mixes, TV dinners, frozen vegetables, canned mushrooms, fish sticks, Jell-O salads, marshmallows, spray-can whipped cream, and other horrible glop. This gave me pause. Would there be a place in the U.S.A. for a book like ours? Were we hopelessly out of step with the times?

I decided to ignore my doubts and push on. There wasn't much else I could do. Besides, I loved *la cuisine bourgeoise*, and perhaps a few others would, too.

Simca, meanwhile, was suffering from *la tension* (high blood pressure and jumpy nerves). This was a sensitive subject for me, as my mother had died young of high blood pressure. "You must pay attention to your health," I cautioned her. Simca didn't take criticism well, so I tried to illustrate my point by telling her about Paul's twin, Charlie Child: "Everything he does is at full speed, like a rocket taking off," I wrote. He lived each moment "as if it were the supreme one, requiring every ounce of energy. You are the same. You have to let a few things . . . slip by you, rather than being pitched at the highest key. . . . Force yourself to relax at times. It is not necessary to do everything as though your life and honour depended on it." I doubt my words had any effect on her.

IN THE SPRING OF 1957, I began to teach cooking classes to a group of Washington women who met on Monday mornings to cook lunch for their husbands. Later that year, I commuted once a month to Philadelphia, to teach a similar class to eight students there. A typical menu would include *oeufs pochés duxelles, sauce béarnaise; poulet sauté portugaise; épinards au jus*, and *pommes à la sévillane*.

I was now an experienced teacher. The night before each class, I would type up the menu and list of ingredients. (Usually I'd forward copies of these menus to Simca, who was teaching a group of U.S. Air

Force wives in Paris.) Teaching gave me great satisfaction, and soon my days fell into a comfortingly regular rhythm.

Most of my time was spent revising and retyping our now dog-eared, note-filled, butter-and-food-stained manuscript. In retesting certain dishes in my American kitchen-laboratory, I discovered that hardly anyone used fresh herbs here, that U.S. veal was not as tender as the French, that our turkeys were much larger than their birds, and that Americans ate far more broccoli than the French did. This on-the-ground reporting would be crucial to the success of our book, I knew, but it could also be exasperating.

"WHY DID WE EVER DECIDE TO DO THIS ANYWAY?" I wailed to Simca, after discovering that my beloved *crème fraîche* was nearly impossible to find in America.

IN JANUARY 1958, Simca and Jean made their first visit to the United States. Jean could only stay a short while, but Simca stayed for three months. She hadn't slowed down one bit, and rushed about visiting friends and former students in New York, Detroit, Philadelphia, and California. In Washington, she and I went on shopping/research expeditions and gave a few lively classes together in our Olive Avenue kitchen, where we demonstrated dishes such as *quiche aux fruits de mer, coq au vin,* and *tarte aux pommes.* She was thrilled by America, and sampled our food and drink with vast enthusiasm, including drugstore tuna fish, frozen blinis, and—her favorite—bourbon!

We had a fine time together, but our manuscript remained far from finished. We had promised to show the Houghton Mifflin editors what we'd written so far, but we were a little nervous, because it was seven hundred detailed pages on nothing but poultry and soups. Added to that, our recipes did not appeal to the TV-dinner-and-cake-mix set. We had discovered this fact, with a bit of a shock, when we attempted to place our work in a few of the mass-circulation magazines. Not one of them was interested in anything we'd done. The editors seemed to consider the French preoccupation with detail a waste of time, if not a form of insanity.

Yet I had run into many Americans who had gone to France and been inspired by the wonderful taste of the food there—"Oh, that juicy roast chicken!" they'd exclaim. "My, that *sole normande!*" Though some returned to the U.S. convinced that such wonders could only be achieved by the magic of being born French, the savvier ones realized that the main ingredient in such succulent dishes was hard work coupled with proper technique.

Unfortunately, this was not a message that the food editors of America wanted to hear or had the technical knowledge to appreciate.

Most of our pupils had traveled and cooked for years, but did not know how to sauté, or cut a vegetable quickly, and had no conception of how to treat an egg yolk properly. I knew—because they told me so—that they wanted this information and were willing to work for it. So I was convinced there would be a market for our work. Would Houghton Mifflin agree?

In the days leading up to our meeting, I rehearsed the arguments I would make in Boston in my correspondence with John Leggett, the publisher's New York editor. He was concerned about the scope and detail of *French Cooking for the American Kitchen.* "Good French food cannot be produced by a zombie cook," I wrote him. To get the proper results, one had to be willing to sweat over it; the preliminaries must be performed correctly and every detail must be observed. "Ours is the only book either in English *or in French* which gives such complete instructions," I explained. It "constitutes a modern primer of classical French cooking—an up-to-date Escoffier, if you will, for the American amateur of the 'be your own French chef' persuasion."

On February 23, the day before our appointment at Houghton Mifflin, it was snowing so hard that all of the trains to Boston were canceled. Simca and I looked at each other. After we had put so many years of hard work into *French Cooking for the American Kitchen,* would a mere blizzard stop us? *Non!* We were determined to deliver what we'd promised.

Late that morning, we boarded a bus. It chugged and slithered northward through the driving snow for hour upon hour, while one or the other of us clutched a cardboard box holding our precious manuscript in our laps. At about 1:00 a.m., we finally straggled into Avis De Voto's house, on Berkeley Street, in Cambridge.

The next day, it was still snowing. Simca and I made our way to 2 Park Street, in Boston, where we mounted a long flight of stairs. Cradling our precious box under my arm, I had no idea how our efforts would be received. In the editorial offices, we finally met Dorothy de Santillana, a nice, straightforward woman who understood cooking and seemed genuinely enthusiastic about *French Cooking for the American Kitchen*. But we did not get a very warm feeling from her male colleagues. One of them muttered something like "Americans don't want an encyclopedia, they want to cook something quick, with a mix."

Simca and I left our seven hundred authoritative pages on soups and poultry with them, slowly descended the long flight of stairs, and returned to Avis's through the snow. Neither of us said much.

A few weeks later, we received a letter from Dorothy de Santillana:

Our most careful group eye has been brought to bear on the fruit of what is self-evidently the most careful labor of love . . . and the problem presented is complex. . . . With the greatest respect for what you have done . . . we must state forthwith that this is not the book we contracted for, which was to be a single volume book which would tell the American housewife how to cook in French.

From here we must talk publishing, not cooking. . . . What we could envisage as saleable . . . is perhaps a series of small books devoted to particular portions of the meal. Such a series would have a logical sequence of presentation . . . such as soups, sauces, eggs, entrees, etc. . . . Such a series should meet a rigorous standard of simplicity and compactness, certainly less elaborate than your present volumes, which, although we are sure they are foolproof, are undeniably demanding in the time and focus of the cook, who is so apt to be mother, nurse, chauffeur, and cleaner as well.

I know this reaction will be a disappointment to you, but I wonder if this isn't the time for you to do some re-thinking yourself on the project which has . . . grown into something much more complex and difficult to handle than the original book.

Ah me, our poor Gargantua. What would become of it?

It was true that we had not delivered the book Houghton Mifflin had contracted for. It was also true that the trend in the U.S.A. was toward speed and the elimination of work, neither of which we had furthered in our seven-hundred-page treatise. And it was true that the publisher's suggestion of a simplified series of booklets aimed at the housewife/chauffeur would appeal to a wide audience. Yet the book Houghton Mifflin envisioned was not the book Simca and I were interested in. We felt that the mass audience was already abundantly served

by women's magazines and most cookbooks. We were far more interested in readers who were devoted to serious, creative cookery. We
knew this was an audience that needed and wanted attention. It would,
however, be a relatively small audience. Furthermore, the publishing
business was in a period of doldrums.

What to do?

Simca and I agreed that, though we would be willing to prune our
manuscript a reasonable amount, our objective remained firm: to present the fundamentals of classical French cooking in sufficient detail
that any loving amateur could produce a perfect French meal. Houghton Mifflin was clearly not interested in this. And it was possible—
maybe likely—that no other publisher would take a flyer on this kind of
book, either. But before relinquishing our dream, we wanted to peddle
the idea around.

With Simca standing over my shoulder, I typed a letter to Mrs. de
Santillana, suggesting we return Houghton Mifflin's $250, the first third
of the advance, and cancel our contract for *French Cooking for the American Kitchen*. "It is too bad that our association must come officially to a
close," I wrote. "But we still have a good 30 or 40 more years of cook
bookery in us, so we may sometime be able to get together again."

Ouf! I went to bed that night feeling empty.

The next day, I crumpled the letter up. Inserting a fresh page into
the typewriter, I wrote in a new vein: "We have decided to shelve our
own dream for the time being and propose to prepare you a short
and snappy book directed to the somewhat sophisticated housewife/
chauffeur."

It had been an extremely difficult decision. But Simca and I had
finally conceded that it made more sense to compress our "encyclopedia" into a single volume, about 350 pages long, of authentic French
recipes—from hors d'oeuvres to desserts—than to hunt for a new publisher right now. "Everything would be of the simpler sort, but nothing
humdrum," I wrote. "The recipes would look short, and emphasis
would always be on how to prepare ahead, and how to reheat. We might
even manage to insert a note of gaiety and a certain quiet chic, which
would be a pleasant change." As we had already tested our recipes, I
promised to have the new manuscript finished within six months, or
less.

Mrs. de Santillana wrote back, approving our new plan.

We knew we'd have to emphasize the simpler *cuisine bourgeoise* dishes over the *grande cuisine*. After all, our readers wouldn't have mortars and pestles for pounding lobster shells, or copper bowls for whipping egg whites, and they weren't used to taking the time and care over sauces that the French were accustomed to. Perhaps that would come with time. For now, I could see clearly that our challenge was to bridge the cultural divide between France and America. The best way to do that would be to emphasize the basic rules of cooking, and impart the things I'd learned from Bugnard and the other teacher-chefs—not least of which was the importance of including *fun* and *love* in the preparation of a meal!

III. OSLONIANS

PAUL HAD DECIDED to retire from government service when he turned sixty, in 1962, in order to devote himself to painting and photography. The next question was: what —and where—would we retire to? We didn't love Washington enough to want to stay there, and we felt that California was too far away from our closest family and friends. We debated the subject back and forth, and after several visits to Avis De Voto in Cambridge, Massachusetts, we said to each other: "Now, *there's* a place we can agree on."

Paul had grown up in and around Boston and taught at the Shady Hill School in the 1930s, and felt comfortable there. I found Cambridge to have a special, charming New England character and to be full of interesting eggheads. Over the Fourth of July weekend, 1958, a real-estate agent friend of Avis's walked us about the narrow, winding streets behind the Harvard and Radcliffe campuses. We didn't see anything that appealed, but as we left, Avis said she'd keep an eye out for us.

Back in Washington, Paul had been given the title "acting chief of the exhibits division," which meant he was the USIA's top exhibits man. It was a temporary post that he held for about six months in 1958. In the meantime, we began to study Norwegian in preparation for our next posting. We were being sent to Oslo, where Paul would become the U.S. cultural attaché, starting in 1959.

While in Washington, I had met John Valentine Schaffner, a New York literary agent who represented James Beard and Mrs. Brown of "the Browns," among others. I asked him about how Simca and I should make ourselves known to our vast potential public. He implied that the professional cooking world (both in the U.S. and in France) was a closed syndicate that was difficult to penetrate. So it may have been, but it was our intention to break into this group on a permanent basis. Clearly, we'd be in a better position to do so once we had a finished cookbook in hand. Simca and I bore down, working our stoves and typewriters to a white-hot heat.

In January 1959, as we were preparing to shove off for Norway, Avis called to say that a "special" house in Cambridge was coming on the market, and that we should drop everything and come right away to see it. It was a day of freezing rain, but we jumped on the train to Boston and had a look at the big, gray-shingled house she had described. It had been built in 1889 by the philosopher Josiah Royce (a native Californian, like me), and stood at 103 Irving Street, a small leafy byway tucked behind Harvard Yard. The house was three stories tall, with a long kitchen and a double pantry, a full basement, and a garden. We walked through it for about twenty minutes, and as Paul tapped the walls and floors to judge their soundness, I stood in the kitchen and imagined myself living there. Another family was touring the house at the same time. While they talked it over in low voices, we decided that we'd never find anything better and bought it on the spot. We paid something like forty-eight thousand dollars for it. It needed updating and improving, but we'd be able to pay for that by renting it out while we were in Norway. Hooray!

As our ferryboat from Denmark made its way up the winding Oslo Fjord in May 1959, we looked at the granite boulders and high cliffs covered with pine trees, sniffed the cool, salty-piney air, and said to each other: "Norway is just like Maine!" Which it was, and wasn't.

You can prepare yourself to enter a new culture, but the reality always takes some getting used to. At that latitude, at that time of year, the surprisingly bright sun didn't set until 10:20 p.m. and rose again almost immediately, at 4:00 a.m., which made sleep difficult. Furthermore, Norwegian beds are covered by a single down coverlet, which is as hot as a baker's oven but only big enough to cover half of one's body. We licked that problem by pulling it up to our chins and piling our car blanket and various bits of clothing onto our legs and feet.

There were hardly any pussycats about, I noticed, but plenty of dogs, and more redheads per square meter than anywhere else I'd ever been.

Every Norwegian seemed to be good-looking and healthy, and to have an air of uncomplicated niceness.

The entire USIA staff in Oslo consisted of only three Americans and one Norwegian secretary. When a big shot like Buckminster Fuller came to town, Paul would have to put aside his usual pile of work to arrange lectures and press coverage and chauffeur the great man around. In the meantime, the U.S. Embassy was moving into a handsome new building designed by Eero Saarinen.

By June, we'd found a lovely house to rent in the suburbs, a two-story white clapboard, rather New Englandy–looking place, complete with a preposterous electric stove, an untuned piano, and ants. I hated ants, and set out to poison the little buggers. There were green hedges and fruit trees and climbing roses. The raspberries were ripening fast, and we had both the large strawberries and the little *fraises des bois*, which were highly perfumed and really good (better than the ones we'd had in France, which tasted woody).

I unpacked my vast *batterie de cuisine*—seventy-four items in total, from cheese graters to copper pots—arranged the kitchen to my liking, and began to take language classes. Soon my Norsk was good enough so

that I could read the newspaper and go shopping. The fish and bread were excellent, as were the strawberries, raspberries, and gooseberries, but we were less impressed with the local meat—which included haunches of moose and reindeer—and the rather wan vegetables.

My favorite place to shop was a fish store with a stupendous window display: three-foot-long salmon crossed over each other, surrounded by salmon trout and interspersed with lobster, mackerel, flounder, and halibut. Above this was a garland of little pink shrimp. I would get to know this shop well, with its jolly fishermen standing around boxes of big crabs, great half-carved sturgeon, and live cod swimming in long tanks made of cement. One afternoon I stopped by when an Englishwoman was trying to take a definitive photograph of a cod. A fisherman obligingly pulled a giant specimen out of the tank, held it in his arms, scratched its belly, and cooed to it; the fish squeakily cooed back to him. What a fine act!

Aside from my French-cooking research for the book, I began to experiment with local produce. I picked red currants and made batches of jelly, tried gravlax for the first time (delicious served with a dill-cream sauce, and Steurder potatoes with cream and mace), and cooked a ptarmigan and a large European grouse called a capercailzie.

As I knew hardly a soul in Oslo, I got a great deal of work done on The Book that summer. Letters between Oslo and Paris flew back and forth at a great rate. After nearly eight years of hard labor, Simca and I could see the end in sight, and spurred each other on to heroic feats of typing.

IV. A GODSEND IN DISGUISE

SEPTEMBER 1, 1959, marked our thirteenth wedding anniversary, and I had just turned forty-seven years old. But the really exciting news was that the revised *French Recipes for American Cooks* was finished at last—*ta-da!*

I sent the manuscripple off to a friend in Washington for an immaculate typing up, and from there it would go to Houghton Mifflin in Boston. The book was now a wholly different beast from our original "encyclopedia" on soups and poultry. It was a primer on *cuisine bourgeoise* for serious American cooks, covering everything from crudités to desserts. But it was still 750 pages long, and I worried how the editors would react. We wouldn't hear their comments for another month, and there was nothing we could do but cross our fingers and hope for the best.

What a strange feeling to be done with The Book. It had weighed so like a stone these many years, you'd think I'd be tripping about in ecstatic jubilation. But I felt rootless. Empty. Lost. I sunk into a slough of discombobulation.

Oh, how I yearned for a passel of blood-brother friends to celebrate with. We had plenty of acquaintances in Oslo, but, as in Plittersdorf, we suffered months and months of nobody to really *hug* but ourselves. This was the thing I hated most about the itinerant diplomatic life.

When I finally got myself invited to a large ladies' lunch, we were served canned shredded chicken in a droopy, soupy sauce, and brownies from a mix. Yuck.

My mood buoyed when I received an enthusiastic note from Dorothy de Santillana at the end of September.

> *I have spent four full days studying the manuscript . . . which is a very long time for any single editorial reading. . . . I was intensely occupied every minute and remain truly bowled over at the intensity and detail with which you have analysed, broken down, and reconstructed every process in full minutiae. I surely do not know any compendium so amazingly, startlingly accurate or so inclusive, for it seems to me almost completely inclusive in spite of your formal announcement that [pâte feuilletée] won't be found!*
>
> *This is work of the greatest integrity and I know how much of your actual life has gone into it. It should be easily recognizeable to anyone.*
>
> *. . . I would like to add that I got out Knopf's most recent entry . . .* Classic French Cuisine *by Joseph Donon, and that compared to you Chef Donon not only doesn't deserve the word classic, he doesn't even deserve the word French, in spite of his Legion of Honour!*
>
> *. . . There is nothing for me to do now except wait for the executives to do their figuring.*

I replied immediately, to tell her how delighted we were to be one step closer to publication and to set the record straight about my co-authors. Louisette, I explained, had suffered "family difficulties" (her husband was an ogre, it turned out, and they were getting divorced), and she had not participated much in the writing process. But Simca and I agreed on the importance of keeping Louisette "on the team," both in deference to the work she'd done, and because of the more practical matter that she was much better socially connected than either of us, both in both France and in the U.S.A.

As for Simca, I wanted to make sure that she got proper credit for her labors. The book, I wrote, "is a joint operation in the truest sense of the word as neither of us would be able to operate in this venture without the other." Simca wrote the entire dessert chapter and included many special twists to make traditional desserts especially delicious—including her *bavarois à l'orange*, her *mousseline au chocolat*, and her magnificent *charlotte Malakoff* with almonds. She had supplied us with unusual sauces, including *sauce spéciale à l'ail pour gigot*, *sauce nénette* (reduction of cream, mustard, and tomato), *chaud-froid*, *blanche neige* (cold cream aspic). It was she who worked out the secret for preventing the cream from curdling in the *gratin jurassien* (sliced potatoes baked in heavy cream—a trade secret from the Baumanière at Les Baux), and she who devised the triumphant recipe for ratatouille, based on her many seasons in Provence.

"It is entirely thanks to Mme. Beck and her life-long interest in cooking that we have not only the usual classical collection of recipes, but many personal and out-of-the-ordinary ones which are deeply French," I wrote. "As far as we know, most are hitherto unpublished."

ON NOVEMBER 6, 1959, I received a letter from Paul Brooks, the editor-in-chief of Houghton Mifflin, in the diplomatic pouch. I picked up the long white envelope and stared at it for a moment. It represented so much to me that I hardly dared to open it. Finally, I did.

The company's executives had met several times about *French Recipes for American Cooks*, he wrote, and after much discussion had reached a decision:

> *You and your colleagues have achieved a reconstruction of process so tested and detailed that there can be no doubt as to the successful outcome of the instructions. Your manuscript is a work of culinary science as much as of culinary art.*
>
> *However, although all of us respect the work as an achievement, it is*

obvious that . . . this will be a very expensive book to produce and the publisher's investment will be heavy. This means that he should be able to define in advance the market for the book, to envisage a large buying public for a cookbook which will have to be high priced because of its manufacturing costs. It is at this point that my colleagues feel dubious.

After the first project grew to encyclopedic size you agreed with us that the book . . . was to be a much smaller, simpler book. . . . You . . . spoke of the revised project as a "short simple book directed to the housewife chauffeur." The present book could never be called this. It is a big, expensive cookbook of elaborate information and might well prove formidable to the American housewife. She might easily clip one of these recipes out of a magazine but be frightened by the book as a whole.

I am aware that this reaction will be a disappointment and . . . I suggest that you try the book immediately on some other publisher. . . . We will always be interested in seeing a smaller, simpler version. Believe me, I know how much work has gone into this manuscript. I send you my best wishes for its success elsewhere.

I sighed. It just might be that The Book was unpublishable.

I wasn't feeling sorry for myself. I had gotten the job done, I was proud of it, and now I had a whole batch of foolproof recipes to use. Besides, I had found myself through the arduous writing process. Even if we were never able to publish our book, I had discovered my raison d'être in life, and would continue my self-training and teaching. French cuisine was nearly infinite: I still had loads to learn about *pâtisserie*, and there were many hundreds of recipes I was eager to try.

But I felt sorry for poor Simca. She and Louisette had started this project ten years earlier, and still had nothing to show for it. "You just picked the wrong American to collaborate with," I wrote her.

ALMOST IMMEDIATELY I got a morale-boosting letter from Avis, our tireless champion, saying: "We have only begun to fight."

She forwarded a lovely consoling letter from Dorothy de Santillana, who wrote: "I hate to think of [Julia and Simca's] disappointment. . . . I feel very badly to see the perfect flower of culinary love, and the solidly achieved work of so many years, go begging. They're such nice authors."

She went on to flesh out the actual reasons behind Houghton Mifflin's decision. It was based on a very cut-and-dried business equation: the cost of production (very high) versus the possible sales of the book (unknown, but probably low). Our competitors were producing gimmicky cookbooks—like Houghton Mifflin's own Texas-themed cookbook—and our more serious approach was considered too much of a risk. Even though our recipes were foolproof, the editors had convinced themselves that our dishes were too elaborate.

"All the men felt the book would seem formidable except to the professional cook, and that the average housewife would choose a competitor for the very reason that it was not so perfect," Dorothy wrote. "They feel she wants 'shortcuts to something equivalent' instead of the perfect process to the absolute, which this book *is*. . . . This manuscript is a superb cookbook. It is better than any I know of. But I could not argue with the men as to its suitability for a housewife-chauffeur."

Was our book ten years too late? Did the American public really want nothing but speed and magic in the kitchen?

Apparently so. The entire recipe for *coq au vin* in one popular cookbook, now in its third printing, read: "Cut up two broilers. Brown them in butter with bacon, sliced onions, and sliced mushrooms. Cover with red wine and bake for two hours." Hm.

Well, maybe the editors were right. After all, there probably weren't many people like me who liked to fuss about in the kitchen. Besides, few Americans knew what French food was supposed to taste like, so why should they want to go to all that silly trouble just to make something to eat?

As for myself, I was not at all interested in anything but French cooking. If we couldn't find a buyer for our opus, then I would just forget about it until we returned to the States.

Charlie Child wrote consolingly: "I think Julie is a natural for TV, with or without [book] publication. But this is only one man's opinion." I laughed. *Me* on *television*? What an idea! We had hardly seen a single program and didn't even own a television set.

THE EDITORS AT Houghton Mifflin had suggested we show *French Recipes for American Cooks* to Doubleday, a big publishing house with its own book clubs. But Avis had another idea. Without consulting me or

Simca (but with our full retroactive approval), she had sent our 750 pages to an old friend, Bill Koshland, whose title was secretary at the Alfred A. Knopf publishing house, in New York.

Koshland was an accomplished amateur cook who had seen part of our manuscript at Avis's, and had asked about it. Knopf was a prestigious house that did not have any new cookbooks on its schedule.

Losing Houghton Mifflin was a "Godsend in disguise," Avis wrote, and publishers like Knopf had far more imagination. "This may take time but you will get published yet—I know it, I know it."

Sleeping on it

CHAPTER 6

Mastering the Art

1. A Lucky Coincidence

IN MAY 1948, a twenty-four-year-old editor at Doubleday named Judith Bailey embarked on a three-week vacation to Europe. She and a Bennington friend sailed steerage-class from New York to Naples, and eventually made their way to Paris. It was Judith's first visit to Europe, and she spoke only schoolgirl French, but was thrilled to be there. Her friend went home, but Judith settled into a small hotel, the Lenox, on the Left Bank, not far from where we'd eventually live on la Rue de l'Université. The days flew by, and the longer she was there the more Judith fell in love with Paris. "I have been waiting for this my whole life," she said to herself. "I just love everything about it."

Two days before she was scheduled to return to her job in America, Judith sat in the Tuileries Gardens reading. She had her return ticket in her purse. The sunset was so beautiful that she began to weep. "Why am I leaving?" she wondered. With a sigh, she stood up, gathered her book, and wandered off. It was only when she turned the corner that Judith realized she'd left her purse, with all of her francs, travelers' checks, passport, and return ticket, in the garden. She rushed back, but it was gone.

She reported the robbery to the police and walked back to the Lenox without a sou to her name. "This is so strange," she mused. "I wonder if somebody is telling me I should stay here?"

Back at the hotel, an old friend from Vermont (Judith's native state) happened to be staying at the same hotel and noticed Judith sitting in her room with the door open. "Judith Bailey!" he exclaimed. "What are you doing here?" He and his pals took her out for dinner. Was this another sign that she should stay? She had also met a young Frenchman, who squired her about to restaurants and was a wonderful cook himself. That clinched it.

Once she had decided that she wasn't returning to New York at all, Judith managed to find work as an assistant to Evan Jones—an American nine years her senior, who was editor of *Weekend*, an American general-interest picture magazine that had grown out of *Stars and Stripes*. *Weekend* did well for a time, but collapsed once the behemoths *Life* and *Look* hit the Paris newsstands. Meanwhile, Judith Bailey and Evan Jones had fallen in love.

While he wrote freelance articles and attempted a novel, Judith worked for a shady American who bought and sold cars for Hollywood stars and other wealthy expats traveling through France. She and Evan rented a little apartment and learned to cook together. Although she didn't have any cookbooks, or the wherewithal to go to a school like the Cordon Bleu, Judith was naturally inquisitive and had a talent for the stove. Like me, she learned by tasting things—the wonderful *entrecôte* in restaurants, the tiny cockles in Brittany. She learned culinary *trucs* by asking questions of all sorts of people, such as the butcher's wife, who showed her the perfect fat to fry *pommes frites* in.

During this time, Paul and I had settled into our apartment at 81 Rue de l'Université. It's quite possible that we passed Judith and Evan on the street, or that we stood next to each other at a cocktail party, for we were leading parallel lives. But we never met in Paris.

Tired of the demanding car-dealer, Judith found new work as an editorial assistant to a Doubleday editor in Paris who was acquiring European books for the U.S. market. One day, she happened to pick up a stray book that her boss was planning to reject. Intrigued by the cover photo of a young girl, she opened the book and read the first few lines. Within pages, Judith found herself so absorbed by the story that she couldn't put it down until she had finished it all. Feeling passionate about the book, she implored her editor to reconsider, which he did. Doubleday bought the book, and it was published it in the U.S. as *Ann Frank: The Diary of a Young Girl*.

By November 1951, Judith and Evan had gotten married and returned to New York. When *Anne Frank* became a worldwide sensation, Knopf, which had rejected the book, offered Judith a job as an editor. Her primary duty was to work with translators of French books acquired by Knopf.

In late 1959, when Bill Koshland showed our manuscript to the editors at Knopf, it was Judith Jones who immediately understood what we were up to. She and Evan tried out a few of our recipes at home, subjecting our work to the operational proof. They made a *boeuf bourguignon* for a dinner party. They used our top-secret methods for making sauces. They learned to make and flip an omelette the way Bugnard had taught me (they practiced the omelette flip using dried beans in a frying pan, as we had suggested, on their little deck; the following spring, they discovered beanstalks sprouting from their roof). They avidly read our suggestions on cookware and wine.

"*French Recipes for American Cooks* is a terrible title," Judith said to her husband. "But the book itself is revolutionary. It could become a classic."

Back at the office, Judith declared to her somewhat skeptical superiors: "We've got to publish this book!"

Angus Cameron, a Knopf colleague who had helped to launch the *Joy of Cooking* at Bobbs-Merrill years earlier, agreed, and together they hatched up all kinds of promotional schemes.

In mid-May 1960, I received a letter from Mrs. Jones in Oslo. Once again I found myself holding an envelope from a publisher that I hardly dared to open. After all these years of soaring hopes and dashed expectations, I was prepared for the worst but was hoping, really hoping, for the best. I breathed deeply, pulled out Mrs. Jones's letter, and read:

We have spent months over [your] superb French cookbook . . . studying it, cooking from it, estimating, and so on, and we have come to the conclusion that it is a unique book that we would be very proud to have on the Knopf list. . . . I have been authorized to make you an offer. . . . We are very concerned about the matter of a title because we feel it is of utmost importance that the title say exactly what this book is which distinguishes it from all the other French cookbooks on the market. We consider it the best and only working French cookbook to date which

will do for French cooking here in America what Rombauer's THE
JOY OF COOKING once did for standard cooking, and we will sell
it that way. . . . It is certainly a beautifully organized, clearly written,
wonderfully instructive manuscript. You have already revolutionized
my own efforts in the cuisine and everyone I have let sample a recipe
or talked to about the book is already pledged not to buy another
cookbook.

I blinked and reread the letter. The words on the page were more generous and encouraging than I ever dared dream of. I was a bit stunned.

When Avis called us transatlantic, she gave a big "Whoop!" and
assured us that Knopf would do a nifty printing job and would know
how to really publish the book the right way.

As for the business side of things, Knopf offered us a fifteen-
hundred-dollar advance against royalties of 17 percent on the wholesale
price of the book (if we sold more than twenty thousand copies, we'd get
a royalty of 23 percent). The book would be priced at about ten dollars,
and would be launched in the fall of 1961. For simplicity's sake, the contract would be with me, and I'd work out the financial arrangements
with Simca and Louisette. Mrs. Jones didn't care for the line drawings
we had submitted (done by a friend), and would arrange to hire the best
artist she could find to do our illustrations. All of these details were
acceptable to us authors, and to our lawyer, and I signed the contract
before anyone could have second thoughts.

There, it was done. Hooray!

Our sweet success was largely thanks to that nice Avis De Voto. She
pushed and hammered and enthused for us for so long. Heaven knows
what would have happened to our book if it were not for her—probably
nothing at all.

It turned out that Mrs. Jones had never edited a cookbook before.
Yet she seemed to know exactly what she liked in our manuscript and
where she found us wanting. She enjoyed our informal but informative
writing style, and our deep research on esoterica, like how to avoid mistakes in a hollandaise sauce; she congratulated us on some of our innovations, such as our notes on how much of a recipe one could prepare
ahead of time, and our listing of ingredients down a column on the left
of the page, with the text calling for their use on the right.

But she felt that we had badly underestimated the American

appetite. "With *boeuf bourguignon*," she noted, "two and a half pounds of meat is not enough for 6–8 people. I made the recipe the other night and it was superb, so much so that five hungry people cleaned the platter." Of course, our servings had assumed that one was making at least a three-course meal *à la française*. But that wasn't the American style of eating, so we had to compromise.

She also felt that we ought to add a few more beef dishes—as red meat was so popular in America—and "hearty peasant dishes." I felt that we had quite a few peasant dishes already—*potée normande* (boiled beef, chicken, sausage, and pork), *boeuf à la mode*, braised lamb with beans, etc.—and that she was being overly romantic about this point. But after a bit of back-and-forth, we included a recipe for cassoulet, that lovely baked-bean-and-meat recipe from southwestern France.

To the untrained American ear, "cassoulet" sounded like some kind of unattainable ambrosia; but in truth it is no more than a nourishing country meal. As with bouillabaisse, there were an infinite number of cassoulet recipes, all based on local traditions.

In my usual way, I researched the different types of beans and meats one could use, and eventually produced a sheaf of papers on the subject at least two inches thick.

"*Non!*" Simca barked at my efforts. "We French—we never make cassoulet like this!"

She dug her heels in over the question of *confit d'oie* (preserved goose) in our list of ingredients. She insisted we must include it, but I pointed out that 99 percent of Americans had never heard of *confit d'oie*, and certainly couldn't buy it. We wanted our directions to be correct, as always, but also to be accessible. "The important item is flavor, which comes largely from the liquid the beans and meats are cooked in," I wrote. "And truth to tell, despite all the to-do about preserved goose, once it is cooked with the beans you may find difficulty in distinguishing goose from pork."

Simca shook her finger at me and insisted: "There is only *one* way to make this dish properly—avec *confit d'oie!*"

This irked. "What earthly good is it for me to do all this research if my own colleague is going to just completely, blithely disregard it?" I retorted.

After much drama, we agreed on a basic master recipe for cassoulet using pork or lamb and homemade sausage, followed by four variations, including one using *confit d'oie*. In the book we explained the dish, gave menu suggestions, discussed the type of beans to use, and provided "a note on the order of battle." This took nearly six pages to accomplish, but we tried to make each word count.

The title of our book caused the biggest headaches. Judith felt that *French Recipes for American Cooks* was "not nearly provocative nor explicit enough." I agreed completely, which set in motion a hunt for a nifty new name. As bounty, I offered friends and family a great big *foie gras en bloc truffé*, straight from France. Who could resist such mouth-watering temptation? All someone had to do to claim the prize, I wrote, was to "invent a short, irresistible, informative, unforgettable, catchy book title implying that ours is *the* book on French cooking for Americans, the only book, the book to supersede all books, the basic French cookbook."

My own suggestion was *La Bonne Cuisine Française*.

Judith felt this wouldn't do, as a French title would be "too forbidding" for the American reader.

Some of the other early contenders included *French Cooking from the American Supermarket*, *The Noble Art of French Cooking*, *Do It Yourself French Cooking*, *French Magicians in the Kitchen*, *Method in Cuisine Madness*, *The Witchcraft of French Cooking*, and *The Passionate French Cook*.

As the apple trees blossomed in Oslo, and Paul and I started to grill outdoors, we debated the merits of poetic titles versus descriptive titles. Who could have predicted that the *Joy of Cooking* would become just the right title for that particular book? What combination of words and associations would work for our tome? We made lists and lists—*The French Chef's Companion*; *The Modern American's Guide to French Cooking*; *How, Why, What to Cook in the French Way*; *Food-France-Fun*—but none seemed to be *le mot juste*.

In New York, meanwhile, Judith was playing with a set of words like pieces of a jigsaw puzzle, trying to get them to fit together. She wanted to convey our idea that cooking was an art, and fun, not drudgery; also that learning how to cook was an ongoing process. The right title would imply scope, fundamentality, cooking, and France. Judith focused on two themes: "French cooking" and "master." She began with *The Master French Cookbook*, then tried variations, like *The French Cooking Master*. For a long time, the leading contender was *The Mastery of French Cooking*. (Judith's tongue-in-cheek subtitle was: *An Incomparable Book on the*

Fundamental Techniques and Traditional Dishes of the French Cuisine Translated into Terms of Use in American Kitchens with American Foods and American Utensils by American Cooks.) Reactions were generally enthusiastic to the title, but the Knopf sales manager worried that mastery is an accomplished thing, and that the title did not tell you how to go about mastering it. Well, then, how about *How to Master French Cooking?* Judith suggested.

Finally, on November 18, 1960, she wrote me to say that she'd settled on exactly the right title: *Mastering the Art of French Cooking.*

I loved the active verb "mastering," immodest as it was, and instantly replied: "You've got it."

At the eleventh hour, Simca declared that she did not care for the title.

"It's too late to change it," I said, adding that only an American ear could catch the subtle nuances of American English. Plus, I said, Knopf knew a lot more about books than we did, and they were the ones who had to sell it. So, in effect, *tant pis!*

Unbeknownst to us, Alfred Knopf, the imperious head of the publishing house, who fancied himself a gourmand, was skeptical that a big woman from Smith College and her friends could write a meaningful work on *la cuisine française.* But he was willing to give it a chance. Then, when Judith announced that we'd decided to call the book *Mastering the Art of French Cooking,* Alfred shook his head and scoffed: "I'll eat my hat if anyone buys a book with that title!"

But then he acquiesced. "All right, let's let Mrs. Jones have a chance."

SEPTEMBER 1, 1960, marked our fourteenth wedding anniversary, but Paul and I had no time to celebrate. After eighteen years in the Foreign Service, he had decided he'd had enough and would retire. Paul could have stayed on to reach the twenty-year mark and earn three thousand dollars a month, if he wanted to. But he didn't. It was a wrenching decision. However, once he'd made it, I noticed an immediate surge in Paul's energy and enthusiasm.

The Knopf contract had been the impetus, but the real reason he quit was that, after twelve years of staunch effort, Paul had been rewarded with exactly one measly promotion and one disgraceful investigation. He was fifty-eight years old and sick of battling narrow-minded bureaucrats in Washington while doing yeoman's work abroad without so much as a "thank you." Furthermore, we both felt it was time to put down roots in our native soil and get to know our family and friends again.

We left government service on May 19, 1961—two years and two days after we had arrived in Oslo. Now we were just plain old U.S. civilians.

In the weeks leading up to our departure, I had been chewing my way through the fifteen pounds of galleys for *Mastering the Art of French Cooking* practically twenty-four hours a day. Proofreading was a perfectly horrible job. I was shocked to discover I'd written things like "¼ cup of almond extract," when I'd meant to say "¼ teaspoon"; or had forgotten to say, "Cover the pot when the stew goes into the oven." How could this ever have happened? Seeing one's inadequate English frozen into type was a lesson in humility.

I worked slowly and methodically. But with an upcoming NATO conference keeping Paul fully occupied until the last moment, our imminent departure for the States, and our looming Knopf deadline, my nerves began to fray. So did Simca's.

She was a dear friend, but horribly disorganized and rather full of herself. She didn't bother to check the copy with care, which led to several difficult moments between us. Our deadline for proofreading was June 10, 1961. As that date drew closer and closer, a flurry of emotional letters winged between Paris and Oslo.

We debated things like a cake recipe Simca had proposed in 1959, but now, in May 1961, had second thoughts about. Noticing the recipe in the galleys, Simca declared: *"Ce gâteau—ce n'est pas français! C'est un goût américain! On peut pas l'avoir dans notre livre!"* ("This cake—it's not French. It's an American taste. We can't have it in the book.")

She didn't think the cake was French, but of course it was. I spent hours checking my datebooks and notes, and reported the facts to her: "On June 3, 1959, you sent me this recipe. I tried it out, it worked well, and we agreed to incorporate it into the manuscript. On October 9, 1960, we met and discussed every recipe together, including this one. On February 20, 1961, I wrote you to confirm this." It was too late to take an entire recipe out of the book. "What you now read in print is what you previously read and approved," I reminded her. "I am afraid

that surprise, shock, and regret is the fate of authors when they finally see themselves on the page."

We had worked so hard, and were so close to the finish line, that our disagreements were a real strain. Yet they could not be simply brushed aside. We did our best to muddle through the give-and-take. But the clock ticked ever louder.

When Simca objected to our section on wine, I wrote back: "It cannot be as incorrect as you now think, or you wouldn't have OK'd it before!"

I was beside myself with frustration over her dithering. To me, *Mastering the Art of French Cooking* was something akin to my firstborn child, and, like any parent, I wanted it to be perfect.

Wise Avis wrote: "Leave us face it. No relationship is flawless. And a relationship like yours with Simca is in many respects like a marriage. Very good ups and very bad downs. But it's been a working relationship, and on the whole, good and productive. And the child you have produced is going to have flaws too, but will also be, on the whole, good. We must settle for what we can get."

11. PRAWNS IN THE MAELSTROM

ONE AFTERNOON in late September 1961, I sat with a printed and bound copy of *Mastering the Art of French Cooking* by Beck, Bertholle, and Child in my lap. It was 732 pages long, weighed a ton, and was wonderfully illustrated by Sidonie Coryn. I could hardly believe the old monster was really in print. Was it a mirage? Well, that weight on my knees must mean something! The book was perfectly beautiful in every respect.

Our official publication date was October 16. Simca would fly to New York for the big day, and Paul and I would leave Cambridge to meet her. We planned to stay in New York for about ten days, to try to meet people in the food-and-wine game and drum up a bit of trade.

Knopf had agreed to take out a few advertisements, but most of the promotion job fell to us. I had no idea how to arrange for publicity, so I wrote friends in business and asked for advice. Frankly, I didn't expect much. Our book was unlike any other out there, and Simca and I were absolutely unknown authors. I doubted whether any newspapers would want to write about us. Besides, I hated the whole idea of selling ourselves. We'd just grit our teeth and try our best.

And as long as we had a real live French woman in the States, we thought we ought to do a quick book tour. But how did one go about that? Simca and I decided to travel to places where we knew people who could put us up for the night and help arrange book signings, lectures, and cooking demonstrations. From New York we'd travel to Detroit, then out to San Francisco, and finally we'd descend to Los Angeles, where we'd stay with Big John and Phila.

Pop was eighty-two years old now. He hardly ever got sick, but lately had been struck by a virus and laid up in bed for two weeks. Otherwise, he had been keeping himself busy fund-raising for Nixon and fulminating against John F. Kennedy. "What this country needs is to get some real businessmen down to Washington to fix things up!" he wrote me. But I didn't think the GOPers were the nation's answer. Poor old Ike wasn't very informed, and after we watched movies of the presidential debates while in Oslo, I couldn't fathom how anyone could vote for that loathsome Nixon. "I will be voting for Kennedy," I informed my father.

LO AND BEHOLD, in its first few weeks in print our little old book caught on in New York. Knopf was hopeful that they had a modest best-seller on their hands. They ordered a second printing of ten thousand copies, and if business continued on as it was, they were prepared to order a third printing.

Simca and I felt very proud and lucky indeed. It must have been that *Mastering* was published at the right psychological moment.

Writing in the *New York Times* on October 18, Craig Claiborne declared:

> What is probably the most comprehensive, laudable and monu-mental work on [French cooking] was published this week. . . . It will probably remain as the definitive work for nonprofessionals.
>
> This is not a book for those with a superficial interest in food. But for those who take fundamental delight in the pleasures of cuisine, "Mastering the Art of French Cooking" may well become a vade mecum in the kitchen. It is written in the simplest terms possible and without compromise or condescension.
>
> The recipes are glorious, whether they are for a simple egg in aspic or for a fish soufflé. At a glance it is conservatively estimated that there are a thousand or more recipes in the book. All are painstakingly edited and written as if each were a masterpiece, and most of them are.

Ouf! We couldn't have written a better review ourselves.

Claiborne sniffed at our use of a garlic press, "a gadget considered in some circles to be only one cut above garlic salt or garlic powder," and thought that our lack of recipes for puff pastry and croissants was "a curious omission." I happened to like garlic presses, but his comment about puff pastry stung a bit. Simca and I had tried and tried, but failed to come up with a workable recipe for *pâte feuilletée* in time for publica-tion. But Claiborne did make special mention of our pages on cassoulet: "Anyone who attempts this recipe will most assuredly turn out a dish of a high and memorable character." I nearly purred at that.

A few days after the *Times* review, Simca and I were interviewed on the radio by Martha Deane, who had a morning news-and-comment broadcast which was much listened to up and down the East Coast. It was the first time we had done anything like this, but Ms. Deane had a natural facility for putting us at ease. We had an informal chat with her for about twenty minutes, with test questions and answers, and then the tape went on and everything we said was for keeps. We didn't worry that our words were being broadcast to the public, and just had a wonderfully good time talking about food and cooking.

Two days later, we went to the NBC studio to do a morning TV program called *Today*. As Paul and I didn't have a television yet, we knew nothing about it, but the Knopf people said the show aired from 7:00 to 9:00 a.m. and was listened to by some four million people. That was a lot of potential readers.

Today wanted us to do a cooking demonstration, and we decided the most dramatic thing we could do in the five minutes allotted to us was to make omelettes. At five o'clock on the assigned morning, Simca and I arrived at the NBC studios in the dark with our black French shopping bag filled with knives, whips, bowls, pans, and provisions. It was then that we discovered that the "stove" they had promised was nothing more than a weak electric hot plate. The damned thing just wouldn't heat up properly for an omelette. Luckily, we had brought three dozen eggs, and had an hour to experiment before the decisive moment. We tried everything we could think of, but it didn't do much good. Finally, we decided we'd just have to fake it and hope for the best.

About five minutes before we were to go on, we put our omelette pan on the hot plate and left it there until it was just about red-hot. At seven-twelve, we were ushered onto the set. The interviewer, John Chancellor, had that same nice quality as Martha Deane—with a deft verbal touch, he put us at ease and bolstered our confidence so that Simca and I had such a good time we didn't care what happened. Well, by heaven, if that one last omelette didn't work out perfectly! The *Today* show went better than we could have hoped for, and it was over before we knew it. We were impressed with the informal and friendly atmosphere of the NBC chaps, not to mention their perfectly timed professionalism. TV was certainly an impressive new medium.

The old publicity express was rumbling along at a good clip now. Somehow, *Life* magazine learned of our book and mentioned it in their pages. Then Helen Millbank, an old Foreign Service friend, arranged to have Simca and me photographed for *Vogue*, where she worked—*ooh-la-*

la! And the best news of all was that *House & Garden*, which had an excellent cooking supplement, asked us to write an article. This was a great boon, as that magazine is where all the fancy food types, like James Beard and Dione Lucas—the English chef and teacher, who had a TV cooking show—appeared.

One night while in New York, we met James Beard, the actual, large, living being, at his cooking school/house at 167 West Twelfth Street. Simca and I felt immediately fond of Jim, as he insisted we call him, and he kindly offered to do what he could to put *Mastering* on the culinary map. He was a man of his word, and introduced us around town to culinary movers-and-shakers, like Helen McCulley, a tiny gray-haired fireball who was the editor of *House Beautiful.* She, in turn, introduced us to a number of chefs, like a young Frenchman named Jacques Pépin, a former chef for de Gaulle who was cooking at Le Pavillon restaurant. And we also met Dione Lucas at the Egg Basket, her little restaurant that had a cooking school in the back. Simca and I sat at the omelette bar, where Lucas put on a wonderful performance while giving us lunch and pointers on doing cooking demonstrations for an audience.

In early November, we flew from Boston, where it was eighty-two degrees, to Detroit, where it was snowing. We stayed in Grosse Pointe with socially prominent friends of Simca's, who invited a big crowd to our demonstration. Although most of the people there knew nothing about *la cuisine française*, they liked our book enough (or followed the herd enough) so that it sold out in local bookstores. We had no idea if these sales had any wider significance, but it was a pleasant surprise in Detroit. It would have been awful to be on a promotion trip for a dead, or dying, duck!

Then on to California, where San Francisco was brilliantly sunny, diamond-clear, cool, and green. On a typical day, we were picked up at nine-forty-five at Dort's house in Sausalito by the local Knopf representative, a Mr. Russell. He drove us to an interview at the *Oakland Times.* Then to the Palace Hotel in San Francisco by noon, where we were interviewed on KCBS Radio. By this point, we were getting much better at answering interviewers' questions, talking more slowly and clearly, and not feeling self-conscious. It was fascinating to see how the radio and newspaper people went about their work. After a quick lunch, Russell drove us back to Sausalito, where we barely had time to wash our hands before Paul and I climbed aboard Dort's Morris Minor and drove

Simca and I being interviewed by Rhea Case at the
Cavalcade of Books in Los Angeles

to Berkeley. There we had a sort of "diplomatic" tea with a Mrs. Jackson, a children's-book author and wife of a famed book editor. Then back to Dort's, where we picked up Simca, and drove into San Francisco for a cocktail party with a mob of university types. Then dinner with a woman who would host a book party for us in Washington, D.C., and who would try to persuade the *Washington Post* to write something about *Mastering the Art of French Cooking.* After dinner we called on an older woman friend, as vigorous as a pirate, and we finally made it home by eleven-thirty. Whew!

On another day, Simca and I set up a stove on the fifth floor of a big department store called the City of Paris, and spent from 10:00 a.m. until 4:00 p.m. making omelettes, quiches, and madeleines, again and again. Screaming at the top of our lungs in order to be heard, we worked practically non-stop and subsisted on whatever we made. It was fun, although we felt like pawns, or prawns, in the maelstrom.

This sort of life was fine for six weeks, but I would not like to be stuck in it continuously. It left no time for work.

When we quit the Foreign Service, Paul and I had said, "Ah, freedom at last—no more of this hurly-burly, thank you very much!" But here we were, shuttling from place to place and hitting deadlines with just seconds to spare. Paul, with his years of experience in exhibits and presentations, helped us immeasurably. Not that Simca and I couldn't take care of ourselves, but to have someone along who didn't have to think about cooking and talking, and who could devote himself entirely to wrangling microphones, stage lights, tables, ovens, etc., allowed us to concentrate on the job at hand.

Just to keep things interesting, we were all ailing—Simca had a leg swell up, Paul suffered a major toothache, and I had a touch of cystitis. "One thing that separates us Senior Citizens from the Juniors is learning how to suffer," Paul noted. "It's a skill, just like learning to write."

By the time we arrived in Los Angeles, Pop had recovered from his flu enough to toss off a few verbal stinkbombs. He needled us as usual about "those people" (i.e., the French), about "the socialist labor unions" (he hated all unions), and about "the Fabian Society in Cambridge" (he disdained the politics of his elder daughter and son-in-law). His views, and general ignorance, were not uncommon in Pasadena. "I've never heard of the Common Market; what is it?" asked a nice and well-educated friend of my parents, a statement that shocked me. Maybe we had lived outside of the U.S.A. for too long, but many of our fellow citizens seemed blissfully unaware of world politics or culture, and seemed exclusively interested in business and their own comfort.

I began to feel nostalgic for Norway, with its good sturdy folk, its excellent educational system, its unspoiled nature, its lack of advertising, and its non-hectic rhythms.

At a cooking demonstration for a women's group in Los Angeles, two ovens, a range, an icebox, and a table, above which was a large mirror tipped at a forty-five-degree angle had been set up, so that the audience could watch our hands and see right into the pots as Simca and I cooked. Unfortunately, the club's leader hadn't bothered to get a single item on the shopping list we had sent her weeks ahead of time. Suspecting as much, we arrived at the theater an hour and a half early, which gave us just enough time to scrounge up the three garbage pails, five tables, rented tablecloth, buckets of ice water, soap, towels, implements, and other items we needed for our demonstration. And it was a good thing, too. About 350 women attended the morning show, and another three hundred arrived in the afternoon. Simca and I demonstrated how to make *quiche au Roquefort, filets de sole bonne femme,* and *reine de Saba* cake. All went smoothly. In between shows, we signed books, sat for interviews, and made the right noises to dozens of VIPs. Meanwhile, the esteemed former American cultural attaché to Norway was crouched behind some old scenery flats trying to wash out our egg- and chocolate-covered bowls in a bucket of cold water.

By December 15, we were back in New York, where generous Jim Beard hosted a party for us at Dione Lucas's restaurant, the Egg Basket. We invited thirty guests, mostly those who had been instrumental to our success, including Avis De Voto, Bill Koshland, and Judith and Evan Jones. Jim saw to it that a small but influential group of food editors and chefs were invited: Jeanne Owen, executive secretary of the Wine and Food Society; June Platt, a cookbook author; and Marya Mannes, a writer for *The New Yorker.*

Dione Lucas had once run the Cordon Bleu's school in London, but she didn't strike us as especially organized, or sober. A few days before the party, the menu hadn't been finalized and arrangements for the wine delivery had yet to be made. Paul and I made an appointment to discuss these details with Ms. Lucas, but when we arrived the Egg Basket was closed and dark. Tacked to the locked door was a note, saying something like "Terribly sorry to have missed you, my son is ill, very ill . . ." Hm. When Judith Jones had lunched at the restaurant two weeks earlier, Lucas had been missing due to "a migraine."

No matter. Simca and I pitched in, and prepared a braised shoulder of lamb at my niece's apartment a few blocks away. Dione Lucas finally appeared, and made a good sole with white-wine sauce, *salade verte,* and *bavarois aux fraises.* The wine arrived intact from Julius Wile, the famous vintner, who was a lively presence. And Avis declared the event "snazzy."

The highpoint of the evening came when Jim Beard stood up and toasted me and Simca with the highest compliment imaginable: "I love your book—I only wish that I had written it myself!"

III. *I'VE BEEN READING*

POP WAS DYING. He had never fully recovered from his flu, and in January 1962 he was hospitalized with a bad mystery ailment: spleen swollen, high white-corpuscle count, perhaps pneumonia. Many tests had revealed little information, although the doctors suspected that they'd found a small tumor at the bottom of his lungs. Phila, one of her daughters, and Dort took turns keeping an eye on him in the hospital. If things took a turn for the worse, I had packed a bag and was ready to fly to Pasadena at a moment's notice.

In the meantime, *Mastering* was in its third printing of ten thousand copies, and I'd received our first royalty payment, a check for $2,610.85. Yahoo! I did some quick calculations, and discovered we were within $632.12 of paying off all of our book expenses. Soon, we would be able to send some real cash money to *ma chérie*, Simca.

John Glenn had circled the globe in his little space capsule (we still didn't have a TV set, and Paul was glued to the radio all day), and I had been invited to go on an egghead television show in Boston to talk about food and *Mastering the Art of French Cooking*.

The show was called *I've Been Reading*, and it was hosted by Professor Albert Duhamel on WGBH, Channel 2, the local public television station. (This lucky break was thanks to our friend Beatrice Braude, who had worked for USIA in Paris, got chewed up by the McCarthy bullies, and now worked as a researcher at WGBH.) I was told that it was unusual for Professor Duhamel to invite a food person on *I've Been Reading*, so my expectations were low. But the interview went extremely well. Instead of the usual five-minute spot, we were given a full half-hour. I didn't know what we'd talk about for that long, so I arrived with plenty of equipment. They had no demonstration kitchen, and were a little surprised when I pulled out a (proper) hot plate, copper bowl, whip, apron, mushrooms, and a dozen eggs. Before I knew it, we were on the brightly lit set and on the air! Mr. Duhamel was calm, clear, and professional; it helped that he loved food and cooking, and had actually read our book. After chatting with him for a bit, I demonstrated the proper technique for cutting and chopping, how to "turn" a mushroom cap, beat egg whites, and make an omelette. There was a large blowup of *Mastering*'s dust jacket projected on a screen behind me, but I was so focused on demonstrating proper knife technique that I completely forgot to mention our book.

Ah me, I had so much to learn!

In response to that little book program, WGBH received twenty-seven more or less favorable letters from viewers. I don't think one of them mentioned our book, but they *did* say things like "Get that woman back on television. We want to see some more cooking!"

By the end of February, the renovation of our kitchen at 103 Irving was finished, and it was a good-looking workroom. We had raised the counters to thirty-eight inches all around, carved out more storage space, and added lights over the work surfaces. Paul chose an attractive color scheme of light blue, green, and black. I hated tile floors, which hurt my feet, so we laid down heavy vinyl, the kind used in airports. There was a thick wood butcher's-block counter and a stainless-steel sink. We had an electric wall oven, and nearby was the professional gas range, in a corner by the door. Over the stove we installed a special hood with two exhaust fans and a utensil rack.

Finally, I arranged all of my pots and pans on the floor the way I liked, and Paul drew their outlines on a big pegboard, so you would know where each one went. Then he mounted the pegboard on the wall, which made my gleaming *batterie de cuisine* look especially handsome.

The kitchen was the soul of our house. This one, the ninth that Paul and I had designed together, was a real wowzer, a very functional space and a pleasure to be in.

While I banged away at recipes suitable for a Washington hostess party for *House & Garden,* Paul devoted an entire day to fixing up a closet in the cellar as a wine *cave.* He even drew up an elaborate chart showing exactly how many bottles of which vintage he had in stock. But when he opened up the cases we'd sent from Norway, he found five bottles had broken—including a fine 1835 Terrantez Madeira, a loss which hurt. "Why did *that* one have to break and not one of the bottles of Jean Fischbacher's homemade *marc,* a fire-water that I detest?" he wailed. "Oh, the injustice."

Mastering the Art of French Cooking continued to sell. With our first royalty check, we bought a book on how not to let plants die (for me), a dry-mount press (for Paul), and the latest edition of Webster's dictionary (for both of us), which led us to scream at each other about the proper use of language. He was a language-by-use type, while I was an against-the-prostitution-of-language type. We also bought our first television set, a smallish square plastic-and-metal box that was so ugly we hid it in an unused fireplace.

Encouraged by the response to our little cooking demonstration on *I've Been Reading*, the honchos at WGBH asked me and the show's director, twenty-eight-year-old Russell Morash, to put together three half-hour pilot programs on cooking. The station had never done anything like this before. But if they were willing to give it a whirl, then so was I.

MY FATHER DIED on May 20, 1962. In the preceding weeks he had lost forty-eight pounds and had grown white and frail; he was a ghost of his former self. The diagnosis was lymphatic leukemia. Dort, John, and I had arrived in L.A. just before he passed away.

I was fond of Pop, in a way. He had been terribly generous financially, but we did not connect spiritually and had become quite detached. He never said much about my years of cookery-work, our book, or my appearances on radio and television. He felt that I had rejected his way of life, and him, and he was hurt by that. He was bitterly disappointed that I didn't marry a decent, red-blooded Republican businessman, and felt my life choices were downright villainous. From my perspective, I did not reject him until the point when I could no longer be honest about my opinions and innermost thoughts with him, especially when it came to politics. As I looked back on it, I think that break—my "divorce" from my father—began with our move to Paris.

I really loved my mother, Caro, and missed her. She was a warm and very human person, though non-intellectual. She died when I was still a semi-adolescent. Yet she—and so many other good people in Pasadena, including Phila—just adored Pop, so he must have had something in there. He had lots of good friends, helped many people, spent hours fund-raising for the Pasadena Hospital and other do-gooding organizations. But he did not communicate well with his children. He was no more sympathetic or decent to John and Dort than he was to me.

I know there were times I could have been better, nicer, more generous toward him, and so forth and so on. But, frankly, my father's death came as a relief more than a shock. I suddenly felt we could go to California whenever we wanted to, without restraints or family trouble.

Big John had not been a churchgoer, so we held his memorial service at the house in Pasadena. About two hundred people were there, and so was his coffin. Phila remained strong and composed throughout. There was a short reading, a hymn or two sung, no eulogy. His body was cremated. We had found his father's ashes in a cardboard box behind a living-room sofa. On a calm bright day, we took the ashes of my grandfather, my mother, and my father on a sailboat out by Catalina Island and strewed them into the sea. My brother read from the Episcopal burial-at-sea service. A few tears were wiped away. *Eh bien, l'affaire conclue.*

iv. *The French Chef*

I KNEW NOTHING at all about television—other than the running joke that this fabulous new medium would thrive on how-to and pornography programs—but in June 1962 I taped the three experimental half-hour shows, or pilots, that WGBH had suggested.

WGBH, Channel 2, was Boston's fledgling public TV station. It didn't have much mazuma and was mostly run by volunteers, but they had managed to cobble together a few hundred dollars to buy some videotape. Russell (Russ) Morash, producer of *Science Reporter,* would be our producer-director, and Ruthie Lockwood, who had worked on a series about Eleanor Roosevelt, would be our assistant producer. Ruthie scrounged up a sprightly tune to use as our theme song. And after considering dozens of titles, we decided to call our little experiment *The French Chef* until we could come up with something better.

Now, would there be an audience out there in TV Land for a cooking show hosted by one Julia McWilliams Child?

The odds were against us. Jim Beard had done some experimental cooking shows sponsored by Borden's Elsie the Cow, but although he had trained as an actor and opera singer, he came across as self-conscious on television. He would spend long silent periods looking down at the food and not up at the camera; or he'd say "Cut here," without explanation, rather than, "Cut it at the shoulder, where the upper arm joins." Unfortunately, his shows never drew a large audience.

Dione Lucas had also done a TV series, but, alas, she was never comfortable in front of the camera, either. Her show fizzled, too.

Our plan was to show a varied but not-too-complicated overview of French cooking in the course of three half-hour shows. We knew this was a great opportunity for . . . *something*, none of us was exactly sure what.

Through some kind of dreadful accident, WGBH's studio had burned to the ground right before we were going to tape *The French Chef* (my own copy of *Mastering* went up in smoke, too). But the Boston Gas Company came to our rescue, by loaning us a demonstration kitchen to shoot our show in. So that we could rehearse, Paul made a layout sketch of the freestanding stove and work counter there, which we brought home and roughly emulated in our kitchen. We broke our recipes down into logical sequences, and I practiced making each dish as if I were on TV. We took notes as we went, reminders about what I should be saying and doing and where my equipment would be: "simmering water in large alum. pan, upper R. burner"; "wet sponge left top drawer."

My trusty sous-chef/bottle-washer, Paul, had his own notes, for he would be an essential part of the choreography behind the camera: "When J. starts buttering, remove stack molds."

There. We had done as much preparation as we could. Now it was time to give television a whirl.

ON THE MORNING OF June 18, 1962, Paul and I packed our station wagon with kitchen equipment and drove to the Boston Gas Company in downtown Boston. We arrived there well ahead of our WGBH crew, and quickly unloaded the car. While Paul parked, I stood in the building's rather formal lobby guarding our mound of pots, bowls, whisks, eggs, and trimmings. Businessmen in gray suits and office girls rushed in and out of the lobby, eyeing me with disapproval. A uniformed elevator operator said, "Hey, get that stuff out of this lobby!"

But how were we to get all of our things down to the demonstration kitchen, in the basement? Resourceful Paul found a janitor with a rolling cart, which we filled with our household goods and clanked down the stairs to the kitchen. There we set ourselves up according to our master plan.

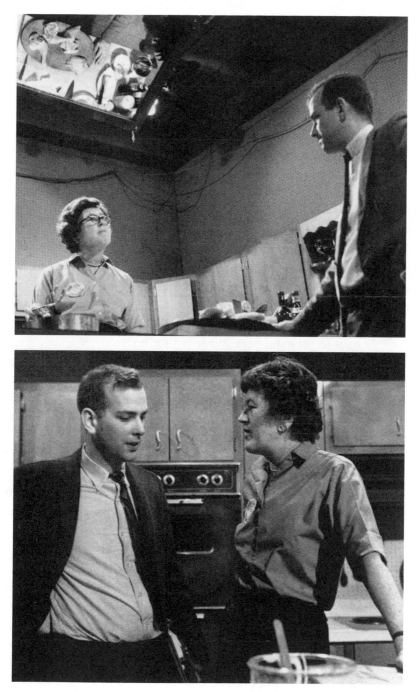

With Russ Morash on the set of The French Chef

Our first show would be called "The French Omelette." Ruthie Lockwood arrived, and we went over our notes and set up a "dining room" for the final scene, where I would be shown eating the omelette. Russ and the camera crew arrived, and we did a short rehearsal to check the lighting and camera angles. He was using two very large cameras, which were attached by thick black cables that snaked up the stairs and out to an old Trailways bus equipped with a generator.

A live show was out of the question—partly due to the limitations of equipment and space, and partly because I was a complete amateur. But we decided to tape the entire show in one uninterrupted thirty-minute take, as if it were live. Unless the cameras broke or the lights went out, there would be no stopping or making corrections. This was a bit of a high-wire act, but it suited me. Once I got going, I didn't like to stop and lose the sense of drama and excitement of a live performance. Besides, our viewers would learn far more if we let things happen as they tend to do in life—with the chocolate mousse refusing to unstick from its mold, or the apple charlotte collapsing. One of the secrets, and pleasures, of cooking is to learn to correct something if it goes awry; and one of the lessons is to grin and bear it if it cannot be fixed.

When we were more or less ready, Russ said: "Let's shoot it!"

I careened around the stove for the allotted twenty-eight minutes, flashing whisks and bowls and pans, and panting a bit under the hot lights. The omelette came out just fine. And with that, WGBH-TV had lurched into educational television's first cooking program.

The second and third shows, "Coq au Vin" and "Soufflés," were both taped on June 25, to save money. We had more time to rehearse these shows, and they went smoother than the first one. Once we had finished taping, our technicians descended on the *coq au vin* like starving vultures.

On the evening of July 26, we ate a big steak dinner at home and, at eight-thirty, pulled our ugly little television out of hiding and switched on Channel 2. There I was, in black and white, a large woman sloshing eggs too quickly here, too slowly there, gasping, looking at the wrong camera while talking too loudly, and so on. Paul said I looked and sounded just like myself, but it was hard for me to be objective. I saw plenty of room for improvement, and figured that I might begin to have an inkling of what I was supposed to do after I'd shot twenty more TV shows. But it had been fun.

The response to our shows was enthusiastic enough to suggest that there was, indeed, an audience for a regular cooking program on public television. Perhaps our timing was good. Since the war, more and more Americans had been traveling to places like France and were curious about its cuisine. Furthermore, the Kennedys had installed a French chef, René Verdon, in the White House. Our book continued to sell well. And television was becoming a hugely popular, and powerful, medium.

WGBH boldly suggested that we try a series of twenty-six cooking programs. We were to start taping in January, and the first show would air in February 1963. And with that, *The French Chef*, which followed the ideas we'd laid out in *Mastering the Art of French Cooking*, was under way.

v. La Peetch

In 1963, I was shooting four episodes of *The French Chef* a week while also writing a weekly food column for the *Boston Globe*. In the fall, we were scheduled to take a break from TV work, and had planned to visit Simca and Jean at their rambling farmhouse in Provence. But as November hove into view, we began to regret it. The quicksand of my cookery-work, Paul's painting and photography projects, and all the many bits of upkeep and improvement that 103 Irving Street required were sucking at our feet.

"I just don't know if we have the time for a trip to France right now," I sighed. Paul nodded.

But then we looked at each other and repeated a favorite phrase from our diplomatic days: "Remember, 'No one's more important than people'!" In other words, friendship is the most important thing—not career or housework, or one's fatigue—and it needs to be tended and nurtured. So we packed up our bags and off we went. And thank heaven we did!

Jean and Simca had been spending more and more time lately at their early-eighteenth-century stone farmhouse, Le Mas Vieux, on a Fischbacher family property known as Bramafam ("the cry of hunger"). It was up a rutted dirt driveway on the slope of a dry, grassy hill outside the little town of Plascassier, above Cannes. In front of the house stood

On the terrace at Bramafam

a lovely tree-shaded terrace that looked across a valley toward the flower fields and tall, swaying cypress trees of Grasse, an area famous for its perfumes.

Le Mas Vieux had been inhabited for twenty-nine years by Marcelle Challiol, a cousin of Jean's, and Hett Kwiatkowska, two women painters who had passed away. Now the house was falling apart. It was extremely rustic, and Simca didn't care much for it at all. But Jean loved it as a retreat from the pressures of perfumery in Paris. Every morning he liked to putter about his garden dressed in a blue bathrobe, whistling tunes and talking to his flowers. As they slowly renovated, adding more rooms, light, and heat, and updating the bathrooms, the old manse slowly won Simca over. As she oversaw renovations, she discovered a small leather sack buried under the stairs; inside of it were a few

Louis XV silver pieces, dating to 1725—"which proves its age," she liked to say. Once all the work was done, Simca discovered that Le Mas Vieux was the perfect place for her to cook, teach, and entertain friends. Suddenly it began to sound as if the renovations had been *her* idea.

Bramafam was gorgeous in November, with lavender bushes and mimosa all about. One afternoon, the four of us shared an idyllic lunch of Dover-sole soufflé with a chilled bottle of Meursault on the terrace. As we sat contentedly in the sun, breathing in the soft, flowery aromas, Paul and I bandied about the idea of buying a simple place of our own nearby. We even took a look at a few properties in the area, but nothing was quite right for us, or quite affordable. Then Jean suggested that we build a small house on a corner of his property. What an idea!

The more we talked about it, the more excited we became. As I've mentioned, Paul and I had long hoped to buy a *pied-à-terre* in Paris, or to build a little getaway cabin somewhere—perhaps in Maine (near Charlie and Freddie), or California (near Dort), or even in Norway (which we still romanticized). But to be in Provence next to Simca would be a dream come true. I could already imagine spending my winter months here, curing the olives from our trees, and cooking *à la provençale*, with garlic, tomatoes, and wild herbs.

Le Mas Vieux sat on about five hectares of land. Jean didn't want to sell off any of the family property, so Paul and I agreed to lease what used to be a potato patch from them, about one hundred yards away from Le Mas Vieux, to construct a house on. Once we had finished using it, the property would revert to the Fischbacher family, with no strings attached. The agreement was made with a handshake. It would be a house built on friendship.

Paul and I envisioned a very simple structure in keeping with the local architecture: a single-level house, with stucco walls and a red-tiled roof. Simca and Jean offered to oversee the construction while we were in the States, and Paul opened a line of credit for them at a nearby bank. We found an accomplished local builder, although Paul had to use every bit of his diplomatic training to convince the man that we did not want a palazzo, but a simple, modest, and as-maintenance-free-as-possible house.

We decided to call it La Pitchoune, or "The Little Thing."

Building La Pitchoune

By 1964, *Mastering the Art of French Cooking*—or *MTAFC*, as we called it—was about to go into its sixth edition (and we were still finding silly errors and making corrections), while *The French Chef* could be seen on public television in more than fifty cities, from Los Angeles to New York. On the spur of the moment, I had decided to end each show with the hearty salutation *"Bon appétit!"* that waiters in France always use when serving your meal. It just seemed the natural thing to say, and our audience liked it. Indeed, I found that I rather enjoyed performing and was slowly getting the hang of it.

The combination of book and TV work, along with the occasional article or recipe, had turned me into a budding celebrity. There were magazine stories about our show, about our home kitchen, about how and where we shopped, and so on. My cooking demonstrations drew larger and larger crowds. "Julia Watchers" began to recognize me on the street, or called our house, and wrote us letters. At first this kind of attention was strange, but I soon adapted (though Paul resented it). I learned not to lock eyes with staring strangers, which only encouraged them. I have always been a ham, but I didn't care much about celebrity one way or the other.

Hardly anyone in France had heard of *The French Chef,* or knew anything about me. I never really discussed the show's success with Simca: it didn't seem important, and I didn't want her to feel overshadowed. I felt that she was such a colorful personality, and so knowledgeable about cooking, that had she been American rather than French she would be immensely well known.

In February 1964, we flew to Paris, and I dropped in on classes at L'École des Trois Gourmandes, ate out with friends, and visited Bugnard—who was as jolly as ever, though crippled by arthritis. Then Paul and I rented a car and drove south to check on the construction of La Pitchoune. I had no worries about the quality of work, as I knew Simca had been hovering over the project like a mother hen over her nest, and had kept a sharp Norman eye on the schedule and costs.

The house was still in a rudimentary condition when we arrived, but I was smitten with "La Peetch" right away. We made a few final decisions on the interior: there would be red tile floors, a fireplace in the long living/dining room, a hallway with a smallish kitchen and my bedroom on the left, and a guest room and Paul's bedroom on the right. (He was a sometime insomniac, and I was known to snore. We decided it was best to spend the nights apart, but we'd put a double bed in Paul's room so that we could cuddle in the mornings.) My room would have a desk and bookshelf; his would have a little fireplace and French doors that opened onto a stone-and-concrete terrace.

"Even in its unfinished state," I wrote Avis, "the house is a jewel."

NINETEEN SIXTY-FIVE was even more hectic than the year before. Paul and I spent long hours with our production team in Boston, working out the scripts and shooting *French Chef* programs at WGBH. In this intensive period, I could feel that I was slowly improving my TV presentation skills. But by the end of the year, Paul and I were both itching to bust out of our same old routine. On the spur of the moment, we decided to spend Christmas in France. "*La belle F.,*" we called it: France was our North Star, our spiritual home. Charlie and Freddie joined us, and we all sailed from New York to Le Havre, then trained it south from

Paris to Nice. At the terminus, we rented a little tin-can-type car, and put-putted slowly to Bramafam.

As we turned in at the gate and bumped our way up the dusty drive-way, we saw, with mounting excitement, a new house on the right-hand brow of the hill. La Pitchoune—it was finished!

The little house was just as we'd dreamed it would be: tan stucco walls, red-tiled roof, two chimneys, wooden shutters, and a stone ter-race. The lights were all turned on. The refrigerator was fully stocked. The windows had curtains. The living room had comfortable chairs. The beds were made up with brand-new sheets. It was chilly outside, but the house had plenty of heat and hot water. Best of all, a great *potée normande* awaited us on the stove. All we had to do was walk inside.

Simca and Jean had been so thoughtful.

A week later, Les Childs and Fischbachers celebrated the New Year together at La Peetch, with a feast of oysters, *foie gras*, and Dom Pérignon. By that time, Paul and Charlie had mounted pegboard on the kitchen wall, outlined my pots and pans, and hung the *batterie de cuisine*. It did my heart good to see rows of gleaming knives and copper pots at the ready. I could hardly wait to get behind the stove.

Paul and I stayed in our satisfying little house for three months, slowly settling into the sedate rhythms of Provence. La Peetch was set into a hill that had been terraced with low stone berms and was studded with olive trees, almond trees, and lavender bushes. The top of the driveway was just big enough to turn around a compact French car in. Our water came from a large concrete tank behind the house. A spread-ing mulberry tree hung over the terrace. Before Charlie and Freddie returned to Lumberville, they helped us to frame the terrace with olive trees and mimosas. And we partially renovated a small stone shepherd's hut, the *cabanon*, to use as a combination wine *cave*/painting studio/guest room.

Simca and Jean had returned to Paris in early January, but she and I wrote back and forth constantly, trading recipes and comparing notes. It was high time, we had decided, to write *Mastering the Art of French Cook-ing*, volume II.

CHAPTER 7

Son of *Mastering*

I. THE IRVING STREET BOULANGERIE

MASTERING WAS A wide-ranging introduction to French cooking, a natural outgrowth of our classes that covered the fundamental techniques of *la cuisine bourgeoise*; Volume II would extend the repertoire, but in a more focused way. In February 1966, Simca and I prepared a detailed outline of our new book, also known around the house as "Son of *Mastering*." We were determined not to repeat recipes that had appeared in the first book, but would occasionally refer our readers back to Volume I for master recipes. As we had generated many perfectly good ideas that did not make it into Volume I, we estimated that Volume II should take us no more than two years to write.

(Louisette did not collaborate with us on Volume II. Now remarried, to Comte Henri de Nalèche, she lived in the beautiful hunting country near Bourges, and had mentioned that she might write her own book.)

The audience we hoped to reach with Volume II would include everyone from amateurs to experienced cooks and even professionals. Unlike Volume I, the new book would embrace the advances in cooking technology that had recently sprung up. In retrospect, we had taken a rather holy and Victorian approach to the virtues of elbow grease in *Mastering*—implying that "only paths of thorns lead to glory," etc. But France had by now stepped into contemporary life, and as teachers intent on reaching a wide audience, so must we. If we made it difficult for people to learn how to cook—insisting, for example, that the only way to beat egg whites was by hand in a copper bowl—then we'd automatically lose much of our potential audience. That made no sense at all. And so we set out to develop our own ways of using labor-saving gadgets—how to beat egg whites or make pastries with a machine, say. And why not? If we could show readers how to make a perfectly delicious apricot mousse with the aid of an electric mixer, then so much the better!

Back when *Mastering* was first published, I was of the opinion that "good breeding" meant never having one's name in print. But now I had learned a bit more about how the world worked. If one wanted to remain gainfully employed as a writer and TV personality, one had to keep one's name in circulation. As a result, I had become shamelessly willing to expose myself—or Simca—to any number of things that would have appalled me just a few years earlier.

At Thanksgiving, 1966, my face appeared on the cover of *Time* magazine (in a painting by Boris Chaliapin) for a story titled "Everyone's in the Kitchen." It was a nice long article about the growing popularity of cooking in America, although I was dismayed that the magazine downplayed Simca's many contributions to our book and did not run a photo they had taken of her teaching a class at L'École des Trois Gourmandes. But the story had a happy effect on sales of *Mastering*. Instead of the usual ten thousand copies for its next printing, Knopf ordered forty thousand this time. We celebrated this lucky boon over turkey with Charlie and Freddie in Lumberville. The other effect of the *Time* cover story, however, was to increase the pressure on us to complete Volume II as quickly as possible. It was time to light the stove and get back to work!

After moving around the world for so long, I was able to work in most places, but nowhere was I more productive than in our little kitchen at La Peetch. From mid-December 1966 through mid-June 1967, Paul and I holed ourselves up there, far from the noise and distraction of the U.S.A. Bumping up the rutted driveway, we were struck, once again, by what Paul termed "the Reverse Hornet-Sting" of the place—the shockingly fresh and inspirational jolt we got from our lovely hideaway. It was the cool, early-morning layers of fog in the valleys; Esterel's volcanic mountains jutting up out of the glittering sea; the warming Provençal sun and bright-blue sky; the odor of earth and cow dung and burning grapevine prunings; the colorful violets and irises and

Sitting for Boris Chaliapin

mimosas; the olives blackening; the sound of little owls talking back and forth; the sea-bottom taste of Belon oysters; the noisy fun of the marketplace; the deeply quiet, sparkling nights with a crescent moon hanging overhead like a lamp. What a place! The very opposite of a hornet's sting, indeed.

Simca and I had beaten a dirt path across the little field between our two kitchens, as we dropped in on each other several times a day to compare notes and taste whatever was on the other's stove. Our work patterns on Volume II were much the same as they had been on the first *Mastering*. Simca was a veritable fountain of recipes and ideas, which she constantly changed or refined. My job was to be the authority on American habits and ingredients, to retest Simca's recipes, to write the text, and (ugh) proofread.

Simca was terrifically productive and inventive. But as I had learned on our first book, I couldn't really trust her on the details. The measurements, precise list of ingredients, and notes on timing that are so important to a successful cookbook were not Simca's forte. In Volume I we had included three recipes that I didn't think worked well, and they galled me every time I saw them. In this book, I vowed, there would be no clunkers!

In order for Volume II to succeed, I was convinced that it had to not only stand on its own two feet but be *better* than Volume I. Part of my concern was that when a recipe failed to produce the desired results I was the one on the spot in the U.S.A. who got blamed for it. Simca didn't really understand this, or perhaps she wasn't sympathetic. At any rate, I went over every single recipe for Volume II myself, sometimes testing dishes ten or fifteen times, to make sure they withstood the operational proof. Sometimes they did not. Once, for instance, Simca suggested a chocolate-cake recipe; I had brought some American chocolate to Plascassier to use in baking, but she never fully tested it, and when I tried it in her recipe it didn't work at all. So I had to stop work on my own recipe, find out what had gone wrong with hers, and rewrite the directions. (Later, in order to really understand chocolate, I invited a Nestlé chemist to 103 Irving Street, and asked him all about the chemical composition of American chocolate, the best way for a home cook to melt it, and so on. It was a fascinating lesson, but Simca had zero interest in that sort of thing.)

I knew my slow, careful approach drove my intuitive co-author crazy, but it was the only way I knew how to work. I was basically writing these recipes for myself. And I was the type of person who wanted to know everything about a dish—what worked or didn't, why, and how to make it better—so that there would be no unsolved questions in our master recipe.

"*Ne te décourages pas, chérie,*" I wrote Simca. "I am just being extremely *difficile,* which we both must be."

A related bit of friction developed when Simca continued to send me recipe after recipe after recipe, even when it was clear that we could hardly use a third of them. She was hurrying off so many suggestions, and each one would take so long to get right, that I only attempted a fraction of her outpouring. This frustrated her, as did my corrections to the recipes we did use. "*Non, non, non!*" she would shout, after I had changed something of hers (to make the recipe work). *"Ce n'est pas français!"*

"Of course, if my method turns out to be wrong, or if your method is better, then I will be happy to change things so that the final recipe is correct," I replied, just as stubborn as she was. "But every recipe in this book must be foolproof!"

I tried to steer Simca's voluminous outpouring in other directions—to *Gourmet* magazine, which was looking for authentic French recipes, or to Jim Beard's cooking school, where she could teach and make her own contacts in the States—but for some reason she didn't pursue these leads wholeheartedly. Paul grew increasingly irritated with her sometimes imperious behavior, and began to refer to her as "Sigh-Moan" Beck. But I valued her as a creative *force de la nature*, and wouldn't allow him to run her down.

Finally, when she proposed using her dozens of unused recipes in a future *Mastering*, Volume III, I had to be frank: "I have no desire to get into another big book like Volume II for a long time to come, if ever. Too much work. I can do nothing else, and I am really anxious to get back again into TV teaching, and out of this little room with the typewriter."

It was in the midst of this whirlwind of experiments, drafts of recipes, and spirited conversation that Judith Jones suggested in her gentle but compelling way that we really owed it to our readers to include a recipe for French bread. Now, this was not a subject that Simca and I had planned to tackle at all. But, of course, Judith was right. One is not really dining *à la française* without proper brioches and croissants for breakfast, or a symmetrically baked, close-grained, beautifully textured sandwich bread for hors d'oeuvres, or a fine baguette to mop up the sauce on one's plate at dinner. "Bread is so quintessentially French—no meal is complete without a baguette," Judith pointed out. "And you can't really buy a decent loaf of French bread here in the States. Why don't you teach people how to make their own?"

Ouf! How were we to create an authentic-tasting French bread in a typical home kitchen? We faced at least two major hurdles: first, American all-purpose flour was different from French flour, and we'd have to accommodate it to traditional baking techniques; second, *boulangers* used traditional bread ovens for baking, and we'd somehow have to create a simulated baker's oven for the typical home kitchen.

And so began the Great French Bread Experiment, one of the most difficult, elaborate, frustrating, and satisfying challenges I have ever undertaken.

I was immersed in our dessert chapter at the time, and delegated the early bread experiments to Paul. He had made his own bread as a young man, and soon he'd turned our kitchen into the Irving Street Boulangerie. The ingredients for bread were always the same: flour, yeast, water, and salt. But the difficulty was that there were ten thousand ways of combining these simple elements. Every little detail was important, we learned: the freshness of the yeast, the type of flour, the time of rising, the way one kneaded the dough, the amount of heat and moisture in the oven, even the weather.

Paul hung rising baguettes in dish towels from closed kitchen drawers. To emulate steam, he squirted the baking loaves with water sprayed from a little rubber spray bottle. By the fall of 1967, he and I were baking loaves (and other things, like croissants) side by side on a daily basis, and giving them to our neighbors to try. We sent sample "baguettes" wrapped in brown paper to Judith, in New York. She later admitted they looked like "the poor twisted limbs of an old olive tree, all gnarled and misshapen." They tasted all right, but they weren't anything like real French bread.

It would eventually take us two years and something like 284 pounds of flour to try out all the home-style recipes for French bread we could find. We used two French textbooks on baking and tutored ourselves on the fine points of yeasts and flours, yet our best efforts still fell short.

Simca had no interest in our breadworks and did not participate at all. But I didn't care if she, or anyone else, was not interested. I was simply fascinated by bread and was determined to learn how to bake it for myself. You have to do it and do it, until you get it right.

One day I read a newspaper article about Professor Raymond Calvel, an eminent baker and teacher at the École Française de Meunerie. When I wrote him, he encouraged me to come to Paris. Paul and I took one of our loaves to show him, as well as the ingredients we used—American all-purpose flour, yeast, and salt. As soon as we walked into his school and saw row upon row of perfectly baked loaves, I felt mortified and tried to throw our amateur efforts away.

In the course of one afternoon, Professor Calvel showed us what we'd been doing wrong, and taught us all about making proper French bread. Every step in his process was different from anything we had

Making baguettes with Professor Calvel

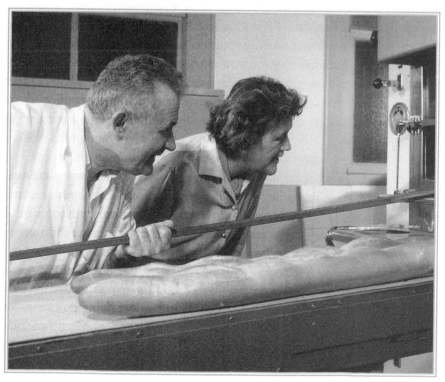

heard of, read about, or seen. His dough was soft and sticky; he let it rise slowly in a cool place, twice, to triple its original volume, because the dough must ripen to develop its natural flavor and proper texture. The way one folded and shaped the loaves was important, Calvel said, as was the flour's gluten content, because, in baking, a gluten cloak encloses the loaf and keeps the proper shape.

I took copious notes on how the dough should look and feel, and the position of the baker's hands, in each step. Paul snapped photographs.

Calvel used a straight razor to slash at an angle the top of the risen loaves before sliding them into the oven. This opened up the bread's gluten cloak and allowed a decorative bulge of dough to swell through the crust.

By the end of the day, our loaves were turning out just right, and I was feeling euphoric. It was as though the sun in all his glory had suddenly broken through the shades of gloom!

Excited, Paul and I rushed back to Cambridge and started baking bread while Professor Calvel's words still rang in our ears.

There remained a few problems to work out.

First, what kind of American flour (which has a higher gluten content than French flour) could be used in place of the softer, unbleached French flour? We conducted numerous experiments, and although Calvel loathed bleached flours, we found that typical all-purpose bleached American flour worked just fine.

Next came the challenge of transforming a home oven into a simulated baker's oven, with a hot surface for the bread to bake on, and some kind of simple but effective steam-generating contraption. These elements were necessary for one to get just the right rise and just the crisp crust of true French bread. Eventually Paul's Yankee ingenuity solved the first problem, when he slid a tile made of asbestos cement onto the oven rack to heat up with the oven: a perfect, affordable baking surface. But creating the all-important burst of steam, which forms the crust, was more difficult. Eventually we discovered that, by placing a pan of cold water in the bottom of the oven, and dropping a very hot brick (or stone, or metal ax-head) into it, one could produce a perfect steam-puff.

Et voilà! We had created the first successful recipe ever for making French bread—the long, crunchy, yeasty, golden loaf that is like no other bread in texture and flavor—with American flour in a home oven. What a triumph!

KNOPF WAS HOPING that we'd finish our manuscript for *Mastering* II by December 1967. But, with our many detours and delays, there was no way we would make that deadline. I wanted to do this book right, and I didn't like to be rushed unduly. It wasn't just the writing that took time. I wanted to explore and explain every ingredient, and make every mistake, so that a recipe could be smoothly translated to the home kitchen.

"When is that second volume of *Mastering* going to be done?" people would ask.

"When it's done," I'd reply.

11. PITCHOUNIANS

ON THE OVERNIGHT FLIGHT from Boston to Paris in December 1968, the plane shuddered, creaked, and bobbed up and down like a lobster boat in a storm. My six-foot-two-inch frame was squinched into a too-tight seat, I didn't sleep a wink and was grumpy when we landed in cloudy, gray Paris. There we boarded a smaller plane, filled with old peasants heading home for the holiday, and flew to Nice. The clouds beneath us remained thick for the entire length of France. But as we neared the Mediterranean, the snowy Alps rose up majestically, and we could see a patchwork of fields below—first white-on-white with snow, then brown with a powder dusting, then all green. Finally, we were racing over the red volcanic rock and turquoise blue water of the coast, as we circled and lost altitude.

Touching down at the sunny Nice airport, we were greeted by colorful pansies, swaying palm trees, and Simca. She began talking, rat-a-tat-tat, as soon as we stepped off the plane. We all trooped into the airport restaurant for our ritual lunch of oysters, *filet de sole*, and sparkly Riesling. The charming waiters flocked to our table and shook our hands like old friends.

"Ahhhh, we're back in France!" Paul said as we drove along country lanes to La Pitchoune. I could feel my shoulders unhunch.

The following night, we were hypnotized by our television, which showed us little humans what our big blue earth looked like from the

With Jeanne Villa

heavens, for the first time, as seen by an American space capsule jetting
to the moon. It was strange and thrilling to be sitting in our cozy
Provençal living room, listening to the astronauts talk loud and clear, as
if Apollo 8 were right next door. On the other end of the technical-
efficiency scale, meanwhile, were the local workmen. Back in April, a
welder had come to measure our terrace for a *canisse* sunshade, an

awning that fits over a metal frame. He was a wonderfully charming chap, who huffed and puffed and talked a lot, and then disappeared. When Paul had tried to stir the man's stumps in June, there was no response. Now it was the end of the year, and the welder and our *canisse* were still MIA. What could we do but shrug? It was annoying but hardly an emergency, like the one at Le Mas Vieux.

Over there, the badly laid water pipes had frozen in the chilly night, and Jean had to drive down to Rancurel's farm to fill trash barrels with water to flush the toilets. Furthermore, he and Simca were furious that their renovations, which were supposed to have been finished by September, were still ongoing. The workmen finally applied the last coat of white paint to the kitchen walls on New Year's Eve.

One of the best things about Bramafam was Jeanne Villa, the roly-poly, pint-sized helper/cook/companion who had faithfully served Simca for forty years. She was a salt-of-the-earth Provençal peasant, who shuffled about in ripped tennis sneakers and a big sunhat, trailed by a menagerie of animals. Jeanne could neither read nor write, but she could communicate with chickens, cats, doves, and dogs. She had a Gabonese parrot, who liked to squawk *"Bonjour, grosse mémère!"* ("Hello, you fat old thing!"). Jeanne was a wonderfully tough old bird who did much of the shopping and upkeep of Le Mas Vieux. She loved to eat, was a natural cook, and was a great source of earthy recipes.

Laurent was the gardener, and he, too, was a leathery old character who loved to talk and worked like an ox. Simca ordered bushels of seeds from catalogues and was a mad planter, but neither she nor Jean cared much for weeding and watering the garden. Jeanne and Laurent kept the Fischbachers' big old property operating smoothly.

Just after Christmas, I bought some flowers in the market at Mouans to spiff up La Peetch for *Vogue*, which was sending a team to do a story on us cookery-bookers at work. The writer, Mary Henry, a blonde, energetic forty-five-year-old American, interviewed Simca, Paul, and me, and took pages of notes in longhand. The photographer, Marc Riboud, a small, twinkle-eyed forty-year-old Frenchman, shot something like two hundred pictures of us with his four Pentax cameras and a bagful of lenses and films that Paul eyed enviously. Later, it would turn out that Simca's feelings had been hurt, as she felt the journalists had focused on me instead of the two of us. I hadn't really noticed it at the time. But when we discussed the matter in private, Paul said, in effect, "I told you so." (He never scolded, but he made his meaning clear.) He claimed that I had protected Simca from the full knowledge of how popular *The French Chef* had become in the U.S.A., and that she was belatedly catching on. I should have given her some warning before *Vogue* showed up on our doorstep, he said.

Perhaps he was right. But Simca was 50 percent of the book, a proud Frenchwoman, and a good friend of mine. I had no intention of making her feel like a second-class citizen.

On December 30, Jim Beard flew into our warm bright Provence from dank London, and as he stepped out of the plane he seemed to expand like a giant sunflower. By now we were all very good friends. A familiar Pitchounian, he sniffed around the house noting minor changes since his visit the year before. Then we sat down and made a list of things to do while he was visiting: cook together, visit restaurants, see the Maeght Museum in Saint-Paul-de-Vence, and go to Monte Carlo.

At seven-thirty the next morning, the last day of the year, Paul threw open the big wooden shutters and let out a startled yell: "Gad!" Our red-brown landscape had been covered in two inches of sparkling white snow. Gobs of the stuff melted off the olive trees as the sun rose and warmed our hillside. Next door, Jean made a racket as he spun the little wheels of his little car uselessly for about ten minutes, until he finally gained traction and slithered down the driveway much too fast with a triumphant look backward at us.

That evening, we welcomed in 1969 with fresh *pâté de foie gras* and champagne at Le Mas Vieux, and didn't get to bed until 1:30 a.m. The cool air, sparkling stars, and semi-white landscape fit the occasion perfectly.

When Jim and I cooked together, we were known as "Gigi," as in "Jim and Julie," with the letter "J" pronounced the French way. We Gigis spent New Year's Day cooking *le dîner de la Nouvelle Année* for seven people—including Les Fischbachers and a gang of local friends. The weather held up splendidly, and we began at 2:00 p.m. with Americanos on our terrace. Moving inside, we had fresh *foie gras panné à l'anglaise et sauté au beurre*, paired with a Chassagne-Montrachet '59. Next came a *filet de boeuf* stuffed with a Catalan mixture of onion, garlic, ham, black olives, thyme, and rosemary, all bound together with egg. It was paired with a 1964 Pommard, and was superb. Then *salade verte, une*

tarte aux pommes, plus cheese and fruit and more wine. The conversation was loud and fun, and mostly about food. It was a leisurely, nearly perfect meal, and we didn't finish until five-thirty that evening. Jeanne Villa helped us cook, serve, and wash up. And then we took a slow walk down the road as the sun dipped behind the hill and the cold air settled into the valley.

Two days later, we drove over to Monte Carlo for lunch at one of my favorite places, the Hôtel de Paris, next to the casino. Entering that hotel was a fascinating dip into La Grande Époque, from the baroque decor to the perfect service. But I had built my expectations so high that the actual experience of the place was an anticlimax. The clientele was mostly ancient and rich, and the food was only so-so. Later, we learned that the hotel had added a new top floor, with striking views of the city and harbor, and a much fresher ambience. *Zut!* We had muffed it! After dinner we dipped into the casino. While Paul and I wandered from Roulette to Chemin de Fer, looking at the people and the enormous naughty paintings of naked ladies, Jim played the slot machines. He claimed he was lucky in casinos. Sure enough, he won fifty-five francs. Then he lost them all. By the end of the evening, he was up two francs from where he had started. "Better than being two francs down!" he said, beaming.

We returned to Cambridge in February, and I dove into deep research on the mysteries of couscous. Originally a North African dish,

Paul making photographs for the illustrator

it had—like Italian spaghetti, American turkey, and English *pouding*—become "French" over the last forty-odd years. (Paul remembered eating heaps of couscous at the Mosquée de Paris back in the 1920s.) As with other national dishes, like bouillabaisse, curry, or paella, every expert claimed to know the "real" recipe, but there was no definitive list of ingredients. Basically, couscous was steamed semolina served with whatever toppings the cook had on hand: lamb, chicken, eggplant, onions, etc.; it was always served with some kind of *sauce au piment bien fort*, plus saffron, cumin, cloves, and so on. After a week of tinkering with various recipes, filling Guinea Pig Number One to the brim with my efforts, and creating a heap of typewritten pages on the subject, I concluded that couscous did not belong in our book after all. It wasn't wasted effort: I knew I'd use this dish at some point, just not in *Mastering*, Volume II.

Meanwhile, Paul and I spent hours doing a photo session showing how to make *boudin blanc* sausages. We tried two methods: one using pig's intestines, the other using cheesecloth. Then we did a shoot of my hands making *un saucisson en brioche*, a wonder-dish that we consumed with a splendid red Burgundy. We had fun, just the two of us, tinkering with food and cameras.

These sausage works were the result of another of Judith Jones's useful suggestions: "Why don't you include a chapter on *charcuterie*?" This, like her suggestion on bread, had come out of Judith's own love of homemade sausage and her frustration at not finding it in American stores. "*Charcuterie* is such an essential flavor of French life," Judith reminded me. "I remember seeing people in Paris in the late 1940s standing in line with their toes sticking out of their slippers, yet willing to pay for fresh *charcuterie*. It would be a real addition to the book."

Chair cuite means meat that is cooked, and traditional *charcuterie* was based on pork in all its forms, from terrines to pâtés to cured hams. But few French householders bothered to make their own *charcuterie* any longer, because it was so easy to go to the specialty shops and buy all manner of terrines, preserved goose, sausages, molds of parsleyed ham, fresh liver pâté, and so on. Nowadays, *charcuteries* had branched out to sell everything from ready-to-heat lobster dishes to salads, canned goods, and liqueurs. We in America didn't have a *charcuterie* store on every other corner, so I set about researching recipes and experimenting with garlic sausages.

I had never made my own sausage before, and was amazed at how deliciously rewarding a simple homemade sausage patty could be. It is only freshly ground pork mixed with salt and spices, after all, but it tasted the way one dreams sausage meat should. And since I was the sausage-maker, I knew exactly what had gone into it. Soon I had home-made links hanging from hooks over the stove and draped from the kitchen door.

The sausage chapter was a very concentrated burst of work, with some splendid eating and one bilious attack along the way. When I typed the final period and sat back in my chair, Paul declared: "Bravo—you deserve a medal-of-honor made of gilded pig tripes!"

III. *LOUP EN CROÛTE*

IN THE SPRING OF 1969, Paul and I were en route from Paris to La Pitchoune when we detoured to Vouzeron, in the Sologne, the little town where Louisette (formerly Bertholle) de Nalèche and her new husband, Henri, lived. The region, in the Cher Department, is noted for its great green forests teeming with animal life. Stag-hunting was still popular there, and it was conducted in the classical manner estab-lished in medieval times. The costumes, protocols, jargon, dogs, special trumpet calls, and elaborate manners remained just as they had in the time of the kings named Louis (XIII, XIV, XV, XVI). Sixteen separate stag-hunts were held in that part of France every year, and for those who partook it was almost a religious way of life. Henri, aka Comte de Nalèche, Louisette's husband, ran one of the sixteen. His pack of eighty-six stag hounds were world-famous because of being so carefully bred that they all looked very much alike. Amazingly, the pack master knew each dog by name. Henri took us for a visit to the kennel and the horse stable and explained about the ceremonial system of killing a wild stag based on the *cor de chasse* trumpets, which are similar to but more beau-tiful than English horns. There were about twenty different trumpet calls, each indicating a stage of the hunt: the dogs are circling; the stag is in the water; the scent is lost; the stag breaks from the forest; etc. It was a weird and fascinating business. As Henri described it, I could sense the life of the court, the separation of courtiers from average citizens, the huge sums it must cost to maintain this ancient hunting tradition.

Louisette seemed very happy indeed. Her house was lovely, with a wide green lawn in the back that had an astonishing 150-year-old cryptomeria pine tree, and a nice feeling of deep French country to it. It suited her.

We drove and picnicked our way to Sancerre, on the upper Loire, which is gracious countryside and good wine country. Continuing in a southeasterly direction along tiny roads, in alternating rain and sun, we made our way to the Auvergne, in the Massif Central. We were amazed to discover that these back roads seemed as empty as they had been in 1949.

We made good time, and arrived at La Peetch a day earlier than planned, which allowed us to dine with Les Fischbachers and catch up on their troubles.

SIMCA, CARRYING A BROKEN wine bottle and glass shards in her right hand, had stumbled, and the glass had sliced down through the space between her thumb and index finger. The cut severed the tendons there, which retracted up inside her hand. She required surgery to find the tendons and sew them together. It was horrid. But the doctor never said "*attention*," so Simca went about her business almost as full-tilt as usual. The suture broke, of course, and had to be resewn. This time she was put in plaster, to hold her hand still, but when the cast came off she was discouraged to find she could barely move her thumb and forefinger. She would require months of therapeutic exercise and re-education, with no guarantee that she would ever regain full function of the fingers in her dominant hand. But with her prodigious energy and iron will, I was confident that La Super-Française could overcome any obstacle.

There were times when Simca's energy beam could be too much. Before cutting her hand, she had planted just about every kind of bush and tree and flower that would grow at Bramafam (and some that wouldn't). Now she was injured, Jean was in Paris, Jeanne had her regular duties to attend to, and Laurent was sick. The upshot was that Paul and I were forced to spend precious vacation hours watering the garden so that it wouldn't broil in the sun.

A little gray pussycat called Minimouche, daughter of Minimère, resumed her life with us just as soon as we arrived. She was very definitely an outdoor cat, who used humans only for food and shelter. But I felt lucky to have any cat company at all. As Thérèse Asche used to say in Paris, "*Une maison sans chat, c'est la vie sans soleil!*" ("A house without a cat is like life without sunshine!") Every morning, Minimouche would dart into the house the instant a shutter was opened, and loudly meow for breakfast. She'd gobble her food down, meow to be let out, and shoot off for a day of chasing lizards. In the evening, she would sit on Paul's lap while we listened to the news on the radio and I cooked dinner. One afternoon, Minimouche brought us a live field mouse and batted it around the kitchen floor. But it managed to escape, and we had a drama worthy of a stag-hunt. We needed a *cor de chasse* to announce each new development: the mouse breaks loose from the cat!; the mouse is hiding under the stove!; the mouse is flushed out with a coat hanger!; etc. *Mon dieu, quel drame!*

IN JUNE, PATRICIA SIMON, a writer for *McCall's* magazine, flew in to write an article about how Simca and I were creating Volume II together. It would be a three-part cover story featuring a number of our latest recipes, timed to the publication of our book. Paul had been hired to photograph us. To make sure things went smoothly, Simca, Paul, and I sat down and planned what we would cook, when to market, and what should be photographed, so there would be no time lost. The next few days would be a bit of a show, of course, but also an important step forward in the Simca-Julia collaboration.

Patricia was shortish, about thirty-two, with dusky skin, and a very soft voice that was sometimes hard to hear. She liked to cook, and took piles of notes about me and Simca, the names of local flowers, the ingredients in various dishes we were working on, and even the contents of our refrigerators. Paul darted around the kitchen, madly photographing us at work. On a balmy afternoon, he shot a few portraits of me holding a spoon and bowl in front of an olive tree, and was very satisfied with the results. But when it came time to shoot Simca, he grew agitated. "She becomes stiff and self-conscious when you point a camera at her," he said later. "She was either hamming it up or freezing. I'm afraid those pictures will be lousy."

A few days later, Simca, Paul, Patricia, and I drove down to La Napoule for lunch at the two-star L'Oasis, Louis Outhier's restaurant.

We penetrated into his beautiful courtyard and were seated at a little white table beneath a leafy trellis, surrounded by geraniums, palms, and a plane tree. It was a splendid lunch, moving from apéritifs to pâté of fresh duck livers and truffles, thick slices of *pain brioche*, a *timbale*, tomatoes and a green salad. But the real reason we were there was for the *loup de mer en croûte:* a Mediterranean sea bass (a large white-fleshed fish with a slightly softer texture than its American cousin) stuffed with herbs and baked in a magnificent brioche crust in the shape of a fish, and served with a *sauce suprême*. This dish was originally conceived by chef Paul Bocuse, but our luncheon at L'Oasis was the first time I'd ever tried it.

The moment it came out of the kitchen—enormous, brown, and glistening—we knew this dish was something special. The maître d'hôtel cut around the edges with an expert sawing motion and lifted the crust off, to reveal the whole *loup* steaming fragrantly. With each helping of fish we received a portion of crust, a big spoonful of the creamy, buttery *suprême*, and another of fresh tomato nicely flavored with shallots and herbs. The crust was thin and gently crunchy, and the fish was beautifully juicy, tender, and lightly flavored with fennel.

If you've been cooking for a long time, you can usually guess how a dish is made. Simca and I studied every detail of this remarkable *loup*, and tried to deduce its secrets. The waiter appeared, and I asked him a few questions, which he was only too happy to answer. "It's delicious," we agreed, as we polished off our lunch. "And it really shouldn't be too difficult to make."

The next day we tried to produce a reasonable facsimile of *loup de mer en croûte* in my kitchen. I measured a whole three-pound sea bass and floured a jelly roll pan. Simca scaled, cleaned, and oiled the fish, then stuffed it with a mixture of parsley, lemon, salt, pepper, and fennel. Using scissors, I cut a fish silhouette out of brown paper and withdrew some brioche dough from the fridge. I rapidly rolled the chilled dough into a thin rectangle, placed the silhouette on top of it, and cut the dough along the paper outline to make a fish shape. Then we laid a second, slightly larger piece of dough over the fish, and tucked it under all around. Finally, we fashioned little fins, eyes, eyebrows, and a mouth out of dough scraps and cut half-moon fish scales into the dough with the large end of a metal pastry tube.

Simca and I debated whether or not to glaze the brioche crust with egg yolk. When Paul suggested we "Submit it to the operational proof!," we decided to do half with glaze and half without, to test the difference.

The *loup* went immediately into the 450-degree oven, and after twenty minutes the crust started to color nicely. We draped a sheet of foil over the top and turned the oven down to 425 degrees. After about forty-five minutes of baking, our fish tasted just as delicious as it had at L'Oasis. The egg glaze, we unanimously agreed, was worth including. (We did not make the *sauce suprême*, though it's perfectly easy to do.)

Simca and I were gleeful and thrilled. What a simple, flavorful, stunning dish to make—just the thing for an informal party for people who care about food. As we sat around discussing how the crust keeps the flesh juicy and full of delicious flavor, we realized that you could wrap all sorts of things in brioche and bake them without their getting soggy. This would require further experimentation!

PATRICIA WOULD STAY with us for a week, and the plan was for me and Simca to cook several meals together using recipes slated for Volume II, to show her—and the readers of *McCall's*—how we collaborated. Paul would photograph us while Patricia would observe. For the first of these meals, we invited some of our former U.S. Embassy colleagues for a luncheon that included four kinds of experimental hors d'oeuvres and a new type of cherry soufflé. But as we ate our breakfast that morning, Simca suddenly called over on the interhouse phone to announce that she and Jean had decided to go to Paris to vote in the national election. This meant she would not be available for the cooking, or the lunch. In fact, she would not return to Bramafam until after Patricia had returned to the States. Hmm.

"She's going *where*?!" Paul said, his eyes going wide. "That's crackers! Patricia has come all the way over here to write an important piece about you, and Simca just throws it away as if it didn't matter. I can't believe it!"

It was hard to disagree with my husband, but I knew from long experience that confronting Simca over this matter would only make her swell up with indignation and wounded pride. It would be a scene. That was hardly the image we wanted to present to *McCall's*. As far as I was concerned, the most important thing to do was to maintain my good relations with Simca. And the best way to do that was to let her go off to Paris without direct confrontation.

Paul remained unconvinced: "You're letting her walk all over you," he muttered.

With Simca gone, I knew it wouldn't be worth cooking the experimental dishes on my own. Not only was the book supposed to be a collaboration, but Simca wouldn't trust my findings if she hadn't been here to observe them herself. She'd insist that we cook everything all over again, which would be a waste of time. So I made other things for lunch. The food came out just fine, and I hoped that Patricia hadn't noticed the deepening furrow in my brow.

"NO MORE GUESTS!" Paul and I said to each other, slumping into our chairs, once Patricia had left. "We need peace and quiet." For the next few days, we did little and thought of nothing. But the summer solstice was approaching, and as we imagined the Norwegians getting drunk and lighting fires along the edges of their fjords, we decided to celebrate in our own way. We invited two other couples, both food-and-wine appreciators, to dinner at La Peetch, and I gave myself a couple of days to create a meal mostly from recipes slated for Volume II.

We started our evening off with iced Clos des Goisses champagne, which Paul served in the big bubbly-glass goblets that we'd bought in Biot, the local glassmaking town. The first course was *tomates farcies à la pistouille:* tomatoes stuffed with chopped eggplant, fresh tomato pulp, basil, and garlic. A poached egg sat on top, like a queen on her throne. Underneath was a lettuce leaf, and the dish was surrounded by freshly made mayonnaise. With this we served a lovely Chablis, Fourchaume 1964. (Paul had discovered this juice at the Cannes *supermarché*, of all places, and it was better than any Chablis we'd had before.)

From there we moved on to *un feuilleton de boeuf en croûte*, a beef tenderloin in a pastry crust. Inspired by our *loup en croûte*, this dish was like a beef Wellington, only it substituted the more handsome, delicious, and non-damply dumpling brioche crust for puff pastry. The tenderloin was sliced into about fifteen pieces and sauced with a heavenly mixture of *duxelle* of mushrooms, ham, *foie gras*, shallots, and Madeira; then the whole was wrapped in brioche and baked. Each slice was served with a bit of crust and stuffing, and a spooning of sauce. An important dish, our *boeuf* was served with the non-distracting *pommes Anna fromagées* and *pointes d'asperges sautées à la chinoise*. This was accompanied by a magnum of velvety Château Haut-Brion, Premier Grand Cru Classé, 1964.

For dessert we had a so-called *pouding pèlerin*, made of ground toasted almonds, kirsch, and apricots with *crème anglaise* in a mold lined with lady fingers toasted in butter and sugar, the whole covered by a *sauce purée aux fraises et framboises*. (The dessert's name refers to the *pèlerins*, the old pilgrims who stuffed their pockets with nonperishables like dried apricots and almonds.) Our *pouding* was accompanied by the nectarlike Château d'Yquem 1962. And we finished with cigars from Havana, brandy, liqueurs, and coffee. Three of the ladies shared cigars, and everyone's faces were aglow. At about 1:30 a.m., the party broke up. What a splendid evening.

Paul was extremely pleased with the 191 photos he'd taken of me and Simca for *McCall's*—at work in our kitchen; shopping in the markets of Grasse and Saint-Paul-de-Vence; eating lunch on a restaurant terrace in Plascassier that overlooks a stunning view of rolling valleys and mountains, with the sea shimmering in the distance. And as far as we knew, Patricia was going to write a marvelous word portrait of us working in sisterly harmony on Volume II.

But in private I had reached a pitch of frustration bordering on despair: Simca simply would not listen to anything I had to say. More than ever, she ignored my infinitely careful measurements, challenged my hard-won findings, and continued to force me to spend hours on recipes she claimed to have tried, only to find that they didn't work at all. It was a sad moment when I realized that collaborating with her actually took longer and caused me more anxiety than working by myself. This perplexed and depressed me. And, for the first time ever, I was looking forward to leaving La Peetch and returning to the U.S.A.

In July 1969, Judith Jones made her way through a driving rain to 103 Irving Street, where she and I huddled over the manuscript for Volume II. Simca and I had been working on the book for three years, and had written only three of our eleven chapters. Knopf was determined to publish Volume II in the fall of 1970, and so Judith had set a hard and firm deadline of March 15, 1970. That seemed like the day after tomorrow. Could we make it?

France beckoned, but we had no time for travel now. We yearned to join Charlie and Freddie in Maine, but it simply wasn't possible. Clackety-clack! went my typewriter, as I bore down.

Working with my editor, Judith Jones

I wrote about all the things a cook can do with crabs. Paul sketched crab parts. And we ate heaps of splendid crab bisque. Then we moved on to eggplant, and after some intensive research I wondered if our skin might be taking on a purplish hue from all the eggplants we consumed. In December, Paul and I sat side-by-side at the long Norwegian table in our kitchen, and sorted through hundreds of envelopes and manila folders filled with Sidonie Coryn's illustrations. There were rough sketches, photocopies of ideas, and finished drawings. We tried to work out the proper flow of visual ideas and to make sure each drawing told the story it should. But Sidonie was not a cook, and apparently had not read the manuscript; she had keyed many of her drawings to the photos instead of to the text. "I feel for her as the illustrator," Paul said. "We're asking for an awful lot." He made corrections on tracing paper to show her how the drawings should look. As for himself, Paul had done ten lobster drawings, a handful of crabs, and was sharpening his pen nibs in preparation for saddle of lamb, a half-boned chicken, a number of beef diagrams, and a step-by-step depiction of how to carve a suckling pig in the French manner.

The book plodded on, and the solitary nature of writing wore on me. "I am closeted with this tiresome Vol. II," I wrote Simca. "This is the last book I shall have anything to do with, I think—too damned much work and no let-up at all."

Judith Jones returned to Cambridge for another editorial check-up in early January 1970. She was wonderfully supportive. About five feet three inches tall, with shoulder-length blond hair, and lively eyes in an expressive face, Judith felt natural to me to work with. She was kind, perceptive, a bit shy, but thoroughly professional, and tough when she needed to be. She had excellent instincts, and had a sure sense of who, what, and where she was. Paul said Judith reminded him of a beautiful Irish fairy queen. Over three long days, she and I made all sorts of important decisions about the book, from the minutiae of font size to the major decision to reduce our planned eleven chapters to seven.

Simca and I began to fret. We learned that a counterfeit version of *Mastering* was being sold in Taiwan for $1.50, and worried about all the snatch grabbing that goes on in the cookbook world. Would someone try to steal our major discovery—how to make real French bread in the home kitchen? There was really nothing we could do to prevent it. And then there were a few recipes we had written five years earlier: we had changed our methods since then, and wanted to rewrite vast sections of the book. Too bad!

"I need at least five years more to get this book right," I wailed, but Judith just smiled and held firm to her deadline. There would be no more additions—no more photographs by Paul, no more drawings by Sidonie Coryn, no more recipes from Simca.

When Simca once again began to complain about things at the very last minute, I wrote her: "Alas, this book may not be as perfect as you might wish, *ma chérie*, but it will be finished."

With two days left, I was still testing in the kitchen, taking notes, and clickety-clacking corrections on my typewriter. I was so busy there wasn't even time to pee!

Then it was March 15, 1970, and I forced myself to hand in the more or less completed manuscript. *Ouf!*

CHAPTER 8

The French Chef in France

1. DOCUMENTARIES

IN 1970, we set out to create our most ambitious *French Chef* series yet. With a bigger budget than ever before (thanks to the happy fact that both Polaroid and Hills Brothers Coffee had signed on to sponsor our show), we were going to shoot thirty-nine new programs, which, for the first time, would all be in color. Since we were doing things differently this time around, I thought it might be fun to record how French food is actually made and sold in France—to show the traditional butchers, olive-oileries, confectioners, triperies, and wine shops that had been my original inspiration. For this, we'd shoot a series of mini-documentaries on thirty-five millimeter film, which we'd later splice into our regular TV programs. So, when I did a show on, say, "How to Bake French Bread," we could insert a sequence showing how a real French *boulanger* made real baguettes in a real baker's oven in Paris.

Although I never mentioned this blatantly, I was convinced that our footage would prove to be an important historical document. Mechanization was taking over the food business, even in France, and it seemed clear to me that many of the artisanal skills we were going to record—the making of glacéed fruits, the hand-cutting of meat, the decorative skills of traditional *pâtissiers*—would disappear within a generation or two. Of course, film itself can fade or break. But if our little documentaries survived, they might be one of the few records showing how food was once made almost entirely by human hands rather than by machines.

I could hardly wait to get started. But that was easier said than done.

In mid-May 1970, a crew of about ten of us gathered at La Pitchoune to map out our shooting schedule. The plan was to start in Provence, then move to Paris, and finish in Normandy. As we had only a few weeks to get everything done, and no chance of returning to France with such a generous budget, we made detailed schedules for each day—down to the hour, and sometimes the minute—to ensure that everything went as smoothly as possible.

We began our first morning of shooting in the market at the Place aux Aires, in Grasse. Peter, our enthusiastic thirty-two-year-old Dutch cameraman, wanted to film me buying fruit, vegetables, flowers, and *crème fraîche*. It all went smoothly until our bright lights and dragging electrical cables bothered one of the market women. She began to wave her arms around and make dramatic faces, while bawling: "Oh no! Enough is enough!" A large crowd pressed around us. "How am I supposed to sell my carrots and be a movie star, too?" she scolded us. "Here I am, surrounded by Hollywood, and only two more hours to sell—how are my customers going to buy anything? Tell me that, Hollywood! Now I'll finish the morning with stacks of stuff on my stand. No! This is too much! Enough!"

It was a legitimate complaint, so we wandered off to shoot elsewhere.

Television production is a lot more tedious than people imagine. Each shot took seconds to watch on TV, and minutes to film, but required hours of preparatory work. When our troops moved into a restaurant, for example, tripods would be erected, light reflectors tilted, spotlights aimed, and rolls of orange electrical cable unspooled. We'd rehearse the scene and begin to shoot, but then my hairdo would have to be rearranged, or we'd have to wait for a cloud to pass. Finally, we'd get the shot we needed, only to break all of our equipment down and move on to the next scene.

It helped that Paul and I were fluent in French and were friendly with many of the local merchants. As Chef Bugnard had tutored me, it was important not to rush, push too hard, or take people's goodwill for granted.

On the morning we invaded Les Oliviers, a restaurant on a hillside near Saint-Paul-de-Vence, Alex, the jolly maître d'hôtel, had set up the restaurant's famous "avalanche" of forty hors d'oeuvres. It was a stunning sight: hot, cold, cooked, raw, mixed, plain, salty, oily, fish, meat, vegetable, and so on. But the food was under big yellow sunshades, and our director, David, grumbled, "This we cannot shoot!"

"But we *must*," cried Peter, the cameraman. "The restaurant's lunch guests will be arriving any minute now, and then it'll be too late!"

"No! Not with this lemon-colored light!"

"Okay, then, take down the umbrellas and shoot with direct sunlight."

"Wait, don't do *that*—the mayonnaise will melt!" interjected Ruthie Lockwood, our producer.

"Brush those flies away—the table looks like a garbage heap!"

The umbrellas came down, the camera went up on Peter's shoulder, the flies were shooed, and we shot the scene. Over and over. "Willie, your feet were sticking out," Peter cried to the soundman, who was hiding under the table with his microphone while Paul and I ate for the camera.

"Let's shoot that sequence again," David sighed.

By three-thirty, we were finished, and our team fell on the "avalanche" like a starving wolfpack.

One day, the crew filmed me driving around Plascassier and visiting our local butcher, Monsieur Boussageon. He ran a nice little shop with his wife and mother-in-law—a trio that, contrary to the usual tradition, worked very well together. We had scheduled to shoot the Boussageons making a *pâté pantin* together, but early that morning his wife gave birth to a little girl—two weeks earlier than expected. Ha! We had to improvise on the fly. With his wife and mother-in-law at the hospital, Boussageon showed us how to make a *pantin:* he used six and a half pounds of pork, veal, and *foie gras* with truffles, done up in a *pâté à croûte*, decorated with dough "leaves" glazed with a whole beaten egg, and cooked for two hours. It was a fabulous display, but in the midst of a particularly good sequence two locals barged into the shop loudly demanding the right to buy blood sausages. At the end of the day, we gratefully bestowed a bottle of champagne upon the wonderfully accommodating Boussageon.

In Marseille we filmed the making of a bouillabaisse, and then took our cameras into the Criée aux Poissons fish market at 4:00 a.m., which was visually splendid. From there we moved to Paris. It was now June, and in rapid-fire succession, we shot segments on frogs' legs at Prunier, cheese at Monsieur Androuet's charming *cave*, hand-carved meat at the Paridoc *supermarché*, pastry decoration at Monsieur Deblieux's *pâtisserie*, and, of course, cookware at Dehillerin's Old Curiosity Shop.

We had planned to shoot the making of *beurre blanc* at Chez la Mère Michel, but when we dropped in for dinner we were badly disappointed, and sadly crossed her off the list. On another evening, Paul and I ate at our old favorite, Le Grand Véfour. We wanted to use the restaurant's venerable sommelier, Monsieur Hénocq, for a show on "Wine and How to Keep It." At eighty-seven, Hénocq remained graceful and charming, but he was going deaf and had taken up long-winded philosophizing. As we left, I embraced Hénocq fondly, but it was obvious that he would not translate well to television.

Even with a dear friend, I could not allow sentiment to cloud our professional standards.

So—what to do about our wine footage?

Halfway up an immensely old, steep street called the Rue de la Montagne-Sainte-Geneviève was a wine store owned by one Monsieur Besse. He was a jolly fellow, with a tired old flapjack of a beret, a gray smock, and a gap where his front teeth had once been. The famous *caves de Monsieur Besse* had been written about many times, but no one had ever tried to record them on film. And for good reason. The *caves* penetrated deep into the earth, each level danker and moldier than the one before, like a series of dungeons connected by narrow tunnels and rotting ladders. Dust, candle-drippings, cobwebs, and *la patine des âges* lay thick on everything. It was a horrible yet fascinating place to explore. Thank goodness we didn't suffer from claustrophobia! There must have been thirty to forty thousand bottles of wine stored in those Stygian depths—although "stored" was not the right word, for there were no shelves, and his bottles were piled haphazardly into mounds on either side of the narrow tunnels up to the top of the stone arches. The jagged edges of broken bottles poked at us in the gloom. Many didn't have labels. There was hardly room to turn around, and if one were to brush against them, the whole jiggery place might crash down.

Paul and I speculated that Monsieur Besse was a "wine miser," who neither drank nor sold most of his collection, but kept amassing bottles to satisfy a personal craving. The catacombs seemed to be an external symbol of some twisted aspect of the Besseian brain.

To film inside Besse's *caves* would require a small hand-held camera and battery-powered lights. At a specialty shop we rented the camera and lights, and began to load them into our little truck. When our director, David, asked the store owner for a receipt, the man handed him a business card. "No, monsieur, I need a receipt to show how much I paid," said David.

The owner's cheeks flamed red and he shouted: "Must I be accused of cheating by every passerby?! If you don't trust me, then I refuse to do business with you!" He and his wife grabbed the cameras and lights, and rushed them inside.

"No! No!" cried Daniel, our local guide. "We've just paid for that. Give it back!" He brought the equipment back outside.

"Take your filthy money!" the owner shouted. "We don't want it!" His wife stuffed the money back into our crew's pockets, while he grabbed his equipment, slammed the door shut, and locked it. And that was the end of that. The famous *caves de Monsieur Besse* remained unfilmed—by us, at least.

By mid-June, the weather in Paris was hot and humid. We kept waiting for a crackling thunderstorm to come along and cool things off, but it just grew hotter and hotter. And now we were delving into what I considered the most important part of the whole expedition: how to make French bread.

The heat was nearly unbearable inside Poilâne's tiny, medieval-style bakery, where we worked from 8:00 a.m. to 7:00 p.m. one day. We filmed every step in the bread-baking process, from the development of the *levain*, to sliding the round loaves into the oven on long wooden paddles, then sliding them out again, and letting the huge golden loaves cool as they gave out wonderful smells. As far as I knew, this step-by-step making of a proper French loaf had never before been filmed.

A few days later, our great bread teacher Raymond Calvel, Professeur de Boulangerie, École Française de Meunerie, gave me a similar step-by-step lesson on making baguettes. We spent all afternoon in his teaching laboratory, while outside the sky roared with thunder and lightning and dripped heavy raindrops. Calvel kneaded, rolled, and slashed the dough. I kneaded, rolled, and slashed. It was an important, triumphant moment, the passing along of one of mankind's oldest life-sustaining traditions, and I prayed we had captured its essence on film.

From Paris we drove to Rouen, to film another of my favorite rituals, the making of pressed duck at La Couronne, the restaurant that would

In Poilâne's bakery

forever remind me of my first meal in France. We warned the owner, Monsieur Dorin, that once we started to shoot there would be no stopping, no matter what. He shrugged, offered to keep his staff late, and said, "I'll stay on the job with you until tomorrow noon, if necessary."

The plan was to eat dinner at the restaurant and begin filming after the last guest had left, around midnight.

That afternoon, Peter, our cameraman, announced that he had an excruciating pain in his left leg. He admitted he'd been suffering throughout the trip, but hadn't mentioned it. Now he was going into the hospital! We were aghast. Without him, we had no show. What to do?

We decided to say nothing to Dorin and to keep our dinner reservation at La Couronne for nine-thirty, as planned. As we ate our way through the fascinating stages of a pressed-duck dinner, we all had our ears strained to hear the telephone. Finally, it rang. The doctors had discovered that one of Peter's vertebrae had been displaced (probably from hoisting the heavy camera to his shoulder), which had pinched his sciatic nerve. He was given injections and pills, and was advised to find a new career.

Temporarily free of pain, Peter leapt into action. He set up his lights and camera and moved furniture around like an athlete.

For visual drama, we decided to set a big fire burning in the medieval fireplace, where three special Rouennaise ducks would be spitted and roasted. (Dorin served thirty ducks a day, and the spit took so long to cook them that they were mostly roasted in the kitchen.) As the heat in the fireplace rose, it turned the blades of a fanlike contraption inside the chimney; this was attached by a chain to the spit, which slowly turned the birds before the fire. Beneath the ducks was a metal trough that collected the drippings, which were scooped up and used to baste.

By 12:30 a.m., the ducks were cooked and we began our demonstration. Dorin was wonderfully relaxed and straightforward in his presentation, as if he were a television veteran. I asked him leading questions, and he answered me in accented English as he deftly dismembered a duck. Peter shot us from many angles and distances. Willie recorded every noise, from the crackle and snap of the fire to the sizzle of the roasting duck flesh and the gush of blood and wine as the silver press crunched down on the carcass. As we finished up, the big old *horloge* chimed 5:00 a.m. outside. The eastern sky was brightening. Cocks began to crow. A light breeze cooled our sweaty, flushed faces. We all felt elated, for we knew we had just shot one of our most successful sequences ever.

After a snooze, Paul, Ruthie, and I drove to the town of Thury-Harcourt, near Caen, where we'd film "All About Tripe" at a restaurant that specialized in that interesting dish. From there, we'd continue on to an ancient abbey in Aulnay, where we'd shoot a bit on Camembert cheese, and conclude with a party in Caen. And then our *French Chef* expedition to France would be complete.

When we arrived in Thury-Harcourt, we were given a message: "Call the Hôtel de la Grande Horloge in Rouen ASAP." Wondering what we'd left behind, we dialed the number. David, our director, answered: "Peter has had a relapse and he can't go on. The pills and shots aren't working on his back. Daniel is driving him to Paris right now. He'll fly home to Amsterdam and go straight into the hospital."

Pouf! That was it. No tripe. No Camembert. No party in Caen.

Within minutes, the *French Chef* team scattered this way and that. Paul and I, meanwhile, felt like a couple of parrots who had just been let out of their cage: "*Now* what?"

II. CONTRETEMPS

I FOUND IT NEARLY impossible to write the introduction to Volume II amid the TV hubbub, and when *McCall's* magazine asked if they could photograph Simca and me cooking together, I had said "No." I simply didn't have the time or energy.

Nevertheless, while we'd been off shooting our documentaries, a team from *McCall's* gathered at La Pitchoune. The magazine hired a French woman food writer to oversee the making of dishes from Volume II, and had contracted Arnold Newman to photograph them. I met the woman at Simca's apartment in Paris. She was charming, but I stood firm: "I am finished working on the book. My time and energies are now devoted entirely to television. I will NOT cook anything for *McCall's*. Furthermore, my husband has already taken hundreds of perfectly good photographs of Simca and me, and I see no point in taking any more."

It was not an uncomplicated situation. Knopf wanted to generate publicity to sell our book, naturally, and *McCall's* was offering a cover story, which would give us a big push. I felt very loyal to our publisher, and to Simca. But I was tuckered out. And so was Paul, who was annoyed that his excellent work had been passed over for reasons we could only guess at. (For one thing, there had been a massive reshuffle of the *McCall's* staff, and the editors who had hired Paul no longer worked there.)

"Why don't we avoid La Peetch altogether, and spend the next two weeks driving slowly through the Massif Central?" he suggested.

"I am not going to be put out of my own house by a bunch of magazine people!" I snapped.

We drove slowly along back roads toward the coast.

IT WAS SUNDAY at La Pitchoune. Our rental-car keys were missing, and we were supposed to take Simca and Jean to the Cannes train station. I was worried about Simca—she had just visited her doctor for the first time in eight years, only to learn that she had heart-valve trouble and was losing her hearing. The doctor had advised her to change her life-style "completely." This was hard to imagine. But my usually vigorous friend was noticeably despondent and diminished. Meanwhile, our little house was covered with cables, boxes, reflectors, and other photographic paraphernalia (somewhere in the midst of which, I just knew, were our car keys). Arnold Newman and a gang of *McCall's* people were crowded into the living room, thinking they had finally coerced me into posing for yet another cover-photo shoot.

"No!" I said.

Paul eyed Patrick O'Higgins, one of the magazine's editors, and reminded him: "Julia has been very clear about this from the start."

With a loud wail, Simca burst into tears. Glancing at me with a hurt expression, she exclaimed: "I had my whole heart set on this picture of you and me together on the cover of the magazine—and now you say *no more photos*! How can you treat me like that?!"

I was speechless. This was the first time in twenty years of collaboration that she had said anything like that. Perhaps the outburst was an emotional reaction to her heart and hearing troubles. Whatever her reasons, I was caught in an impossible situation. I fumed for several minutes, but finally relented. For the rest of the afternoon, Simca and I stood and sat in various poses while Newman snapped off 175 traditional look-at-the-camera portraits.

The next day, salty old Jeanne Villa took Patrick O'Higgins to the

Marché aux Fleurs in Grasse and bought a car-full of flowers and veg-etables. These were to decorate the dining room at Rancurel's restau-rant, across the river. The idea was to create a hearty, country *"fête champêtre"* as background for dishes from Volume II that Rancurel and Boussageon would cook and Arnold Newman would photograph. For atmosphere, they invited a dozen local people to partake of the meal. Jeanne and Laurent made one "couple," and they were joined by Cantan the contractor, Lerda the carpenter, Ceranta the electrician, their wives, plus a few others. Everyone got tight, screamed with laughter, told dirty jokes, ate huge amounts of food, and sang loudly. The kids from the kitchen sneaked in and poked their fingers into the whipped cream on top of the cake.

III. MOVIE NIGHT

MASTERING THE ART OF FRENCH COOKING, Volume II, was pub-lished on October 22, 1970, nine years after Volume I. Knopf had decided on a first printing of a hundred thousand copies, and Simca and I did a quick publicity tour across the country. About two weeks after the book launch, our colorful new *French Chef* TV series began broadcast-ing—featuring the documentary footage we'd shot in France—on PBS stations across the country. The first show was on bouillabaisse, and the reviews were mostly favorable. What a terrific way to launch our book!

The first inkling of trouble arrived one evening in January 1971, when Judith Jones went to a dinner party in Manhattan. She happened to be seated next to a doctor from Mount Sinai Hospital, who men-tioned that he was part of a team researching the possibility that asbestos was a carcinogen. A little bell went off in the back of Judith's mind. *"Asbestos* . . . Hmm . . . Julia recommends using a piece of asbestos cement to create a bread-baking surface in her simulated baker's oven in Volume II!"

We had indeed. The next day, Judith telephoned the hospital and located the doctor in charge of the asbestos research. Without telling him exactly why she was interested, she asked about their findings. The doctor said something like: "We have reason to believe that there may be a causative relationship between certain types of cancer and asbestos, and we advocate not using it in connection with any form of food preparation. Asbestos cement may be less harmful than plain asbestos, because it is compacted with cement, but we do not wish to theorize about this until our research is complete."

"About how long will that be?" Judith asked.

"Oh, about five years," he replied.

"Thank you," Judith said. She hung up and immediately called us in Cambridge.

Quel désastre! We had already recommended using tile made of asbestos cement in the book, and now we were days away from taping our two bread shows for TV. But we couldn't recommend using a potentially carcinogenic tile in our simulated baker's oven! What to do?

We had eight days to find a substitute. Any new tile must be affordable and available to the average American; it must be tough enough to get very hot and not split when cold water was dropped on it; it must adapt to bread loaves and ovens of various sizes; it must not weigh too much; and its glaze must be "high-fired" (baked at over 2,250 degrees), so as to avoid lead poisoning.

At 103 Irving Street, Paul spent hours researching all manner of tiles, in various sizes, thicknesses, and prices: silicon-carbide plaques for $19.00 each, Pyrex slabs for $14.50, and slate for $5.15. The first two were too expensive, and when we tested a piece of slate it split in the oven's heat.

On Friday night, February 5, I made bread on three different tiles: quarry tile, tortoise-glaze tile, and firebrick splits. All three produced excellent loaves. None broke. Hooray!

Then we had a long talk with Dr. Rothschild, a lead-poisoning expert at Sloan-Kettering Hospital. Not only was he a charming and careful scientist, but he and his wife had already read Volume II, bought a sheet of asbestos cement, and successfully made a loaf of French bread. He said that he didn't think there was much, if any, danger from asbestos cement, but he would test it anyway.

In taping the first bread show, we decided not to mention asbestos tile on air; we would simply suggest that people use ordinary red floor tiles. Judith reached much the same conclusion about the book. It was selling well, and in subsequent printings of Volume II, she made several corrections, one of them a quiet altering to red floor tile or quarry tile for use in the simulated baker's oven. We never got any letters on the subject, and I'm not sure anybody even noticed. I began to suspect that

French bread was the recipe I worked hardest on that the fewest people bothered to try!

The taping of our bread shows went off quite well, though there was one last scare to get through. Hanging over the set were sixty-five very hot lights that burned like the Saharan sun. Arrayed in front of me were several bowls of rising dough, so I could show how bread dough should look at different stages. But the heat from the lights got the yeast going and, as they say, "Time and rising dough wait for no man!" Then I misplaced my reading glasses, on camera, and couldn't read the little labels on the bowls. I kept up my patter, but picked up the wrong bowl of dough to demonstrate with. When I began to knead it, the dough didn't behave the way it was supposed to. But I was already deep into my explanation, and managed to muddle through the scene. *À la fin*, the loaves rose perfectly just before going into the oven, and everything worked out fine at exactly 28.57 minutes.

Whew!

But there was no time to rest. We were on to the next show, and the next—"Pizza Variations," "Chocolate Cake," "Pressed Duck," "Working with Chocolate," etc. It was a hectic spring, fully taken up with rehearsing and shooting two *French Chef* programs every week, reviewing our French footage, and so on.

IN MAY 1971, Paul and I slipped away from the telemaelstrom to the peace and quiet of La Pitchoune. After landing in Nice, we celebrated with our traditional lunch at the *aérogare*. The food was perfect, the wine was perfect, and the service was perfect. Ahhh! Where else in the world would you find airport food of such quality? As always, this ritual meal signified an internal shifting of gears: it reminded us not only to slow down, but to open up our senses. "You're not in the U.S.A. anymore, kids," it seemed to say. "You are here in *la belle France*! *Faites attention!*"

At first we thought we might spend a week or two roaming the Côte d'Azur, but once we settled into our satisfying little house there was no question, we'd stay put. Our zest was worn out. We needed to be incognito, do nothing but sleep late, eat well, and enjoy the sound of the cuckoos and the smells of the countryside. But we were so keyed up that it took at least a week to adjust to our peaceful surroundings.

La Peetch was as cold and dark as a dungeon. It took hours to get the radiators working, sweep out the cobwebs, and replace the burned-out lightbulbs. The carpenter and mason had done their work, but the plumber and electrician had yet to appear—and when they did, they discovered that our new dishwasher had the wrong voltage and was missing certain pieces. What with the holidays of Ascension and Pentecôte upon us, no work could be done for days. We shrugged. The big new parking lot at the top of the driveway looked magnificent, and behind the stone wall a line of pretty rosemary sprigs was sprouting. It had been an unusually cold winter in our corner of Provence, and all of the mimosas and a good many other plants had been killed off or badly stunted; now the survivors were full of bright-green shoots, and there was a profusion of enormous orange and yellow rosebuds.

Before we'd arrived, the *International Herald Tribune* had published an article by a former Paris embassy colleague of Paul's, who wrote about knowing us in the old days and how to find La Pitchoune. This was irritating, especially after two sets of American tourists and a Canadian family in a minibus drove right up our driveway asking for us. As instructed, Jeanne and Laurent told them, "The Childs aren't here." It seemed to do the trick.

We had two of our TV shows, "Spinach Twins" (shot at La Pitchoune) and "Meat Loaf" (shot *chez* Boussageon, the butcher), made into sixteen-millimeter sound-and-color films. One evening, we invited a group of the locals over for a movie night. The audience numbered about a dozen, including Jeanne Villa, the Boussageons, the Lerdas, Umberto, Gina, Les Fischbachers, and so on. At nine, just before the lights went down, there was slight nervous tension in the air: our guests were not used to being invited into an American's home, and they had probably never seen themselves in a movie before. They all smiled stiffly and sat ramrod-straight in their seats. The lights dimmed, and as they watched me, Simca, and themselves in the sequences shot *right here*, no one budged a muscle.

The lights came up, we served champagne, and suddenly everyone was talking boisterously. It was interesting to note that the women scarcely wet their lips, while the men indulged in at least three or four glasses of champers each.

By eleven-forty-five that night, we were ready for bed, as I'm sure the early-rising locals were, too. Only, they didn't know what the protocol was for departing politely, so they just sat there waiting for some kind of mysterious signal. We didn't know what the signal might be, either. Finally, Paul pulled Jean Fischbacher into the kitchen and in a whisper asked him to leave first. Entering the living room, Jean said in a loud voice: "Well, thanks a lot, it's been a very good evening!" As he ushered Simca toward the door, the entire crowd rose out of their seats as one and rumbled outside in happy confusion.

CHAPTER 9

From Julia Child's Kitchen

1. *Ma Chérie*

IN JUNE 1971, *Réalités* sent a writer-photographer team to interview me at La Pitchoune, and, bearing in mind Simca's hurt feelings over the *Vogue* and *McCall's* stories, I insisted that we include her for lunch. It was important to show the two of us working together as a team, I felt.

"Simca will ride in on that interview like one of Patton's tanks—innocently, to be sure, but with total egocentricity," Paul warned. "I mean, she hasn't even tried out your recipes, not even for French bread. It's incredible!"

"Not entirely true," I replied. "But it is a fact that she has never considered me a cook worth bothering about."

I sighed. Simca was my "French sister." I responded tremendously to her verve and creative flair, and I was grateful for her generosity with La Pitchoune. But there was no doubt that she and I had grown further and further apart. Maybe it was inevitable. I called her La Super-Française in part because she was typical of the old school: her opinions were fixed; she wouldn't listen; *she* told *you* what was what. That left no room to bat around ideas or have any real conversation.

A few months later, I was standing with Judith Jones in my Cambridge kitchen when I opened a letter from Simca. In it she criticized a recipe from *Mastering*, Volume II, saying something like, "*C'est pas français!* You Americans can't possibly understand that we French would *never* use beef drippings to baste with!"

For years I had brushed off Simca's slights and insults, but now I was sick of it. This letter was the final straw. I was so angry that I threw the pages to the floor and stomped on them. "No more!" I swore. "I won't be treated this way any longer."

Judith raised her eyebrows.

"That's it," I declared. "End of collaboration!"

SIMCA AND I never had a frank discussion about our contretemps. There was no need to. After so many years of working together, we knew each other inside and out. Now we were graduating from each other and going our separate ways—me to my television teaching and books, she to her private life and cooking classes. Still, she would always remain my *"adorable grande chérie bien aimée."*

Simca was sixty-six years old, and after twenty-two years in professional cooking, she said, she "wanted a rest." But she wasn't really the resting type. In a stroke of good fortune, Judith Jones made a contract with her to write a book of her own. *Simca's Cuisine* would be a combination of stories about her life with menus and recipes from her favorite regions of France—Normandy (her native *terroir*), Alsace (where Jean was from), and Provence (where they lived together). Her book, Simca wrote in the Foreword, was for those who were "no longer quite beginners, who adore to cook and partake of *la véritable cuisine à la française*—the true French cuisine." It was also a good repository for some of her many recipes we did not have space for in our two *Masterings*.

Writing an entire book on her own proved to be tough going. Part of the problem was that it was to be written in English, for the American market, and Simca didn't have as full a grasp of the language as she thought she did. I lent a helping eye and tongue where I could, but did not involve myself in any meaningful way. Eventually Patricia Simon—the American who had written about us for *McCall's*—was hired to help midwife *Simca's Cuisine.* With a good deal of encouragement from Judith (to whom the book was dedicated), they eventually finished. It was a very French book, with ambitious menus that demanded a lot from the American cook. But it was charming and packed full of Simca's creativity. I even recognized a few of Jeanne Villa's earthy touches woven in.

Simca's Cuisine was published in 1972. Sales were decent, but not as brisk as Simca had hoped for. Publishing is a tricky business, and for better or worse sales are closely tied to an author's celebrity. I tried to console her by pointing out that even the great Jim Beard's *Beard on Food* had not sold all that well.

BY NOW JIM was a regular guest at La Pitchoune. He was bald, stood about six feet two inches tall, and must have weighed at least 260 pounds. He was a kind, funny man with a remarkable palate. Whenever I was stumped on a cooking question, I'd call Jim, who knew most of the answers off the top of his head, or, if not, who to ask.

When Jim Beard arrived at La Pitchoune in January 1971, he looked heavier and more tired than usual. He had been traveling practically non-stop for months, doing cooking demonstrations, teaching classes, and writing food articles all over America. He had come to visit us in France to take a break. The usual pattern was that, after a few days of R & R at La Peetch, his vigor would bounce back. But this time he never felt quite right. Concerned, Paul and I drove him to Grasse, where Dr. Pathé bluntly told him: "Monsieur Beard, you are overweight and over-strained. You must make major changes in your life-style *immédiatement*, or you will certainly suffer *une crise cardiaque!*" That put the fear of God in him, and within six months Jim had dieted off some sixty pounds.

That October, we had scheduled a lunch date with him in New York. But at four-thirty in the morning, Jim was awakened by sharp chest pains. He just lay in his bed, breathing heavily, not daring to move. Finally, a friend forced him to call his doctor, and Jim was whisked off to the hospital. There he was hooked up to a machine, which probably saved his life.

It was a close call. We were now at that age where some of our oldest and best friends were "slipping off the raft," as the saying goes, and heading into the great blue yonder. Paul Mowrer, our beloved friend from the Paris days, had died over the summer.

To forestall the inevitable, Paul and I went in for our annual physical. I was fifty-nine, and the doctor said my health was fine. Paul was sixty-nine, and the doctor said to him: "Your electrocardiogram could be printed in a medical textbook. . . . Everything about your condition is just great." (Now, that's my idea of a good doctor!)

IN JUNE 1972, Jim Beard once again flew in for a rest stay at La Peetch. He was coming from Norway this time, where he had traveled about advising the 'Weegians on how to please the American palate. He stayed at Le Mas Vieux, partly because the bedrooms were more Jim-sized than at our house, and partly to keep Simca company.

She had broken her right leg and had been housebound in a wheel-chair for forty days; her spirits were in the dumps, and she was desperate for fresh air and visitors.

The evening Jim arrived, the weather was gorgeous and the frogs' chorus croaked loudly in the background. Jeanne produced a lovely tar-ragon chicken, and we had a fun conversation around the dinner table, mostly about food. As the night wore on, the sometimes stern and intense Simca suddenly burst forth with a girlish *joie-de-vivre*.

Every morning, Jim wafted slowly across the field to La Peetch, dressed in a vast, billowing Japanese kimono, for breakfast. We'd sit on the terrace in the shade of the olive tree, drinking Chinese tea and eat-ing fruit, while chatting about cooking, restaurants, and wine. Jim knew what everyone in the food world was doing, and filled us country bump-kins in on all the big-city gossip.

One midmorning, we climbed into our little French rental car—Paul behind the wheel, Jim seated Buddha-like next to him (still in kimono), and me accordioned into the backseat. Then we bumped down our old rutted driveway—the kind of road known as "a jeepable track" during the war—around the corner and up the hill to Plascassier. While Paul emptied our big paper sacks full of trash at the local garbage depository, I bought two rabbits from Boussageon, and Jim chatted with passing Plascassiens, many of whom he recognized from his previous visits. From there we drove on to Grasse.

What a fabulous city! Jim and I bought fruit in the Place aux Aires, while Paul snapped pictures with his trusty Rolleiflex, and then we strolled slowly through the crowded medieval streets, taking in the lay-ers of history and smell and sound. We returned to the car laden with swollen shopping bags, and transferred the perishables to our "traveling fridge," a large Styrofoam box lined with bags of ice cubes—an excellent system for preserving things like fresh fish or greens in the heat. That afternoon, we Gigis experimented in the kitchen with a beer-and-flour batter for deep-frying the big orange zucchini blossoms we'd bought. They made lovely crisp eating.

11. CHEF

ONCE A YEAR, a fascinating cooking contest was held in Paris: to the victor went the lifelong right to put the initials "MOF" after his name. These magical letters stood for "Meilleur Ouvrier de France"—which roughly translates to "Best Chef in France." And in the competitive and rigidly hierarchical world of *la cuisine française* there was absolutely no higher glory. The challenge was to cook a whole meal drawn from the classical repertoire. Everyone cooked the same dishes, and the menu was announced a week ahead of time, so that there were no surprises. The competition took most of a day, and was open to any chef who dared pit his skills against the best in France. The judges were a group of former contest-winners and venerable cooks. They watched every step in the competitors' preparation of the dishes, and judged them as much on presentation as on taste. The contest was avidly followed by the public and widely reported on. It was said that triumph in the MOF was more prestigious for a chef than earning a Ph.D. was for a graduate student, because in the cooking competition there could be only one winner.

That year, 1972, there were forty-eight contestants, and at the end of the day the winner proved to be none other than Roger Vergé, chef of Le Moulin de Mougins. How lucky for him—and for us! The Moulin was our favorite restaurant in all of the Côte d'Azur, or perhaps in all of France, and it was right down the road.

A culinary star, Chef Vergé, had spent time in the States and knew all about James Beard (he had even seen an episode or two of *The French Chef*, which hardly anyone else in France had heard of). When he learned that Jim was in town, he asked us to make sure to stop by and say hello. So one day Paul, Jim, and I drove to his restaurant in Mougins, a small hilltop town long favored by artists.

Chef Vergé and his wife, Denise, were a charming couple, the most attractive of the well-regarded chefs we had met. He was in his early forties, with thick hair and a bushy mustache turning prematurely gray, and a melodious voice. Not especially tall or big in stature, Chef Vergé had tremendous charisma. His personality was on display everywhere at the Moulin: in his great skill in the kitchen, his handpicked wine list, his brigade of personally trained young men, his clearly thought-out conception of what a first-class dining room should look like, and his ability to live up to that ideal on a daily basis. (A little-known fact about this "chef to the stars and artists" was that he judged people by their hands: out of some personal superstition, he shied away from those with small hands—something I didn't have to worry about.)

Madame Vergé, a tiny and pretty woman, always made one feel welcome in the dining room, even on days when the chef was away. Ever energetic, she did the restaurant's flowers, and ran a boutique in Mougins, where she sold antiques, tabletop decor, and Vergé's gourmet products. Above the shop, Vergé had a second restaurant, L'Amandier, and a cooking school.

The Moulin was a remarkable and thoroughly satisfying experience, and I asked Vergé how he had created such a place.

For over a year, the chef said, he had looked and looked for just the right building in just the right town in just the right region to establish his restaurant. After nearly settling on a place in Aix-en-Provence, and spending several months there checking into the markets, transportation, and the kind of clientele he might expect, he had settled on Le Moulin de Mougins in 1968. For many years the building had been an olive-oil mill, before turning into what was known as *un cinq à sept* (a disreputable inn, where men took their girlfriends from five to seven o'clock in the evening). Now, of course, the Vergés had completely renovated the building and furnished it tastefully. It had two large dining rooms inside, an ample bar, and a few rooms upstairs (no longer available by the hour!). The two terraces were wonderful places to eat, with widely spaced white tables covered with pink linen tablecloths and shaded by big umbrellas. Behind the restaurant were several very tall and very ancient olive trees. At the bottom of the hill was a thick dell, with willow trees and a jaunty little brook.

For lunch we ate a lobster dish with a rich red-wine reduction. As we finished our coffee, Chef Vergé emerged from the kitchen and joined us for a glass of champagne. We introduced Jim, and then fell straight into food talk—the challenges of getting stars from Michelin (he had two and was headed for his third), the satisfactions and pitfalls of running a successful restaurant, the budgetary balance one must strike between staff, the kitchen equipment, the dining-room decoration, and so on. At one point I mentioned something that had been bothering me lately: "You know, Chef, over the past five years or so, I feel your famous French chickens, the *poulets de Bresse*, have not been as good as they used to be."

"*Oui*, it's true," he replied. "But I have found one little place in L'Allier that still produces good chickens." As he toured us through the kitchen and introduced us to his smiling staff, Chef Vergé opened a door into a room-sized refrigerator, pulled out a fresh chicken from L'Allier, wrapped it in foil, and presented it to us. In a final act of kindness, he refused to allow us to pay the bill.

Paul and I began to see Chef Vergé frequently, and the better I got to know him, the more I thought of him as a quintessential example of

With Chef Vergé at his restaurant

what a true chef should be. He was a living link to the greats of the past, the kind of dedicated cuisinier that had so inspired my love of France and its food. And, like Curnonsky, Vergé could not have come from anywhere but France.

At five-thirty one evening, the chef and his wife joined us for cocktails on the terrace at La Pitchoune. We had brought a big Virginia ham from the States, and hoped they would be interested in that typically American fare. I had used a bit of it to make a *jalousie au fromage et jambon de Virginie*, a cheese-and-ham tart in puff pastry, which we served with a bottle of Dom Pérignon 1964 that Jim Beard had left for us.

I had long ago decided not to go into the restaurant trade myself, because it required total commitment; furthermore, in a restaurant one is restricted to cooking what's on the menu, and I preferred to experiment with many different dishes. Still, I always wondered, "What if I had . . . ?" I was curious to know how others had done it.

"How did you become a restaurateur?" I asked Vergé.

"Well, I was raised in the Allier Department with eight brothers and sisters. And for us, food was more important than anything else in our life," he explained. His village was populated by typical country people—wine-growers, poultry farmers, cheesemakers, orchardists, fishermen, hunters, farmers, *marchands de bétail*, etc. There were no movies or television, or even any organized sports there, so eating and drinking (and sex, evidently) were their main diversions.

"One of my grandfathers would wake up at four a.m., drink a cup of black coffee, and eat a whole roast chicken. Then he'd drink a second cup of coffee and eat a second chicken. Mind you, this was before breakfast, just to start the day right . . . and *every* day, too!"

As he said this, I couldn't help noticing that both Chef Roger and petite Denise had eaten two enormous helpings of *jalousie* each.

Sundays were the day of real feasting *chez* Vergé, and all the generations of his family would gather. "My mother and aunt would rise early and spend the whole day cooking," he said. "We'd start eating and drinking around ten o'clock Sunday morning, and we wouldn't stop till about five." At that point, the men would all troop out into the village, where they'd spend an hour or two in a café drinking apéritifs. The women washed up and began cooking dinner. "One of my uncles—he must have been seventy-five at the time—would get so drunk that he'd fall on the floor. When the eating and drinking started up again, my aunt would take a pair of scissors and cut a vein in his ear. By the time he'd bled enough, he'd get up and join right in with the rest of us!" Those epic Sunday dinners would go till midnight.

"My uncle, he was a very robust man who lived to be eighty-four, you know. Everybody in town was *big*—red faces, strong people, hard workers. No one in my family ever heard of dieting. When I see some of the skinny little people in my restaurant pecking at their food like sparrows, I remember our village, where everyone ate heaps of sausages and pâtés and beef, and fish, and pheasants, and geese, and venison, and chicken. Not too many vegetables, of course. Mostly meat."

"So you learned to cook by watching your mother and aunt?"

"They put a bench right up next to the stove for me to stand on, so I could see everything they were doing. Sometimes I would stir the pots, or hold a casserole, and of course I was tasting everything and listening to all their talk. So when I turned seventeen it was only natural that I should apprentice myself to a chef, and that's how it all began."

III. HEARTBREAK

IN AUGUST 1974, it was ninety-nine degrees and humid at La Pitchoune, and despite a cure of iced champagne poor Jim Beard was not faring well at all. But it was Paul who awoke at 4:00 a.m., coughing and choking with a gusher of a nosebleed. We stanched the flow, cleaned him up, and changed the sheets. The next morning, he was struck again. And just before lunch, he had a third nosebleed attack. This was not normal. We called the local doctor, who suggested putting ice on Paul's nose, keeping his head elevated, and a few other basic remedies. The gushers stopped.

We had never been to La Peetch in August before, but I was taking a break from telly work and meanwhile working on my latest book, *From Julia Child's Kitchen*. That evening, we held a party on our terrace. There were nine guests, including the American cookbook-writer Richard Olney, a friend of Jim's who had come over from his house in Solliès-Toucas. The menu included *oeufs en gelée*, roast leg of lamb, *haricots panachés* (shell beans and string beans), and cheeses. For dessert, I unveiled a long-worked-on and finally-presented-to-the-public *tarte au citron*, which was marvelous. Paul served a succession of wonderful wines. His nose behaved.

"Well, sure, you can *call* it a heart attack if you want to, but that phrase has many meanings," the doctor said. "Why did it happen? We don't really know. But we'll give him every test we can think of." It was October now, and we were back in Cambridge. Paul had suffered an infarction, a slowly developing heart condition.

It wasn't a roaring lion of a heart attack, such as you see in the movies, he said. Rather, it was a blockage of the arteries that had sneaked up on him "on tiny padded feet, like a field mouse."

Starting in about 1967, Paul recalled, he had felt very slight chest pains. They would disappear, and when his heart was tested, the doctor said: "Congratulations, you have the heart of an athlete in his thirties!" But after his nosebleeds at La Pitchoune in 1974, Paul started feeling the pains every day. He told our doctor in Boston about it that fall, and was immediately whisked into the Intensive Care Unit, where they detected two blocked blood vessels. Using veins from his legs, the doctors performed a new kind of operation, a bypass. After the surgery, Paul was trussed up with tubes like *un pigeon désossé*, and remained miserably bedridden for weeks. Furthermore, something about the operation (perhaps a lack of oxygen to the brain) had left him with a case of mental scrambles. He confused numbers and names, and his beautiful handwriting degenerated into scribbles.

My poor husband, he who took such pride in lifting heavy suitcases and felling massive trees, hated to be so weak and confused. I hated it, too.

I went to visit Paul at the hospital every day, sometimes twice a day. But I had much left to do on *From Julia Child's Kitchen*—and thank heavens I did! As always, my work gave my life form, forced me to be productive, and helped me to keep a good balance. I was very lucky indeed. Without a challenging project like a cookbook to work on, I could well have gone cuckoo in those dark months of Paul's hospitalization.

THIS NEW BOOK had started out as a kind of *French Chef Cookbook*, Volume II, and was based on our seventy-two color-TV shows. But once I started in on writing it, the book turned into something quite different: a personal meander full of stories, recipe tangents, and summarizing comments about my twenty-five years in the kitchen. It was my most personal book, and the most difficult book I've ever written. Perhaps that's why I'd come to consider it my favorite.

In a way, *From Julia Child's Kitchen* represented a great liberation for me. It included the lessons I'd learned from classical French cuisine, while putting my cooking know-how to work in new directions. With Judith Jones's strong encouragement, I branched into Indian curries, New England chowders, Belgian cookies, and tinkered with new gadgets like the microwave oven. As was my habit, I delved into the proper hard-boiling of eggs and the various ways to soufflé those tricky busters, potatoes.

My hope was that readers would use *From Julia Child's Kitchen* as if it were a private cooking school. I tried to structure each recipe as a class. And the great lesson embedded in the book is that no one is *born* a great cook, one learns by *doing*. This is my invariable advice to people: Learn how to cook—try new recipes, learn from your mistakes, be fearless, and above all have fun!

Epilogue

FIN

PAUL ALWAYS FELT that closing up La Pitchoune after a stay was "a symbolic death." But that seemed awfully gloomy to me. I didn't think of closing our house for a few months as a "death" at all. To me, life moves forward. Leaving La Peetch now just meant that there would be a good reason to come back the next time. And go back we all did, year after year.

In 1976, Jean and Simca gave up their little apartment in Neuilly, outside of Paris, and moved down to Le Mas Vieux full-time. Every summer she conducted cooking classes there, mostly for Americans, who loved her accessible and genuinely French recipes. And in ensuing years both she and Louisette would write two recipe books apiece.

Then came a period when our intimate friends and family began to slip off into the Great Blue Yonder. Charlie and Freddie died of heart attacks. Jim Beard died in 1985, at age eighty-one. Jean Fischbacher died the following year, at age seventy-nine. Simca, living alone in Le Mas Vieux, refused to put herself into a retirement home or to hire a nurse. I worried about *ma belle soeur*; but, as always, she was determined to do things her own way.

"I do often think of we childless ones, with no offspring to lean on," I wrote Simca. "Avis, for instance, who evidently has only a year or so to live with her internal cancer, has her grandchildren to take her shopping, etc. *Eh bien*, we shall take care of ourselves . . . which we do very well. But I realize at our time of life the great difference between ourselves and those who have produced!" There were melancholy moments when I wished I had a daughter of my own to share things with.

But we cooks are a hardy lot: Escoffier survived to be eighty-nine, after all, and my old chef Max Bugnard lived to be ninety-six. Perhaps Simca and I would make it to eighty-five, or even ninety.

Simca was eighty-seven years old in June 1991, when she fell in her bedroom at Le Mas Vieux and caught a chill, which led to a terrible pneumonia. Although she held on for another six months through force of will, La Super-Française finally succumbed that December. "We have lost a remarkable person who was a fond and generous sister to me," I wrote with a heavy heart.

Paul never fully recovered from the effects of his heart troubles, and slowly became *un vieillard*. In 1989, he suffered a series of strokes, which, on top of prostate problems, made travel an ordeal. He was brave about it, but the aging process was rotten. It no longer made sense for him to get up at 5:00 a.m. so that I could do cooking demonstrations and TV shows in places like New York and Washington, D.C. I sharply cut back my work and travel schedule.

And I came to a decision. Without Paul to share the house with, or my *grande chérie* Simca, or all of our other favorite friends and family, it had come time to relinquish La Pitchoune.

People seemed surprised when I told them that it wasn't an especially difficult or emotional decision. But I have never been very sentimental. La Pitchoune was a special place, but the heart had gone out of it for me now. It was the people I shared it with, more than the physical property, that I would miss.

Besides, Provence was no longer the quiet refuge we had all loved. It had become hideously expensive (a head of lettuce cost twice as much in Cannes as in Cambridge), and the coastline was more jammed than ever. Houses were multiplying on the hillsides, and the winding country roads were clogged with streams of cars and enormous trucks. Our little village of Plascassier, which had always had a butcher, baker, vegetable shops, and electrician, now had no little businesses left at all; everyone went to the big supermarket down the hill. As Paul had accurately predicted years earlier, the place was turning into southern California. And *that* I could walk away from *sans regret*.

In June 1992, Dort's daughter Phila, her husband, and baby boy joined me for a final, month-long stay at La Peetch. The house was filled with familiar smells and memories, but, rather than dwell on them too much, I preferred to keep busy. Friends dropped by; I played a round of golf (my favorite game); we took long walks, marketed, and ate very well in Cannes and Nice and Grasse. There was little water pressure at the house, and I had to take sponge baths the whole time, but one gets used to that. Every night I would set the alarm for 2:00 a.m. so that I could call Paul, who was now ninety years old and living in a nursing home outside of Boston.

In a leisurely way, Phila and I packed up my *batterie de cuisine*, Paul's paintings and photographs, and our glassware from Biot. We left Simca's furniture and tidied up all the legal and financial loose ends, in order to return the house to Jean's family—just as Paul and I had promised we would nearly thirty years earlier.

As the month drew to a close, I was feeling upbeat, and was surprised when Phila began to cry. I asked her what was wrong. "Oh, I'm all stirred up because this is the last time we will be here like this," she said.

"That's true," I replied. "But I will always have such wonderful memories of the Peetch."

"But aren't you going to miss it?"

I shrugged, and said: "I've always felt that when I'm done with something I just walk away from it—*fin!*"

On our last day at La Pitchoune, we invited a group of friends over for dinner. I lit a match and turned on the four-burner *cuisinière;* the stove made a dramatic *pouf!* noise when the gas lit, which scared everyone but made me smile. Then I cooked a *boeuf en daube à la provençale*, a splendid braised pot roast with wine, tomatoes, and *herbes de Provence*. Yum! It was a jolly meal indeed, and a fitting way to close the curtain.

Just before going to bed that night, I stood on the terrace in the dappled shadows of the mulberry tree. A pale moon hung in the sky over the red-tiled roof. A cool breeze brushed my face and rustled the trees on the hillside across the valley. I inhaled the sweet scent of flowers, listened to the nightingale-and-frog chorus, and felt the familiar rough stones under my bare feet. What a lovely place.

The next morning, it was a classic Provençal day—sunny and cool, with a sharp blue sky. After breakfast, I handed the keys to La Pitchoune over to Jean's sister. Then we climbed into the car and bumped down the dusty, rutted driveway for the very last time.

I TRIED TO HOLD on to my impressions, but it was hopeless, as if I were trying to hold on to a dream. No matter. France was my spiritual homeland: it had become part of me, and I a part of it, and so it has remained ever since. Now I was moving forward again, into new experiences, in new places, with new people. There was still so much to learn and do—articles and books to write, perhaps another TV show or two to try. I wanted to go lobster-fishing in Maine, visit a Chicago slaughterhouse, teach kids how to cook. I viewed our recipes as a sacred trust, a set of rules about the right way and wrong way to approach food, and I felt a duty to pass this knowledge on. In short, my appetite had not diminished!

In Paris in the 1950s, I had the supreme good fortune to study with a remarkably able group of chefs. From them I learned why good French food is an art, and why it makes such sublime eating: nothing is too much trouble if it turns out the way it should. Good results require that one take *time* and *care*. If one doesn't use the freshest ingredients or read the whole recipe before starting, and if one rushes through the cooking, the result will be an inferior taste and texture—a gummy beef Wellington, say. But a careful approach will result in a magnificent burst of flavor, a thoroughly satisfying meal, perhaps even a life-changing experience.

Such was the case with the *sole meunière* I ate at La Couronne on my first day in France, in November 1948. It was an epiphany.

In all the years since that succulent meal, I have yet to lose the feelings of wonder and excitement that it inspired in me. I can still almost taste it. And thinking back on it now reminds me that the pleasures of the table, and of life, are infinite—*toujours bon appétit!*

INDEX

✣ ✣ ✣

Page numbers in *italic* refer to illustrations.

ILLUSTRATION CREDITS

ALL OF THE PHOTOGRAPHS reproduced in this book are by Paul Child, with the exception of those provided with the permission and courtesy of the following: Robert K. Brigham, Fish & Wildlife Service, U.S. Department of the Interior (page 261); Jack Case (page 235); the collection of Julia Child (pages 2, 4, 30, and 77); the Child family (pages 80 and 159–162); Dorothy Cousins (page 85); Mark Kauffman, Time Life Pictures/Getty Images (pages 88 and 102); Lee Lockwood (page 262 [both]); Hans Namuth (page 293); WGBH (page 271).

A NOTE ABOUT THE AUTHORS

JULIA CHILD was born in Pasadena, California. She was graduated from Smith College and worked for the OSS during World War II in Ceylon and China, where she met Paul Child. After they were married they lived in Paris, where she studied at the Cordon Bleu and taught cooking with Simone Beck and Louisette Bertholle, with whom she wrote the first volume of *Mastering the Art of French Cooking* (1961). In 1963, Boston's WGBH launched *The French Chef* television series, which made her a national celebrity, earning her the Peabody Award in 1965 and an Emmy in 1966. Several public television shows and numerous cookbooks followed. She died in 2004.

ALEX PRUD'HOMME, Paul Child's grand-nephew, is a freelance writer whose work has appeared in *The New York Times*, *The New Yorker*, and other publications. He is the author of *The Cell Game* and the co-author (with Michael Cherkasky) of *Forewarned*. He lives with his family in Brooklyn, New York.

A NOTE ON THE TYPE

This book was set in Janson, a typeface long thought to have been made by the Dutchman Anton Janson, who was a practicing typefounder in Leipzig during the years 1668–1687. However, it has been conclusively demonstrated that these types are actually the work of Nicholas Kis (1650–1702), a Hungarian, who most probably learned his trade from the master Dutch typefounder Dirk Voskens. The type is an excellent example of the influential and sturdy Dutch types that prevailed in England up to the time William Caslon (1692–1766) developed his own incomparable designs from them.

Composed by North Market Street Graphics,
Lancaster, Pennsylvania
Printed and bound by Berryville Graphics,
Berryville, Virginia
Designed by Virginia Tan